RECAP

APPLY

REVIEW

SUCCEED

REVISION GUIDE

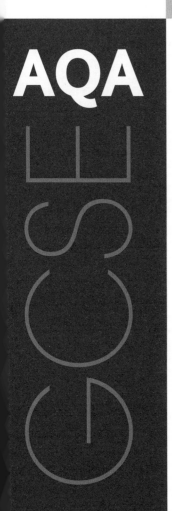

AQA GCSE

Religious Studies A (9 – 1)
Christianity & Buddhism

Marianne Fleming
Nagapriya
Peter Smith

OXFORD
UNIVERSITY PRESS

OXFORD
UNIVERSITY PRESS

Great Clarendon Street, Oxford, OX2 6DP, United Kingdom

Oxford University Press is a department of the University of Oxford. It furthers the University's objective of excellence in research, scholarship, and education by publishing worldwide. Oxford is a registered trade mark of Oxford University Press in the UK and in certain other countries

British Library Cataloguing in Publication Data
Data available

978-0-19-842285-3

10 9 8 7 6 5 4

Paper used in the production of this book is a natural, recyclable product made from wood grown in sustainable forests. The manufacturing process conforms to the environmental regulations of the country of origin.

Printed in Great Britain by Bell & Bain Ltd, Glasgow

Links to third party websites are provided by Oxford in good faith and for information only. Oxford disclaims any responsibility for the materials contained in any third party website referenced in this work.

Please note that the Practice Questions in this book allow students a genuine attempt at practising exam skills, but they are not intended to replicate examination papers.

ACKNOWLEDGEMENTS

The publishers would like to thank the following for permissions to use their photographs:

Cover: Peter Adams/Getty Images

Artworks: QBS Learning and Jason Ramasami

Photos: p16: Renata Sedmakova/Shutterstock; **p17:** GrahamMoore999/iStockphoto; **p44 (T):** prapann/Shutterstock; **p44 (B):** Pascal Deloche/Getty; **p45:** Godong/Alamy Stock Photo; **p46:** dangdumrong/Getty; **p47:** Fred de Noyelle/Getty; **p49:** Ville Palonen/Alamy Stock Photo; **p51:** georgeclerk/iStock; **p52:** 3DMI/Shutterstock; **p55:** Godong/Alamy Stock Photo; **p56:** r.classen/Shutterstock; **p58:** southtownboy/iStock; **p59 (T):** vladru/iStock; **p59 (B):** Antonprado/iStock; **p60:** DR Travel Photo and Video/Shutterstock; **p61:** NICK FIELDING/Alamy Stock Photo; **p66:** saiko3p/Shutterstock; **p67:** Luckykot/iStock; **p68:** maked/iStock; **p70:** NICK FIELDING/Alamy Stock Photo; **p71:** Hemis/Alamy Stock Photo; **p74:** mr_owlman/Shutterstock; **p84:** areeya_ann/Shutterstock; **p96:** mshch/iStock; **p98:** janrysavy/iStock; **p108:** SteveAllenPhoto/Getty; **p111:** cinoby/iStock; **p112:** rrocio/iStock; **p130:** querbeet/iStock; **p137:** adventtr/iStock; **p143:** Jeff J Mitchell/Getty; **p145:** Serena Taylor/Getty.

Carrotflower font © Font Diner – www.fontdiner.com

FSC® C007785

We are grateful to the authors and publishers for use of extracts from their titles and in particular for the following:

Scripture quotations [marked NIV] taken from the **Holy Bible, New International Version Anglicised** Copyright © 1979, 1984, 2011 Biblica. Used by permission of Hodder & Stoughton Ltd, an Hachette UK company. All rights reserved. 'NIV' is a registered trademark of Biblica UK trademark number 1448790. Excerpts from **The Group of Discourses**, translated by K. R. Norman (Pali Text Society, 2015). Reproduced with permission from the Hon. Pali Text Society. Excerpts from **The Story of Gotama Buddha: The Nidāna-kathā of the Jātakaṭṭhakathā**, translated by N.A. Jayawickrama. (Pali Text Society, 1990). Reproduced with permission from the Hon. Secretary, Pali Text Society.

Excerpts from **The Word of the Doctrine: Translation of Dhammapada**, translated by K.R. Norman, (Pali Text Society, 1997). Reproduced with permission from the Hon. Secretary, Pali Text Society. Excerpts from **The Connected Discourses of the Buddha: A New Translation of the Samyutta Nikaya**, translated by Bhikkhu Bodhi (Wisdom Publications, 2005). Copyright holder not established at time of going to print. Excerpts from **The Middle Length Discourses of the Buddha: A New Translation of the Majjhima Nikaya**, translated by Bhikkhu Nanamoli and Bhikkhu Bodhi, (Wisdom publications, 2005). Copyright holder not established at time of going to print.

AQA: *Paper 1A: Specimen question paper*, (AQA 2017). Reproduced with permission from AQA. **AQA:** *Paper 1A: Additional specimen question paper*, (AQA 2017). Reproduced with permission from AQA. **Bhadantacariya Buddhaghosa:** *The Path of Purification: Visuddhimagga*, translated by Bhikkhu Nanamoli (Buddhist Publication Society, 1991). Reproduced with permission from the Administrative Secretary, Buddhist Publication Society. **The Church of England:** Lines from the *Creeds,* the *Lord's Prayer,* the *marriage rite* and the *baptism rite*. (The Archbishops' Council, 2017). © The Archbishops' Council. Reproduced with permission from The Archbishops' Council. **The Church of England:** *Marriage, Family & Sexuality Issues,* https://www.churchofengland.org/our-views/marriage,-family-and-sexuality-issues/family.aspx (The Archbishops' Council, 2010). © The Archbishops' Council. Reproduced with permission from The Archbishops' Council. **His Holiness Tenzin Gyatso the Dalai Lama:** speech, New Delhi, India, February 4th 1992, (Dalai Lama, 1992). Reproduced with permission from His Holiness The Dalai Lama. **His Holiness Tenzin Gyatso the Dalai Lama:** *My Land and My People,* (Srishti Publishers, 2002). Reproduced with permission from His Holiness The Dalai Lama. **His Holiness Tenzin Gyatso the Dalai Lama:** speech, Inter-faith Seminar, Ladakh Group, August 25th 2005, (Dalai Lama, 2005). Reproduced with permission from His Holiness The Dalai Lama. **His Holiness Tenzin Gyatso the Dalai Lama:** *Compassion and the Individual,* https://www.dalailama.com/messages/compassion-and-human-values/compassion (The Office of His Holiness the Dalai Lama, 2016). Reproduced with permission from His Holiness The Dalai Lama. **The House of Bishops of the Church of England:** *Civil Partnerships- A pastoral statement from the House of Bishops of the Church of England,* July 25th 2005. https://www.churchofengland.org/sites/default/files/2017-11/House%20of%20Bishops%20Statement%20on%20Civil%20Partnerships%202005.pdf (Archbishops' Council, 2005) Reproduced with permission from the Archbishops' Council. **B. H. Gunaratana:** *Meditation in Everyday Life from Mindfulness in Plain English: Updated and Expanded Edition,* (Wisdom Publications, 2011). Copyright holder not established at time of going to print. **D. Khyentse Rinpoche and P. Sangye:** *The Hundred Verses of Advice: Tibetan Buddhist Teachings on What Matters Most,* translated by Padmakara Translation Group (Shambhala Publications, 2006). Reproduced with permission from Shambhala Publications. **The Methodist Church in Britain:** *Methodist Conference 2009,* Motion 203, (The Methodist Church in Britain, 2009). © Trustees for Methodist Church Purposes. Reproduced with permission from The Methodist Church in Britain. The Methodist Church in Britain. **D. Morgan:** quote, (D. Morgan). Reproduced with permission from Rev. Daishin Morgan, courtesy of the Prior at Throssel Hole Buddhist Abbey. **Pope Francis:** *Address to a meeting at the ponitifcal academy of scinces,* October 2014. (The Vatican, 2014) © Libreria Editrice Vaticana. Reproduced with permission from The Vatican. **A. Sumedho:** *The Four Noble Truths,* (Amaravati Publications, 1992). Reproduced with permission from Amaravati Publications. **Thich Nhat Hanh:** *The Heart of Buddha's Teaching,* (Parallax Press, 1996. Paperback edition 1999, 2015 Random House). Reproduced with permission from Parallax Press. **The United Nations:** *The Universal Declaration of Human Rights,* (UDHR) (United Nations, 1948). Reproduced with permission from United Nations. **The Salvation Army:** *Positional Statement: Euthanasia and Assisted Suicide,* July 2013, http//www.salvationarmy.org/ihq/ipseuthanasia (The Salvation Army, 2013). Reproduced with permission from the General of The Salvation Army.

We have made every effort to trace and contact all copyright holders before publication, but if notified of any errors or omissions, the publisher will be happy to rectify these at the earliest opportunity.

Contents

PART ONE: THE STUDY OF RELIGIONS 12

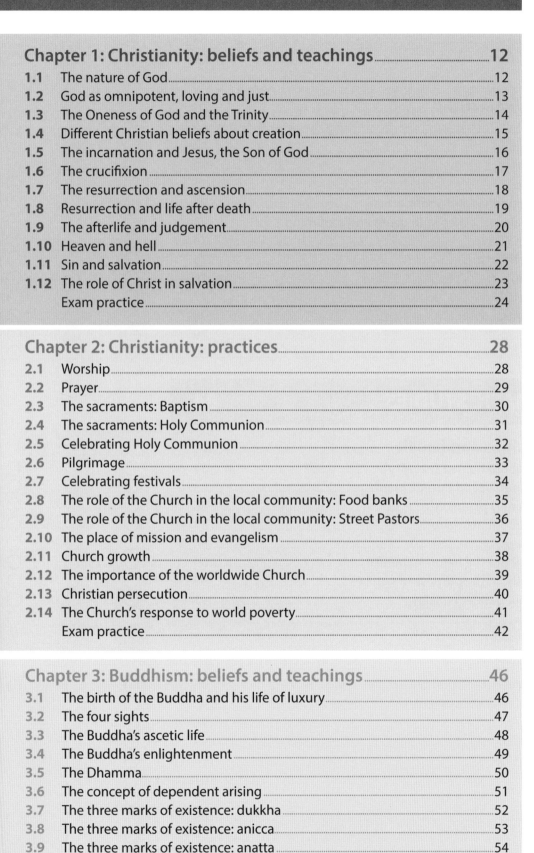

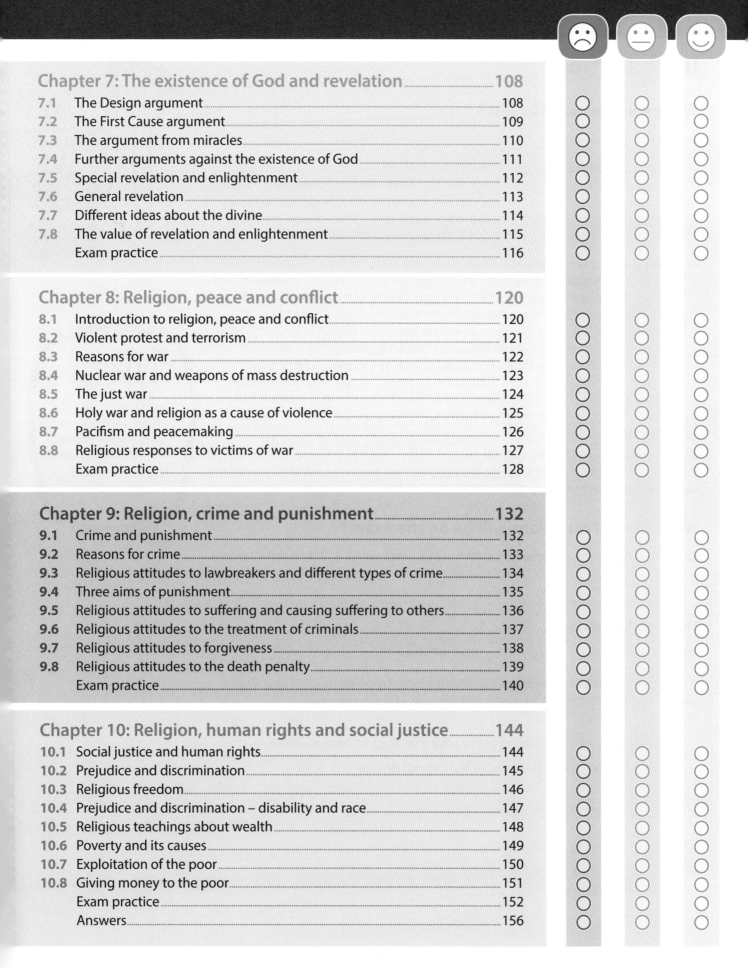

Introduction

What will the exam be like?

For your GCSE Religious Studies exam, you will sit two papers.

- **Paper 1 will cover the study of religions.** You will need to answer questions on the beliefs and teachings, and practices, of **two** world religions. There will be separate question and answer booklets for each religion. Chapters 1 and 2 of this revision guide will help you to answer questions on Christianity for Paper 1. Chapters 3 and 4 will help you to answer questions on Buddhism.

- **Paper 2 will cover thematic studies.** There are six themes on the paper. You will need to **choose four themes**, and answer all the questions for each chosen theme. You will need to know about religious beliefs and viewpoints on themes and issues. Except in those questions where the main religious tradition of Great Britain is asked for, you can use beliefs from any religion in your answer. For example, you might want to focus on Christianity, including viewpoints from different traditions within Christianity, such as Catholic or Protestant views. Or you might want to include beliefs from across six religions, including Christian, Buddhist, Hindu, Muslim, Jewish or Sikh viewpoints. Chapters 5 to 10 of this revision guide cover the six themes, focusing on Christian and Buddhist perspectives.

If you are studying **St Mark's Gospel**, then the six themes will appear in Section A of Paper 2. You will need to choose **two themes**. You will then also need to answer the **two questions on St Mark's Gospel** from Section B.

> **TIP**
>
> Each paper is 1 hour and 45 minutes long, and you'll need to answer four full questions. Aim to spend 25 minutes on each question.

What kind of questions will be on the exam?

Each question on the exam will be split into five parts, worth 1, 2, 4, 5 and 12 marks.

The 1 mark question

The 1 mark question tests knowledge and understanding.

It is always a **multiple-choice question** with four answers to choose from. It will usually include the command words: '**Which one of the following…**'

> Which **one** of the following is the idea that God is three-in-one?
>
> Put a tick (✔) in the box next to the correct answer.
>
> | | | |
> |---|---|---|
> | **A** | Atonement | ☐ |
> | **B** | Incarnation | ☐ |
> | **C** | Salvation | ☐ |
> | **D** | Trinity | ☐ |
>
> **[1 mark]**

How is it marked?

1 mark is awarded for a correct answer.

The 2 mark question

The 2 mark question tests knowledge and understanding.

It always begins with the command words 'Give two...' or 'Name two...'

> Give **two** ways in which religious believers help victims of war.
>
> **[2 marks]**

TIP

The examiner is expecting two simple points, not detailed explanations. You would get 2 marks if you answered "1) praying for victims; 2) providing food and shelter". You don't need to waste time by writing in full sentences and giving long explanations.

How is it marked?
1 mark is awarded for 1 correct point.
2 marks are awarded for 2 correct points.

The 4 mark question

The 4 mark question tests knowledge and understanding.

It always begins with the command words '**Explain two...**'

It might test your knowledge of how a religion influences individuals, communities and societies. Or it might ask for similarities or differences within or between religions.

TIP

Here, 'contrasting' means different. The question is asking you to explain two different ways in which Holy Communion is celebrated.

> Explain **two** contrasting ways in which Holy Communion is celebrated in Christianity.
>
> **[4 marks]**

How is it marked?
For the first way, influence or similar/contrasting belief:

- 1 mark is awarded for a simple explanation
- 2 marks are awarded for a detailed explanation.

For the second way, influence or similar/contrasting belief:

- 1 mark is awarded for a simple explanation
- 2 marks are awarded for a detailed explanation.

So for the full 4 marks, the examiner is looking for two ways/influences/ beliefs and for you to give detailed explanations of both. The examiner is expecting you to write in full sentences.

What is a detailed explanation?
An easy way to remember what you need to do for the four mark question is:

Make one point	Develop it

Make a second point	Develop it

TIP

One point you might make to answer this question is to say "Catholics celebrate Holy Communion by receiving offerings of bread and wine." This would get you 1 mark. For a second mark you could develop the point by giving further information: "During the service they believe the bread and wine become the body and blood of Jesus Christ."

There is more you could probably say, but as you'd get 2 marks for this, it would be better to turn your attention to thinking about a second contrasting way in which Holy Communion is celebrated, and then developing that second point.

But how do you develop a point? You might do this by:

- giving more information
- giving an example
- referring to a religious teaching or quotation.

The 'Great Britain' question

Sometimes there may be additional wording to the 4 mark question, asking you to **'Refer to the main religious tradition of Great Britain and one or more other religious traditions.'**

Explain **two** similar religious beliefs about abortion.

In your answer you should refer to the main religious tradition of Great Britain and one or more other religious traditions.

[4 marks]

The main religious tradition of Great Britain is Christianity, so in your answer **you must refer to Christianity**. You can refer to **two different denominations within Christianity**, or you can compare **a Christian belief with that from another religion,** such as Buddhism, Hinduism, Islam, Judaism or Sikhism.

For theme C: the existence of God and revelation, the wording will say: 'In your answer you should refer to the main religious tradition of Great Britain **and non-religious beliefs.'** You must refer to Christianity and a non-religious belief.

This type of question will only be asked about certain topics. We point them out in this Revision Guide using this feature:

You might be asked to compare beliefs on contraception between Christianity (the main religious tradition in Great Britain) and another religious tradition.

TIP

You can't, for example, refer to two different groups within Buddhism, or compare Buddhism and Islam. There must be a reference to Christianity or you won't get full marks for this question however detailed your answer is.

The 5 mark question

The 5 mark question tests knowledge and understanding.

Like the 4 mark question, it always begins with the command words **'Explain two...'** In addition it will also ask you to **'Refer to sacred writings or another source of religious/Christian belief and teaching in your answer.'**

Explain **two** reasons why Christians pray.

Refer to sacred writings or another source of Christian belief and teaching in your answer.

[5 marks]

How is it marked?

For the first reason/teaching/belief:

- 1 mark is awarded for a simple explanation
- 2 marks are awarded for a detailed explanation.

For the second reason/teaching/belief:

- 1 mark is awarded for a simple explanation
- 2 marks are awarded for a detailed explanation.

Plus 1 mark for a relevant reference to sacred writings or another source of religious belief.

So for the full 5 marks, the examiner is looking for two reasons/teachings/beliefs and for you to give detailed explanations of both, just like the 4 mark question. **For the fifth mark, you need to make reference to a writing or teaching that is considered holy or authoritative by a religion.** The examiner is expecting you to write in full sentences. You might aim to write five sentences.

What counts as 'sacred writings or another source of religious belief and teaching'?

Sacred writings and religious beliefs or teachings might include:

- a quotation from a holy book or religious text, such as the Bible or the Dhammapada
- a statement of religious belief such as the Apostles' Creed
- a prayer such as the Lord's prayer
- a statement made by a religious leader, for example the Pope or the Dalai Lama.

TIP

If you can quote exact phrases this will impress the examiner, but if you can't then it's fine to paraphrase. It's also ok if you can't remember the exact verse that a quotation is from, but it would be helpful to name the holy book, for example, to specify that it is a teaching from the Bible.

The 12 mark question

The 12 mark question tests analytical and evaluative skills. It will always begin with a statement, and then ask you to **evaluate the statement**. There will be bullet points guiding you through what the examiner expects you to provide in your answer.

From Paper 1:

> 'The Bible tells Christians all they need to know about God's creation.'
>
> Evaluate this statement. In your answer you should:
>
> - refer to Christian teaching
> - give reasoned arguments to support this statement
> - give reasoned arguments to support a different point of view
> - reach a justified conclusion.
>
> **[12 marks]**
> **[+3 SPaG marks]**

TIP

The examiners are not just giving marks for what you know, but for your ability to weigh up different sides of an argument, making judgements on how convincing or weak you think they are. The examiner will also be looking for your ability to connect your arguments logically.

From Paper 2:

'War is never right'

Evaluate this statement. In your answer you:

- should give reasoned arguments in support of this statement
- should give reasoned arguments to support a different point of view
- should refer to religious arguments
- may refer to non-religious arguments
- should reach a justified conclusion.

[12 marks]

[+3 SPaG marks]

TIP

For Paper 2, on thematic issues, you can use different views from one or more religions, and you can also use non-religious views.

How is it marked?

Level	What the examiner is looking for	Marks
4	A well-argued response with two different points of view, both developed to show a logical chain of reasoning that leads to judgements supported by relevant knowledge and understanding. ***References to religion applied to the issue.***	10–12 marks
3	Two different points of view, both developed through a logical chain of reasoning that draws on relevant knowledge and understanding. ***Clear reference to religion.***	7–9 marks
2	One point of view developed through a logical chain of reasoning that draws on relevant knowledge and understanding. OR Two different points of view with supporting reasons. ***Students cannot move above Level 2 if they don't include a reference to religion, or only give one viewpoint.***	4–6 marks
1	One point of view with supporting reasons. OR Two different points of view, simply expressed.	1–3 marks

TIP

This question is worth the same amount of marks as the 1, 2, 4 and 5 mark questions combined. Try to aim for at least a full page of writing, and spend 12 minutes or more on this question.

Tips for answering the 12 mark question

- **Remember to focus your answer on the statement you've been given**, for example 'War is never right.'

- **Include different viewpoints, one supporting the statement, one arguing against it** – for example one viewpoint to support the idea that war is *never* right, and an alternative viewpoint to suggest that war is sometimes necessary.

- **Develop both arguments showing a logical chain of reasoning** – draw widely on your knowledge and understanding of the subject of war, and try to make **connections** between ideas. Write a detailed answer and use evidence to support your arguments.

- **Be sure to include religious arguments** – a top level answer will explain how religious teaching is relevant to the argument.

- **Include evaluation** – you can make judgements on the strength of arguments throughout, and you should finish with a justified conclusion. If you want to, you can give your own opinion.

- **Write persuasively – use a minimum of three paragraphs** (one giving arguments for the statement, one for a different point of view and a final conclusion). The examiner will expect to see extended writing and full sentences.

Spelling, punctuation and grammar

Additional marks for **SPaG – spelling, punctuation and grammar** will be awarded on the 12 mark question.

A maximum of 3 marks will be awarded if:

- your spelling and punctuation are consistently accurate

- you use grammar properly to control the meaning of what you are trying to say

- you use specialist and religious terminology appropriately. For example, the examiner will be impressed if you use appropriately the term 'resurrection' rather than just 'rising from the dead'.

In Paper 1, SPaG will be awarded on the Beliefs question for each religion.

In Paper 2, SPaG will be assessed on each 12 mark question, and the examiner will pick your best mark to add to the total.

TIP

Always try to use your best written English in the long 12 mark questions. It could be a chance to pick up extra marks for SPaG.

How to revise using this book

This Revision Guide takes a three step approach to help with your revision.

RECAP	This is an overview of the key information. It is not a substitute for the full student book, or your class notes. It should prompt you to recall more in-depth information. Diagrams and images are included to help make the information more memorable.
APPLY	Once you've recapped the key information, you can practise applying it to help embed the information. There are two questions after each Recap section. The first question will help you rehearse some key skills that you need for the questions on the exam that test your knowledge (the 1, 2, 4 and 5 mark questions). The second question will help you rehearse some key skills that you will need for the 12 mark question, which tests your evaluative skills. There are suggested answers to the Apply activities at the back of the book.
REVIEW	At the end of each chapter you will then have a chance to review what you've revised. The exam practice pages contain exam-style questions for each question type. For the 4, 5 and 12 mark questions, there are writing frames that you can use to structure your answer, and to remind yourself of what it is that the examiner is looking for. When you've answered the questions you can use the mark schemes at the back of the book to see how you've done. You might identify some areas that you need to revise in more detail. And you can turn back to the pages here for guidance on how to answer the exam questions.

The revision guide is designed so that alongside revising *what* you need to know, you can practise *how* to apply this knowledge in your exam. There are regular opportunities to try out exam practice questions, and mark schemes so you can see how you are doing. Keep recapping, applying and reviewing, particularly going over those areas that you feel unsure about, and hopefully you will build in skills and confidence for the final exam.

Good luck!

1.1 The nature of God

Essential information:

☐ Christianity is the main religion in Great Britain.

☐ Christianity has three main traditions: Catholic, Protestant and Orthodox.

☐ Christianity is **monotheistic**, meaning that Christians believe in one Supreme Being, **God**.

Different branches of Christianity

CHRISTIANITY

Catholic – based in Rome and led by the Pope.

Orthodox – split from Catholic Christianity in 1054 CE and practised in Eastern Europe.

Protestant – split from Catholic Christianity in the 16th century and branched out into different **denominations** (distinct groups), e.g. Baptist, Pentecostal, Methodist, United Reformed Churches. Protestants agree that the Bible is the only authority for Christians.

TIP

If you are asked about similarities and differences in a religion, try to remember that even though Christianity has different denominations, they all share the same belief in God.

What do Christians believe about God?

- There is only one God:

> ❝ We believe in one God ❞
> *The Nicene Creed*

- God is the creator and sustainer of all that exists.
- God works throughout history and inspires people to do God's will.
- People can have a relationship with God through prayer.
- God is spirit (John 4:24) – neither male nor female – but has qualities of both.
- God is **holy** (set apart for a special purpose and worthy of worship).
- Jesus is God's son – the true representation of God on earth (Hebrews 1:3).

TIP

See page 13 for more Christian beliefs about God.

A Christians believe that there is only one God. Refer to scripture or another Christian source of authority to support this idea.

B 'Christianity is a major influence on people's lives.'

Write a paragraph to **support this statement**.

1.2 God as omnipotent, loving and just

Essential information:

Christians believe:

☐ God is **omnipotent**, almighty, having unlimited power.

☐ God is **benevolent**, all-loving and all-good.

☐ God is **just**, the perfect judge of human behaviour who will bring about what is right and fair or who will make up for a wrong that has been committed.

Some qualities of God

Omnipotent	Benevolent	Just
• God is the Supreme Being who is all-powerful. • God has unlimited authority.	• God uses his power to do good. • God shows his love by creating humans and caring for them. • God showed his love by sending God's Son, Jesus, to earth.	• God is a just judge of humankind. • God will never support injustice, ill-treatment, prejudice or oppression.

The problems of evil and suffering

The problems of evil and suffering challenge belief in these qualities of God:

- If God is benevolent, **why does God allow people to suffer**, and to hurt others?
- If God is omnipotent, **why does God not prevent evil and suffering**, such as the suffering caused by natural disasters?
- If God is just, **why does God allow injustice** to take place?

Christians believe a just God treats people fairly, so they trust God even when things seem to be going wrong.

TIP

See page 111 for more arguments in response to these challenges to belief in God.

(A) Give **two** ways in which Christians believe God shows his benevolence.

(B) Write the response a Christian would make to someone who said that a loving God would not allow suffering. Think of **two** arguments and develop them.

TIP

In the 12 mark exam answer, using the key terms 'omnipotent', 'benevolent' and 'just' where appropriate, and spelling them correctly, may gain you more marks for SPaG.

RECAP

Essential information:

☐ Christians believe there are three persons in the one God: Father, Son and Holy Spirit. This belief is called the **Trinity**.

☐ Each person of the Trinity is fully God.

☐ The persons of the Trinity are not the same.

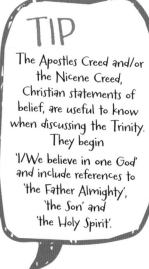

TIP

The Apostles Creed and/or the Nicene Creed, Christian statements of belief, are useful to know when discussing the Trinity. They begin 'I/We believe in one God' and include references to 'the Father Almighty', 'the Son' and 'the Holy Spirit'.

The Trinity

- God is understood by Christians as a relationship of love between Father, Son and Holy Spirit.
- In describing God as Trinity, 'person' does not mean a physical being, although Jesus did have a physical presence in history.

God the Father, the creator of all life, acts as a good father towards his children. He is all powerful (omnipotent), all loving (omnibenevolent), all knowing (omniscient) and present everywhere (omnipresent).

THE FATHER

IS NOT IS IS NOT

GOD

IS IS

THE SON   THE HOLY SPIRIT

IS NOT

God the Son became incarnate through Jesus who was both fully human while on earth and fully God at all times. Jesus is called the **Son of God** to show his special relationship to God the Father.

God the Holy Spirit is the unseen power of God at work in the world, who influences, guides and sustains life on earth.

APPLY

A Here are **two** Christian beliefs about the Trinity. Develop each point with further explanation or a relevant quotation:

1. *"The Trinity is the Christian belief that there are three persons in the one God."* _____

_____

2. *"One of the persons of the Trinity is God the Father."* _____

_____

B Here are some arguments that could be used to evaluate the statement, 'The Trinity is a helpful way of describing God.' Sort them into arguments in support of the statement, and arguments in support of different views. **Write your own justified conclusion.**

1. The Trinity is a helpful idea because it describes God as a loving relationship of persons.	5. If God is One, then how can God have three persons?
2. The love of God the Son is shown in Jesus' mission and sacrifice.	6. The Holy Spirit is the outpouring of love between Father and Son that encourages Christians to love their neighbour.
3. The Trinity seems contradictory.	7. Jesus was a Jew and believed in the oneness of God.
4. The love of God the Father is shown in his sending his Son to earth to save humankind.	8. The Trinity is not helpful to people of other faiths as they may think that Christians believe in three different Gods.

RECAP

Essential information:

☐ Christians believe in **creation** by God, the act by which God brought the universe into being.

☐ God, the Father, chose to design and create the earth and all life on it.

☐ The Holy Spirit was active in the creation (Genesis 1:1–3).

☐ The **Word**, God the Son or Jesus, was active in the creation (John 1:1–3).

☐ The Trinity, therefore, existed from the beginning and was involved in the creation.

Creation: *Genesis 1:1–3*

> **In the beginning, God created the heavens and the earth.** Now the earth was formless and empty, darkness was over the surface of the deep, and the Spirit of God was hovering over the waters. And God said, "Let there be light," and there was light.
>
> *Genesis 1: 1–3 [NIV]*

- Many Christians believe that the story of the creation in Genesis, while not scientifically accurate, contains religious truth.
- Some Christians believe that God made the world in literally six days.
- God created everything out of choice and created everything 'good'.
- Christians believe that God continues to create new life today.
- Although God the Father is referred to as the creator, the Holy Spirit was active in the creation, according to Genesis.

Creation: *John 1:1-3*

> **In the beginning was the Word, and the Word was with God, and the Word was God.** He was with God in the beginning. Through him all things were made; without him nothing was made that has been made.
>
> *John 1: 1–3 [NIV]*

- In John's gospel, everything was created through the Word, who was both with God and was God.
- The Word refers to the Son of God who entered history as Jesus.
- Christians believe that the Son of God, the Word of God, was involved in the creation.

TIP
See pages 96 and 100 for more detail on different Christian beliefs about creation.

APPLY

(A) Explain **two** ways in which belief in creation by God influences Christians today.

(B) Here is an argument in support of the statement, 'The Bible is the best source of information about the creation.'

Evaluate the argument. Explain your reasoning.

"The Bible contains the truth about the creation of the world by God. God is omnipotent, so God can just say 'Let there be light' and it happens. The Bible is God's word, so it is true. Other theories about the creation, like evolution and the Big Bang theory, have not been proved."

TIP
Show the examiner that you are aware of contrasting views within Christianity about the way Genesis 1 is interpreted, that is, between those who take the story literally and those who do not.

RECAP

Essential information:

☐ Christians believe that Jesus was God in human form, a belief known as the **incarnation** (becoming flesh, taking a human form).

☐ Christians believe that Jesus was the Son of God, one of the persons of the Trinity.

The incarnation

> ❝This is how the birth of Jesus the Messiah came about: His mother Mary was pledged to be married to Joseph, but before they came together, **she was found to be pregnant through the Holy Spirit.**❞
>
> *Matthew 1:18 [NIV]*

- On separate occasions an angel appeared to Mary and Joseph explaining that it was not an ordinary conception and it was not to be an ordinary child.
- The gospels of Matthew and Luke explain that Mary conceived Jesus without having sex.
- The virgin conception is evidence for the Christian belief that Jesus was the Son of God, part of the Trinity.
- Through the incarnation, God showed himself as a human being (Jesus) for around 30 years.

> ❝**The Word became flesh** and made his dwelling among us.❞
>
> *John 1:14 [NIV]*

Son of God, Messiah, Christ

- Jesus was fully God and fully human, which helps explain his miracles and **resurrection** (rising from the dead).
- His words, deeds and promises have great authority because they are the word of God.
- Most Jews expected a Messiah who would come to save Israel and establish an age of peace, but do not believe that Jesus was that person.
- Christians believe that Jesus is the Messiah, but a spiritual rather than a political one.
- Gospel writers refer to Jesus as the Christ ('anointed one' or Messiah), but Jesus warned his disciples not to use the term, possibly because his opponents would have him arrested for **blasphemy** (claiming to be God).

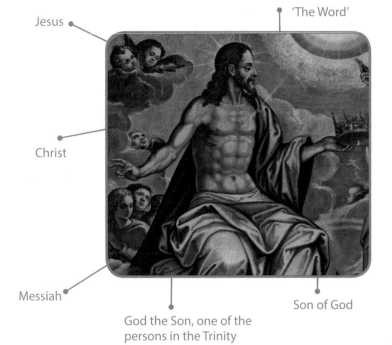

Jesus ·
'The Word' ·
· Christ
· Messiah
Son of God
God the Son, one of the persons in the Trinity

APPLY

(A) Explain **two** Christian beliefs about Jesus' incarnation. **Refer to sacred writings in your answer.**

(B) **Develop this argument** to support the statement, 'The stories of the incarnation show that Jesus was the Son of God' by explaining in more detail, adding an example, or referring to a relevant religious teaching or quotation.

"The stories of the incarnation in the gospels of Matthew and Luke show that his mother, Mary, was a virgin. Joseph was not the natural father of Jesus. Jesus' conception was through the Holy Spirit, so really God was his father. That is why he is called the Son of God."

TIP

In a 5 mark question, you need to give a detailed explanation of each belief and then support your answer by quoting from scripture or sacred writings for full marks. The sacred writings may refer to just one of the beliefs or to both of them.

RECAP

Essential information:

- [ ] Jesus was sentenced to death by Pontius Pilate, a death by **crucifixion** (fixed to a cross).
- [ ] Jesus forgave those who crucified him and promised one of the men crucified with him that he would join God in paradise.
- [ ] Jesus' body was buried in a cave-like tomb.

Jesus' crucifixion – what happened?

- Although Jesus was fully God, he was also fully human so suffered pain and horror.
- Jesus' last words before dying were:

> **"**Father, into your hands I commit my spirit.**"**
>
> *Luke 23:46* [NIV]

- A Roman centurion acknowledged Jesus was innocent, and said he was the Son of God (Mark 15:39).
- The Roman guards made sure Jesus was dead.
- Joseph of Arimathea was permitted to bury Jesus in a cave-like tomb, rolling a large stone to block the entrance.
- Jesus' burial was rushed because the Sabbath was about to begin.

Jesus' crucifixion – why is it important?

- Jesus' sacrifice on the cross gives hope to Christians that **their sins will be forgiven if they sincerely repent**.
- Christians believe that **God understands human suffering** because Jesus, who is God, experienced it.
- **Christians accept that suffering is part of life**, just as it was a part of Jesus' life.

TIP

See page 23 for more detail on why the crucifixion was important.

APPLY

A Here are two ways in which Jesus' crucifixion influences Christians today:

1) Their sins are forgiven.
2) They have hope when they are suffering.

Develop both points by **explaining in more detail or by adding an example.**

TIP

Keep rereading the statement to make sure you are answering the question asked.

B Read the following response to the statement, 'The crucifixion is the most important belief for Christians.' Underline the **two** best arguments. Explain how this answer could be improved.

"Jesus was arrested in the Garden of Gethsemane and brought to trial, first before the Jewish Council and then before the Roman Governor, Pontius Pilate. In the gospels it says that Pontius Pilate did not think Jesus was guilty of anything, so he didn't want to have him killed. Instead he had him flogged. The Jewish leaders called for Jesus' death, so Pilate gave in to their wishes and sentenced Jesus to death. After about six hours of agony on the cross, Jesus died. A Roman centurion said that because Jesus was innocent, he must surely be the Son of God. When Jesus died, he took the sins of everyone on himself. This is called the atonement. If Jesus had not died, he would not have risen from the dead."

RECAP

Essential information:

- ☐ The gospels say that after Jesus died and was buried, he rose from the dead. This event is known as the **resurrection**.

- ☐ The **ascension** of Jesus took place 40 days after his resurrection, when he returned to God the Father in **heaven**.

- ☐ There would be no Christian faith without the resurrection.

The resurrection of Jesus – what happened?

- Early on Sunday morning, some of Jesus' female followers, including Mary Magdalene, visited the tomb to anoint Jesus' body.
- Jesus' body was not there.
- Either a man or two men, who may have been angels, told the women to spread the news that Jesus had risen from the dead.
- Over the next few days, Jesus appeared to several people including Mary Magdalene and his disciples. He told them he had risen from the dead, as he predicted he would before the crucifixion.

> **❝** And if Christ has not been raised, our preaching is useless and so is your faith. But Christ has indeed been raised from the dead... For as in Adam all die, so in Christ all will be made alive. **❞**
>
> *1 Corinthians 15:14, 20, 22* [NIV]

TIP

This quote shows that Christianity would not exist without the resurrection. It also shows that the resurrection is important because it is significant evidence for Christians of the divine nature of Jesus.

The ascension of Jesus – what happened?

- After meeting with his disciples and asking them to carry on his work, Jesus left them for the last time, returning to the Father in heaven. This event is called the ascension.

> **❝** While he was blessing them, he left them and was taken up into heaven. **❞**   *Luke 24:51* [NIV]

The significance of these events for Christians today

The significance of the **resurrection**:	The significance of the **ascension**:
• Shows the power of good over evil and life over death. • Means Christians' sins will be forgiven if they follow God's laws. • Means Christians will be resurrected if they accept Jesus, so there is no need to fear death.	• Shows Jesus is with God in heaven. • Paves the way for God to send the Holy Spirit to provide comfort and guidance.

APPLY

A Give **two** reasons why the disciples believed Jesus was alive after his resurrection. (AQA Specimen question paper, 2017)

B 'The resurrection is the most important belief for Christians.'

Develop this response to the statement, by adding a relevant religious teaching or quotation.

"Without the resurrection, there would be no Christian faith. Jesus' death would have been the end of all the hopes the disciples placed on him. He would have been just like all the other innocent victims put to death for their beliefs."

1.8 Resurrection and life after death

RECAP

Essential information:

☐ Jesus' resurrection assures Christians that they too will rise and live on after death.

☐ Christians have differing views about what happens when a person who has died is resurrected.

☐ Belief in resurrection affects the way Christians live their lives today.

Different Christian views about resurrection

Some Christians believe a person's soul is resurrected **soon after death**.	Other Christians believe the dead will be resurrected at **some time in the future**, when Jesus will return to judge everyone who has ever lived.
Catholic and Orthodox Christians believe in bodily resurrection. This means resurrection is **both spiritual and physical**: the physical body lost at death is restored and transformed into a new, spiritual body.	Some other Christians believe resurrection will **just be spiritual**, not physical as well.

> ❝ So will it be with the resurrection of the dead. The body that is sown is perishable, it is raised imperishable; it is sown in dishonour, it is raised in glory; it is sown in weakness, it is raised in power; it is sown a natural body, it is raised a spiritual body. If there is a natural body, there is also a spiritual body. ❞
>
> *1 Corinthians 15:42–44 [NIV]*

TIP
This quote explains some of the differences between a living body and a resurrected body. For Catholics and Orthodox Christians, it suggests there is a physical element to resurrection, as it talks about the resurrected body being a 'body', even if it is a spiritual one.

Impact of the belief in resurrection

- inspires Christians to live life in the way God wants them to, so they can remain in his presence in this life and the next
- means life after death is real
- gives hope of a future life with Jesus

A belief in resurrection...

- shows Christians how much God loves them
- gives confidence in the face of death

APPLY

(A) Explain **two** ways in which a belief in resurrection influences Christians today.

(B) The table below presents arguments for and against the belief in bodily resurrection. **Write a paragraph** to explain whether you agree or disagree with bodily resurrection, having evaluated both sides of the argument.

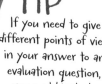
TIP
If you need to give different points of view in your answer to an evaluation question, you could include contrasting non-religious perspectives as well as religious perspectives.

For	Against
Jesus rose from the dead and appeared to his disciples.	Science has shown the body decays after death, so there cannot be a physical resurrection.
The gospels insist he was not a ghost, as he ate with them and showed his wounds to them.	Some people are cremated so their bodies no longer exist.
Yet he could appear and disappear suddenly, so it seems that his body was transformed.	Stories of the resurrection appearances may have been exaggerated.
Paul says 'the body that is sown is perishable, it is raised imperishable', suggesting the natural body is raised as a spiritual body, but a body nevertheless.	The disciples may have felt Jesus' presence spiritually rather than seeing him physically.
Catholic and Orthodox Christians believe people's bodies are transformed into a glorified state in which suffering will not exist.	Christians believe in the soul and it is the soul that rises again, not the body.

1.9 The afterlife and judgement

Essential information:

☐ Christians believe in an **afterlife** (life after death) that depends on faith in God.

☐ The afterlife begins at death or at the **Day of Judgement**, when Jesus will come to judge the living and the dead.

☐ Judgement will be based on how people have behaved during their lifetimes, as well as their faith in following Jesus. This has an effect on how Christians choose to live their lives today.

The afterlife

Christian beliefs about life after death vary, but many believe that:

- They will be **resurrected** and receive **eternal life** after they die.
- This is a gift from God, and **dependent on faith in God**.
- They will be **judged by God** at some point after they die, and either rewarded by being sent to heaven or punished by being sent to hell.
- This judgement will happen either **very soon after death** or **on the Day of Judgement**. This is a time in the future when the world will end and Christ will come again to judge the living and the dead.

Some of these beliefs about the afterlife are found in the **Apostles' Creed**, which is an important statement of Christian faith:

> **"** He ascended into heaven, and is seated at the right hand of the Father,
> and he will come to judge the living and the dead:
> I believe in…
> the resurrection of the body;
> and the life everlasting. **"**
>
> *The Apostles' Creed*

Judgement

- Christians believe that after they die, God will judge them on their **behaviour and actions** during their lifetime, as well as their **faith in Jesus** as God's Son.
- In the Bible, Jesus' **parable of the Sheep and the Goats** describes how God will judge people.
- This parable teaches Christians that **in serving others, they are serving Jesus**, so this is the way they should live their lives.

> **"** For I was hungry and you gave me something to eat, I was thirsty and you gave me something to drink, I was a stranger and you invited me in, I needed clothes and you clothed me, I was ill and you looked after me, I was in prison and you came to visit me. **"**
>
> *Matthew 25:35–36* [NIV]

JUDGEMENT

for good actions and behaviour

for faith in God and Jesus

- Before he died, Jesus told his disciples he would prepare a place for them in heaven with God. He also made it clear that **having faith in him and following his teachings** was essential for being able to enter heaven when he said:

> **"** I am the way and the truth and the life. No one comes to the Father except through me. **"** *John 14:6* [NIV]

A Explain **two** Christian teachings about judgement. **Refer to sacred writings or another source of Christian belief and teaching in your answer.**
(AQA Specimen question paper, 2017)

B **Evaluate the statement,** 'The afterlife is a good way to get people to behave themselves and help others.' Refer to two developed Christian arguments, and two developed non-religious arguments. **Write a justified conclusion.**

TIP

When writing a justified conclusion, do not just repeat everything you have already said. Instead, weigh up the arguments and come to a personal view about their persuasiveness.

1.10 Heaven and hell

Essential information:

☐ Many Christians believe God's judgement will result in eternal reward or eternal punishment.

☐ **Heaven** is the state or place of eternal happiness and peace in the presence of God.

☐ **Hell** is the place of eternal suffering or the state of being without God.

What happens after God's judgement?

- After God's judgement, Christians believe they will either **experience eternal happiness in the presence of God** (heaven), or **be unable to experience God's presence** (hell).
- Catholics believe some people might enter an intermediate state, called purgatory, before they enter heaven.
- Knowledge of these states is limited and linked to imagery from the past.

Heaven and purgatory

- **Heaven** is thought to be either a **physical place** or **spiritual state** of peace, joy, freedom from pain and a chance to be with loved ones.
- Traditional images of heaven often show God on a throne with Jesus next to him and angels all around him, or a garden paradise.
- Christians differ in their views about **who is allowed into heaven**, where there may be:
  - only Christians (believers in Jesus)
  - Christians and other religious people who have pleased God by living good lives
  - baptised Christians, regardless of how they lived their lives.
- However, many Christians believe heaven is a reward for **both faith and actions** – not just one of these – as the parable of the Sheep and the Goats seems to show (see page 20).
- **Purgatory** is an intermediate state where souls are cleansed in order to enter heaven. This is a Catholic belief.

Hell

- **Hell** is seen as the opposite of heaven – a state of existence without God.
- It is often pictured as a **place of eternal torment** in a fiery pit ruled by Satan (a name for the Devil), who is the power and source of evil.
- However, many people question whether a loving God would condemn people to eternal torment and pain in hell.
- Christians who believe God would not do this see hell as an **eternal state of mind** of **being cut off from the possibility of God**.
- Hell would then be what awaits someone who did not acknowledge God or follow his teachings during their life.

(A) Give **two** reasons why some people do not believe in hell.

(B) **Make a list of arguments** for and against the idea that heaven and hell were invented to encourage people to behave themselves.

TIP
If this question said 'some Christians', you should offer Christian objections to the idea of hell. 'Some people' means you can give non-religious reasons if you wish.

Essential information:

☐ **Sin** is any thought or action that separates humans from God.

☐ **Original sin** is the in-built tendency to do wrong and disobey God, which Catholics believe all people are born with.

☐ The ways Christians can be saved from sin to gain salvation include following God's **law**, receiving God's **grace**, and being guided by the **Holy Spirit**.

The origins and meanings of sin

A sin is any **thought or action that separates humans from God**. Sinful thoughts (such as anger) can lead to sinful actions (such as murder).

- Some sins, like murder or assault, are illegal.
- Other sins, like adultery, are not illegal but are against the laws of God.

Christians believe that all humans commit sins. Some Christians (particularly Catholics) also believe humans are born with an in-built tendency to sin, called **original sin**.

- The idea of original sin comes from Adam and Eve's disobedience of God, when they ate the fruit of the tree of knowledge of good and evil which was forbidden by God. This was the first (original) sin.
- The result of their sin was separation from God, and the introduction of death into the world.

Christians believe **God gave people free will**, but they should use their freedom to make choices God would approve of, otherwise they will separate themselves from God. God provides people with the guidance to make good choices in his law, for example the Ten Commandments (Exodus 20:1–19), the Beatitudes (Matthew 5:1–12) and other Christian teachings.

Salvation

- **Salvation** means to be saved from sin and its consequences, and to be granted eternal life with God.
- Salvation **repairs the damage caused by sin**, which has separated people from God.

There are two main Christian ideas about how salvation can come about:

- Through **doing good works** – the Old Testament makes it clear that salvation comes through faith in God and obeying God's law.

> **"**In the same way, faith by itself, if it is not accompanied by action, is dead. **"**
> *James 2:17* [NIV]

- Through **grace** – salvation is given freely by God through faith in Jesus. It is not deserved or earned, but is a free gift of God's love.

> **"**For it is by grace you have been saved... **"**
> *Ephesians 2:8* [NIV]

- Christians believe it is the **Holy Spirit** who gives grace to Christians and continues to guide them in their daily lives, to help them achieve salvation.

A Explain **two** Christian teachings about the means of salvation. **Refer to sacred writings or another source of Christian belief and teaching in your answer.** (AQA Specimen question paper, 2017)

B 'As nobody is perfect, it is impossible not to sin.' **Evaluate this argument** and explain your reasoning.

"It is perfectly possible to live a good life without sin. Jesus lived his life without sin. Many saints have lived good and courageous lives without acting badly to other people. It is true that nobody is totally perfect, but that's different. Sin separates you from God and goes against God's law, and there are many people who stay close to God and keep his commandments, so I disagree with the statement."

1.12 The role of Christ in salvation

Essential information:

☐ Christians believe that salvation is offered through the life and teaching of Jesus.

☐ Jesus' resurrection shows that God accepted Jesus' sacrifice as **atonement**. This means that through the sacrifice of his death, Jesus restored the relationship between God and humanity that was broken when Adam and Eve sinned.

The role of Jesus in salvation

Christians believe Jesus' life, death and resurrection had a crucial role to play in God's plan for salvation because:

- Jesus' crucifixion **made up for the original sin** of Adam and Eve.
- The death of Jesus, as an innocent man, was necessary to **restore the relationship between God and believers**, to bring them salvation.
- Jesus' resurrection shows the goodness of Jesus defeated the evil of sin. It was proof that God had accepted Jesus' sacrifice on behalf of humankind.
- Jesus' resurrection means humans can now receive forgiveness for their sins.
- Jesus' death and resurrection made it possible for all who follow his teachings to **gain eternal life**.

> **TIP**
> This quote shows the Christian belief that death came into the world as a punishment for sin, but salvation is offered through the life and teaching of Jesus.

> 66 For the wages of sin is death, but the gift of God is eternal life in Christ Jesus our Lord. 99
> *Romans 6:23* [NIV]

Atonement

- Atonement **removes the effects of sin** and allows people to restore their relationship with God.
- Many Christians believe that through the sacrifice of his death, Jesus took the sins of all humanity on himself and paid the debt for them all. He **atoned for the sins of humanity**.
- This sacrifice makes it possible for all who follow Jesus' teachings to **receive eternal life** with God.

> 66 […] if anybody does sin, we have an advocate with the Father – Jesus Christ, the Righteous One. He is the atoning sacrifice for our sins, and not only for ours but also for the sins of the whole world. 99
> *1 John 2:1–2* [NIV]

Jesus' death + grace and good works

sin   atonement

(A) Give **two** reasons why the death and resurrection of Jesus is important to Christians.

(B) Here are some sentences that could be used to evaluate the statement, 'Salvation is God's greatest gift to humans.'

Sort them into arguments in support of the statement, and arguments in support of different views. Try to put them in a logical order. What do you think is missing from these statements to make a top level answer? Explain how the answer could be improved.

> **TIP**
> To remember the meaning of 'atonement', think of it as 'at-one-ment', because Jesus' death and resurrection make people at one with God.

1. Atheists do not consider salvation important because they do not think there is a God who saves people.	5. Without salvation, humankind would have to pay the price of human sin.
2. God shows his great love for people by sending his Son to save us.	6. People may doubt the truth of Jesus' resurrection so they don't see the need for a belief in salvation.
3. Even some religious people may think there are greater gifts to humans, such as nature or life itself.	7. Some people may question whether God is loving if God demands the death of his Son in payment for human sin.
4. Everyone needs forgiveness from God.	8. Humans should be grateful every day of their lives for Jesus' sacrifice on their behalf.

Test the 1 mark question

1 Which **one** of the following is the idea that God became human in Jesus?

[A] Atonement   [B] Incarnation   [C] Resurrection   [D] Creation   **[1 mark]**

2 Which **one** of the following is the idea that God is loving?

[A] Omniscient   [B] Omnipotent   [C] Benevolent   [D] Immanent   **[1 mark]**

Test the 2 mark question

3 Give **two** ways that Christians believe salvation can come about.   **[2 marks]**

1) _____

2) _____

4 Give **two** Christian beliefs about life after death.   **[2 marks]**

1) _____

2) _____

Test the 4 mark question

5 Explain **two** ways in which a belief in Jesus' crucifixion influences Christians today.   **[4 marks]**

● **Explain one way.**	One way in which a belief in Jesus' crucifixion influences Christians today is that they believe that the crucifixion was a sacrifice Jesus chose to make for them
● Develop your explanation with more detail/an example/ reference to a religious teaching or quotation.	in order to give them the opportunity to be granted forgiveness by God, so they can live in confidence that their sins have been forgiven.
● **Explain a second way.**	A second way in which a belief in Jesus' crucifixion influences Christians today is that it helps Christians who are suffering because they know Jesus suffered as well.
● Develop your explanation with more detail/an example/ reference to a religious teaching or quotation.	For example, Christians who are suffering persecution for their faith will be comforted to know that Jesus understands what they are going through because he too was innocent and suffered for his beliefs.

6 Explain **two** ways in which the belief in creation by God influences Christians today.   **[4 marks]**

● **Explain one way.**	
● Develop your explanation with more detail/an example/ reference to a religious teaching or quotation.	
● **Explain a second way.**	
● Develop your explanation with more detail/an example/ reference to a religious teaching or quotation.	

TIP

The student has explained the influence a belief in Jesus' crucifixion has on a Christian's <u>attitude</u> (their confidence in being forgiven and their comfort in dealing with their own suffering). You could also discuss the influence of this belief on a Christian's <u>life</u> (e.g. it might encourage them to spread the message of Jesus or to make the sign of the cross when they pray to remind themselves of Jesus' sacrifice).

7 Explain **two** ways in which the belief that God is loving influences Christians today.   **[4 marks]**

1 Exam practice

Test the 5 mark question

8   Explain **two** Christian beliefs about salvation.

Refer to sacred writings or another source of Christian belief and teaching in your answer.   **[5 marks]**

● **Explain one belief.**	*One Christian belief about salvation is that salvation can be gained through good works.*
● Develop your explanation with more detail/an example.	*These good works may be following teachings such as the Ten Commandments, the Golden Rule and 'love your neighbour'. Worshipping and praying regularly also help Christians to earn salvation.*
● **Explain a second belief.**	*A second Christian belief about salvation is that it is gained through grace.*
● Develop your explanation with more detail/an example.	*God gives salvation to people who have faith in Jesus. It is a gift for the faithful.*
● Add a reference to sacred writings or another source of Christian belief and teaching. If you prefer, you can add this reference to your first belief instead.	*Paul wrote in his letters that it is through grace, which is a gift from God, that people are saved, not simply through their good works.*

> **TIP**
> The references to scripture here count as development of your first point.

9   Explain **two** Christian teachings about God.

Refer to sacred writings or another source of Christian belief and teaching in your answer.   **[5 marks]**

● **Explain one teaching.**	
● Develop your explanation with more detail/an example.	
● **Explain a second teaching.**	
● Develop your explanation with more detail/an example.	
● Add a reference to sacred writings or another source of Christian belief and teaching. If you prefer, you can add this reference to your first teaching instead.	

> **TIP**
> You only need to make one reference to scripture in your answer. It can support either your first or your second point.

10   Explain **two** Christian teachings about atonement.

Refer to sacred writings or another source of Christian belief and teaching in your answer.   **[5 marks]**

Test the 12 mark question

11 'The stories of the incarnation prove that Jesus was the Son of God.'

Evaluate this statement. In your answer you should:

- refer to Christian teaching
- give reasoned arguments to support this statement
- give reasoned arguments to support a different point of view
- reach a justified conclusion.

[12 marks]
Plus SPaG 3 mark▶

REASONED ARGUMENTS IN SUPPORT OF THE STATEMENT ● **Explain why some people would agree with the statement.** ● Develop your explanation with more detail and examples. ● Refer to religious teaching. Use a quote or paraphrase or refer to a religious authority. ● **Evaluate the arguments.** Is this a good argument or not? Explain why you think this.	*Christians believe in the incarnation. This means that God took human form in Jesus. The stories of Jesus' birth show he was not conceived in the normal way. The fact he was conceived through the actions of God and born of a virgin proves that he was special and if God was involved it is likely that Jesus was his son. However, even though he was a physical person, he was also God at the same time. John's gospel calls Jesus 'the Son of God' and says he was the Word made flesh, living among us. This supports the idea that Jesus was both God and human.*
REASONED ARGUMENTS SUPPORTING A DIFFERENT VIEW ● **Explain why some people would support a different view.** ● Develop your explanation with more detail and examples. ● Refer to religious teaching. Use a quote or paraphrase or refer to a religious authority. ● **Evaluate the arguments.** Is this a good argument or not? Explain why you think this.	*Many people do not agree that Jesus was conceived through the actions of God and believe that Mary, his mother, was not a virgin. If the stories of the incarnation are not correct, they cannot be used as evidence that Jesus was the Son of God although his actions showed he was very special.*
CONCLUSION ● **Give a justified conclusion.** ● Include your own opinion together with your own reasoning. ● **Include evaluation.** Explain why you think one viewpoint is stronger than the other or why they are equally strong. ● Do not just repeat arguments you have already used without explaining how they apply to your reasoned opinion/conclusion.	*It may be true that the title 'Son of God' does not mean that there is such a close relationship between Jesus and God. It is possible that he was chosen by God, maybe when he was baptised, to do good works on earth and tell people about Christianity without there being a family relationship between himself and God. If this is true, there is no such thing as incarnation as far as Jesus is concerned.*

TIP
The question is about stories (plural) so it would improve the answer to mention details of Jesus' conception in the gospels of Matthew and Luke.

TIP
This argument could be developed further for more marks. For example, after the sentence that ends 'not a virgin' you might add 'Mary was engaged to Joseph, making it possible that Joseph was Jesus' father.'

TIP
The conclusion shows logical chains of reasoning. It evaluates different interpretations of the title 'Son of God' in relation to the stories of the incarnation. The examiner will want to see that you can link ideas together when developing your argument, and not just repeat what you have said already.

12 'There is no such place as hell.'

Evaluate this statement. In your answer you should:

- refer to Christian teaching
- give reasoned arguments to support this statement
- give reasoned arguments to support a different point of view
- reach a justified conclusion.

TIP

Spelling, punctuation and grammar is assessed on each 12 mark question, so make sure you are careful to use your best written English.

[12 marks]
Plus SPaG 3 marks

REASONED ARGUMENTS IN SUPPORT OF THE STATEMENT ● **Explain why some people would agree with the statement.** ● Develop your explanation with more detail and examples. ● Refer to religious teaching. Use a quote or paraphrase or refer to a religious authority. ● **Evaluate the arguments.** Is this a good argument or not? Explain why you think this.	
REASONED ARGUMENTS SUPPORTING A DIFFERENT VIEW ● **Explain why some people would support a different view.** ● Develop your explanation with more detail and examples. ● Refer to religious teaching. Use a quote or paraphrase or refer to a religious authority. ● **Evaluate the arguments.** Is this a good argument or not? Explain why you think this.	
CONCLUSION ● **Give a justified conclusion.** ● Include your own opinion together with your own reasoning. ● **Include evaluation.** Explain why you think one viewpoint is stronger than the other or why they are equally strong. ● Do not just repeat arguments you have already used without explaining how they apply to your reasoned opinion/conclusion.	

TIP

It's essential to include evaluation because this is the key skill that you are being tested on in the 12 mark question. You can evaluate after each viewpoint, and/or at the end as part of your justified conclusion.

13 'The best way to gain salvation is to obey God's law.'

Evaluate this statement. In your answer you should:

- refer to Christian teaching
- give reasoned arguments to support this statement
- give reasoned arguments to support a different point of view
- reach a justified conclusion.

[12 marks]
Plus SPaG 3 marks

Check your answers using the mark scheme on pages 161–162. How did you do? To feel more secure in the content you need to remember, re-read pages 12–23. To remind yourself of what the examiner is looking for, go to pages 6–11.

2 Christianity: practices

2.1 Worship

RECAP

Essential information:

☐ **Worship** is the act of religious praise, honour or devotion. It is a way for Christians to show their deep love and honour to God.

☐ Worship can take different forms, including liturgical, non-liturgical and informal worship.

☐ **Private worship** is when believers praise or honour God in their own home.

Why do Christians worship?

| To praise and thank God | To ask for forgiveness | To seek God's help for themselves or others | To deepen their relationship with God and strengthen their faith |

Different forms of worship

Type of worship	What form does it take?	Examples	Why is it important for Christians?
liturgical worship is a church service that follows a set structure or ritual	• takes place in a church • priest leads the congregation and may perform symbolic actions • formal prayers with set responses • Bible passages are read out, there may be a sermon • music and hymns	the Eucharist for Catholic, Orthodox and Anglican Churches	• worldwide set order for service that is familiar to everyone • ritual passed down through generations gives a sense of tradition • Bible readings follow the Christian calendar and teach Christian history and faith
non-liturgical worship is a service that does not follow a set text or ritual	• takes place in a church • often focused on Bible readings followed by a sermon • may also have prayers and hymns but there is no set order, the number and type can change from week to week	services in non-Conformist churches, e.g. Methodist, Baptist, United Reformed	• services can be planned and ordered to suit a certain theme • non-Conformist churches place an emphasis on the word of God in the Bible
informal worship is a type of non-liturgical worship that is 'spontaneous' or 'charismatic' in nature	• community or house churches meet in private homes and share food • Quaker worship is mainly silent, people speak when moved by God to offer their thoughts or read from the Bible • 'charismatic' worship may involve dancing, clapping, calling out and speaking in tongues	community or house churches, Quaker worship, charismatic ('led by the spirit') worship of the Pentecostal Church	• the style of worship in house churches is similar to the worship of early Christians • people can share readings and prayers and can take an active part in church by calling out or speaking without formal training • service may have an emotional impact with a feeling of personal revelation from God

APPLY

(A) Going on pilgrimage, celebrating festivals and religious art are also forms of worship. Give **two** more ways that Christians worship.

(B) 'Worship is most powerful when believers follow a set ritual.'

List arguments to support this statement and arguments to support a different point of view.

TIP

The arguments should apply to Christianity. Try to use religious language (see key terms in red).

Essential information:

- [ ] **Prayer** is communicating with God, either silently or through words of praise, thanksgiving or confession, or requests for God's help or guidance.

- [ ] Christians may use **set prayers** that have been written down and said more than once by more than one person. An example is **the Lord's Prayer**, which is the prayer Jesus taught to his disciples.

- [ ] Christians may also use **informal prayers** (made up by an individual using his or her own words) to communicate with God. Some Christians find they can express their needs to God more easily by using their own words.

The importance of prayer

encourages reflection in the middle of a busy life

enables Christians to talk and listen to God

gives strength in times of trouble

Why is prayer important?

helps Christians to keep a close relationship with God

gives a sense of peace

helps Christians to accept God's will even if it means suffering

The Lord's Prayer

> " Our Father in heaven, hallowed be your name,
> your Kingdom come, your will be done,
> on earth as in heaven.
> Give us today our daily bread.
> Forgive us our sins
> as we forgive those who sin against us.
> Lead us not into temptation, but deliver us from evil.
> For the kingdom, the power, and the glory are yours
> now and for ever. Amen. "
>
> *The Lord's Prayer*

- When Jesus' disciples asked him to teach them how to pray, he answered with the Lord's Prayer.
- Christians see it as a **model of good prayer**, as it combines praise to God with asking for one's needs.
- It reminds Christians to **forgive others in order to be forgiven**, since prayer is only effective if people's relationships with others are right.
- It reminds Christians that **God is the Father of the whole Christian community**, and it can create a sense of unity when everyone in the congregation says it together.
- The Lord's Prayer is often used in worship and is nearly always said at Holy Communion, baptisms, marriages and funerals. It is also used in schools and in commemoration services in Britain.

(A) Give **two** reasons why the Lord's Prayer is important to Christians.

(B) 'Private worship has more meaning for a Christian than public worship.' (AQA Specimen question paper, 2017)

Develop this argument to support the statement by explaining in more detail, adding an example, or referring to a relevant religious teaching or quotation.

"An individual Christian can choose how they want to worship in private, whereas in public worship they have to follow what everyone else is saying and doing. Therefore private worship has more meaning because they can put their heart and soul into it."

TIP
Always analyse the statement carefully. For example, here 'has more meaning' might depend on an individual's reasons for prayer.

Essential information:

☐ **Sacraments** are holy rituals through which believers receive a special gift of grace (free gift of God's love). Some Christian denominations recognise seven sacraments while others acknowledge fewer.

☐ **Baptism** is the ritual through which a person becomes a member of the Church. It involves the use of water to symbolise the washing away of sin.

☐ **Infant baptism** is for babies and young children. **Believers' baptism** is for people who are old enough to understand the significance of the ritual.

The sacraments

- **Catholic and Orthodox** Christians recognise **seven** sacraments: baptism, confirmation, Holy Communion, marriage, Holy Orders, reconciliation and the anointing of the sick.
- Many **Protestant** churches recognise **two** sacraments – baptism and Holy Communion – because they believe Jesus taught people to undertake these.
- Some churches that practise believers' baptism consider it to be important but not a 'sacrament'.
- Some churches, like the Quakers or Salvation Army, do not see any ritual or ceremony as being a 'sacrament'.

Baptism

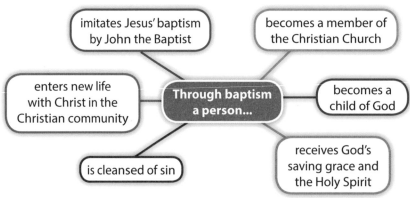

imitates Jesus' baptism by John the Baptist

becomes a member of the Christian Church

enters new life with Christ in the Christian community

Through baptism a person...

becomes a child of God

is cleansed of sin

receives God's saving grace and the Holy Spirit

Infant baptism and believers' baptism

	Practised by	Reasons why	What happens
Infant baptism	Catholic, Orthodox, Anglican, Methodist, and United Reformed Christians	• Removes original sin (Catholic and Orthodox belief). • Allows the child to be welcomed into the Church as soon as possible. • The parents can thank God for their new baby and celebrate with family and friends.	• The priest or minister pours blessed water over the baby's head and says, 'I baptise you in the name of the Father, and of the Son, and of the Holy Spirit.' • Godparents and parents promise to bring up the child as a Christian. • The child is welcomed into the Christian community.
Believers' baptism	Baptists, Pentecostalists	• People should be old enough to consciously make a mature decision about their faith. • The decision to live a life dedicated to Jesus is what saves a person, rather than the baptism itself.	• The person is fully immersed in a pool which symbolises cleansing from sin and rising to new life in Christ. • When asked whether they are willing to change their lives, the person gives a brief testimony of their faith in Jesus. • The person is baptised 'in the name of the Father, and of the Son, and of the Holy Spirit.'

Ⓐ Explain **two** contrasting ways in which Christians practise baptism and develop each point.

Ⓑ 'Parents should not have their children baptised if they have no intention of bringing them up as Christians.'

Evaluate this statement.

2.4 The sacraments: Holy Communion

Essential information:

☐ **Holy Communion** (also known as the Eucharist) is the sacrament that uses bread and wine to celebrate the sacrifice of Jesus on the cross and his resurrection.

☐ It recalls the Last Supper of Jesus, using his words and actions.

☐ Christians interpret the meaning of Holy Communion in different ways, but all agree that it brings them closer to each other and to God.

The meaning of Holy Communion

Holy Communion is a service which celebrates and gives thanks for the sacrifice of Jesus' death and resurrection (see pages 17–18). It has different meanings for different Christians:

- **Catholics, Orthodox Christians** and **some Anglicans** believe the bread and wine become **the body and blood of Christ**. This means Jesus is fully present in the bread and wine. This is a divine mystery that helps believers share in the saving sacrifice of Jesus' death and resurrection.
- **Protestant Christians** celebrate Holy Communion as a **reminder of the Last Supper**. They do not believe the bread and wine become the body and blood of Christ. Instead, the bread and wine remain **symbols of Jesus' sacrifice**, which helps believers to reflect on its meaning today.

> 66 For whenever you eat this bread and drink this cup, you proclaim the Lord's death until he comes. 99
>
> *1 Corinthians 11:26 [NIV]*

The impact of Holy Communion

For many Christians, Holy Communion is at the centre of their lives and worship. It affects individuals, local communities and the wider society in a number of ways:

Individuals	Communities	Wider society
• Christians **receive God's grace** by joining in the sacrifice of Jesus. • This helps to strengthen their faith. • They become closer to God.	• Holy Communion **brings the community of believers together** in unity by sharing the bread and wine. • This can provide support and encouragement for those going through a difficult time.	• Holy Communion **acts as a call to love others in practical ways**. • It encourages Christians to work for equality and justice for all. • Many churches collect money during the service to help support those in need, such as the poor or homeless.

Ⓐ Explain **two** ways in which Holy Communion has an impact on the lives of believers.

Ⓑ Use the table below with arguments about the statement, 'It is more important to help the poor than to celebrate Holy Communion.'

TIP
Decide on two ways and explain each. Do not simply list a number of ways without developing any of your points.

Write a paragraph to explain whether you agree or disagree with the statement, having evaluated both sides of the argument.

In support of the statement	Other views
The poor need urgent help, particularly if they are living in less economically developed countries, so of course it is more important to help them than to receive Holy Communion. Christians are taught to love their neighbour so that must come before their own needs. Remembering Jesus' death and resurrection through Holy Communion is nice, but not very useful to anyone. It's just focusing on the past when people should be thinking about the present.	It doesn't need to be such a stark choice. After all, when Christians break bread together at Holy Communion they remember that people in the world are starving and they try to help them. Many churches collect money for the poor during the service of Holy Communion, so celebrating this sacrament encourages people to care for others, not just themselves. 'Eucharist' means 'thanksgiving', so it makes Christians grateful for God's love and this makes them want to share it.

2.5 Celebrating Holy Communion

RECAP

Essential information:

☐ In most churches the Holy Communion service has two parts: the ministry of the Word (which focuses on the Bible), and the ministry of Holy Communion (the offering, consecrating and sharing of bread and wine).

☐ Christians have different practices when it comes to celebrating Holy Communion.

Differences between Holy Communion services

- In the **Orthodox Church**, Holy Communion is called the Divine Liturgy, and is believed to recreate heaven on earth. Much of the service is held at the altar behind the iconostasis, which is a screen that represents the divide between heaven and earth. The priest passes through the iconostasis using the Royal Doors.
- Holy Communion in the **Catholic and Anglican Churches** is very similar. The main difference is that Catholics believe the bread and wine turn into the body and blood of Christ, whereas many Anglicans believe Jesus is only present in a spiritual way when the bread and wine are being eaten.

Further examples of how Holy Communion services differ from each other include the following:

Orthodox Divine Liturgy	Catholic Mass and Anglican Holy Communion	Holy Communion in the United Reformed Church
Liturgy of the Word: • There are hymns, prayers and a Bible reading. • The priest comes through the Royal Doors to chant the Gospel. • There may be a sermon. **Liturgy of the Faithful:** • The priest receives wine and bread baked by church members. • Prayers are offered for the church, the local community and the world. • Behind the iconostasis, the priest says the words of Jesus at the Last Supper. • Most of the bread is consecrated as the body and blood of Christ. • The priest distributes holy bread and wine on a spoon. • Prayers of thanksgiving are said. • Unconsecrated pieces of bread are given to people to take home, as a sign of belonging to the Christian community.	**Liturgy of the Word:** • There are three Bible readings, a psalm and a homily. • The Creed is said. • Prayers are said for the Church, the local community, the world, and the sick and the dead. **Liturgy of the Eucharist:** • In the Anglican Holy Communion, people give a sign of peace to each other. • Offerings of bread and wine are brought to the altar. • The priest repeats the words of Jesus at the Last Supper over the bread and the wine. • People say the Lord's Prayer. • In the Catholic Mass, the sign of peace is given at this point. • People receive the bread and wine. • The priest blesses people and sends them out to live the gospel.	• The service begins with a hymn and prayer of praise and thanksgiving. • Bible readings and a sermon are given. • Prayers for the world and the needs of particular people are said. • The minister repeats the words and actions of Jesus at the Last Supper. • There is an 'open table' so anyone who wishes may receive Holy Communion. • Sometimes the bread is cut beforehand, other times it is broken and passed around by the congregation. • Wine is sometimes non-alcoholic and is usually distributed in small cups. • The service ends with a prayer of thanksgiving, a blessing, and an encouragement to go out and serve God.

APPLY

(A) Explain **two** contrasting ways in which Holy Communion is celebrated in Christianity. (AQA Specimen question paper, 2017)

(B) **Write a paragraph** in response to the statement, 'Holy Communion services should focus more on the Liturgy of the Word than on the Holy Communion itself.' **Develop your reasons** and include a reference to scripture or religious teaching in your answer.

TIP
Holy Communion services have many similarities. Be sure to choose aspects that show a real contrast.

RECAP

Essential information:

☐ A **pilgrimage** is a journey made by a believer to a holy site for religious reasons. As well as making a physical journey to a sacred place, the pilgrim also makes a spiritual journey towards God.

☐ A pilgrimage gives many opportunities for prayer and worship, and is itself an act of worship and devotion.

☐ Two popular pilgrimage sites for Christians are Lourdes (a town in France) and Iona (a Scottish island).

The role and importance of pilgrimage

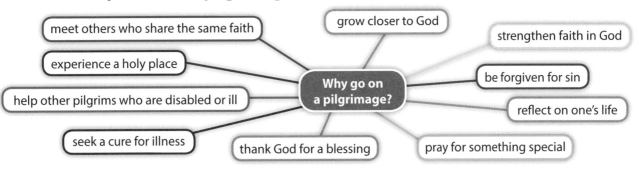

meet others who share the same faith

grow closer to God

strengthen faith in God

experience a holy place

be forgiven for sin

Why go on a pilgrimage?

help other pilgrims who are disabled or ill

reflect on one's life

seek a cure for illness

thank God for a blessing

pray for something special

A pilgrimage can impact on a Christian's life in a number of ways. It can:

- give them a better understanding of their faith
- renew their enthusiasm for living a Christian life
- help them to see problems in a new light
- help them to feel cleansed from sin
- help them to feel more connected to the Christian community
- give them a good feeling about helping other pilgrims who are disabled or ill.

Places of Christian pilgrimage

Place	Significance	Activities
Lourdes (a town in France)	• Where Mary is said to have appeared in a number of visions to a young girl called Bernadette. • Mary told Bernadette to dig in the ground, and when she did a spring of water appeared. • The water is believed to have healing properties, and a number of healing miracles are claimed to have taken place here.	• Pilgrims go to Lourdes to bathe in the waters of the spring, or to help other pilgrims who are ill or disabled to bathe in the waters. • Pilgrims also pray for healing or forgiveness. • They may recite the rosary together.
Iona (an island off the coast of Scotland)	• Where St Columba established a monastic community in the 6th century AD. • The community now has an ecumenical centre where pilgrims can stay.	• Because it is quiet, peaceful and a place of natural beauty, pilgrims can spend time praying, reading the Bible, and reflecting or meditating. • Pilgrims can also attend services in the abbey church, take part in workshops, and visit the island's holy or historic sites.

APPLY

A Explain **two** contrasting examples of Christian pilgrimage. (AQA Specimen question paper, 2017)

B 'There is no difference between a pilgrimage and a holiday.'

Develop this argument against the statement by explaining in more detail, adding an example or referring to Christian teaching.

"Although a pilgrimage can seem a lot like a holiday, especially if you travel abroad, there is a big difference. A pilgrimage is a spiritual journey that people undertake for religious reasons rather than just to sightsee."

TIP

You need to explain why the examples are contrasting, rather than just describing the two places, so be sure to explain the different reasons why pilgrims go there.

RECAP

Essential information:

☐ A **festival** is a day or period of celebration for religious reasons.

☐ Festivals help Christians to remember and celebrate the major events in their religion – particularly the life, death and resurrection of Jesus.

☐ **Christmas** commemorates the incarnation and the birth of Jesus. Celebrations begin on 25 December and last 12 days, ending with Epiphany (which recalls the visit of the wise men).

☐ **Easter** celebrates the resurrection of Jesus from the dead. Celebrations begin before Easter Sunday and finish with the feast of Pentecost.

Christmas

Christmas **commemorates the incarnation of Jesus**, which is the belief that God became human in Jesus (see page 16). The celebrations reflect Christian beliefs and teachings in the following ways:

* **lights** represent Jesus as the light coming into the world of darkness
* **nativity scenes** show baby Jesus born into poverty
* **carol services** with Bible readings remind Christians about God's promise of a saviour and the events of Jesus' birth

* **Midnight Mass** reflects the holiness of the night and the joy Christians feel at Jesus' birth
* **Christmas cards and gifts** recall the wise men's gifts to Jesus
* Christians **give to charity** in this time of peace and goodwill because God gave humanity the gift of Jesus, his Son.

Easter

Easter is the most important Christian festival, which **celebrates Jesus' rising from the dead**.

Holy Week (the week before Easter Sunday) remembers the events leading up to Jesus' crucifixion, including his arrest and trial.

* On **Saturday night**, some churches hold a special service to celebrate Christ's resurrection.
* Orthodox Christians walk with candles in procession, then enter the dark church as if going into Jesus' empty tomb.
* The priest announces 'Christ is risen!' to which people answer 'He is risen indeed.'
* Catholics and Anglicans have a vigil that begins in darkness, before the Paschal candle is lit to symbolise the risen Christ. The service ends with Holy Communion.

On **Good Friday** (the day Jesus was crucified), there are special services and processions led by a person carrying a cross.

* On **Easter Sunday**, churches are filled with flowers and special hymns are sung to rejoice at Jesus' resurrection.
* Services are held at sunrise, and shared breakfasts include eggs to symbolise new life.

> **❝** Christ is risen from the dead, trampling down death by death, and upon those in the tombs bestowing life. **❞**
> *Traditional Orthodox hymn at the Easter Divine Liturgy*

APPLY

Ⓐ Give **two** ways in which Christians celebrate the festival of Easter.

Ⓑ 'Christmas is no longer a religious festival.' Evaluate this statement.

2.8 The role of the Church in the local community: Food banks

Essential information:

☐ **The Church** is the holy people of God, also called the Body of Christ, among whom Christ is present and active.

☐ **A church** is a building in which Christians worship.

☐ Individual churches and the Church as a whole help the local community in a variety of ways, including the provision of **food banks**. These give food for free to people who cannot afford to buy it.

What does the Church do?

Individual churches and the Church as a whole help the local community in many ways.

Individual churches:

- educate people about Christianity (e.g. Bible study groups)
- are meeting places for prayer and worship
- provide activities for younger people (e.g. youth clubs)
- are places where Christians can socialise and obtain spiritual guidance.

The Church:

- supports local projects such as food banks
- provides social services such as schooling and medical care
- helps those in need
- campaigns for justice.

> ❝ And God placed all things under his [Jesus'] feet and appointed him to be head over everything for the church, which is his body. ❞
>
> *Ephesians 1:22–23* [NIV]

> **TIP**
> You could use this quote in your exam to show that Christians think of the Church as the followers of Jesus, who together are the body of Christ on earth.

Examples of the Church helping the local community

The Trussell Trust and The Oasis Project are two organisations that help the local community by providing food banks and other services. The work of these charities is based on Christian principles (such as the parable of the Sheep and the Goats).

The Trussell Trust
• A charity running over 400 food banks in the UK.
• These provide emergency food, help and support to people in crisis in the UK.
• Non-perishable food is donated by churches, supermarkets, schools, businesses and individuals.
• Doctors, health visitors and social workers identify people in crisis and issue them with a food voucher.
• Their aim is to bring religious and non-religious people together to help end poverty and hunger.

The Oasis Project
• A community hub run by Plymouth Methodist Mission Circuit.
• Provides an internet café, creative courses, a job club, training opportunities, a meeting place and a food bank.
• Spiritual and practical help is given to those in need because of ill health, learning disabilities, domestic violence, substance abuse, low income and housing problems.

> **TIP**
> You will not be asked about these particular organisations in your exam, but if you learn what they do, you will be able to give detailed examples of how the Church helps in the local community.

APPLY

Ⓐ Give **two** meanings of the word 'church'.

Ⓑ Here is a response to the statement, 'There will always be a need to feed hungry people in Britain.' Can you improve this answer by including religious beliefs?

"At first this statement appears untrue. No one should be hungry in Britain as there is a welfare state. People who can't work to feed themselves or their families can apply for benefits."

"However, I agree with the statement because people can suddenly be faced with bills they can't pay, or lose their jobs, or become ill so they can't work. It may take many weeks to apply for benefits and be accepted, so what do they do in the meantime? If they don't have much savings they will be really hard up and need the help of food banks."

2.9 The role of the Church in the local community: Street Pastors

Essential information:

☐ Christians should help others in the local community because Jesus taught that people should show **agape** love (a Biblical word meaning selfless, sacrificial, unconditional love).

☐ Christians believe it is important to put their faith into action. They do this through many organisations and projects that help vulnerable people in the community.

☐ **Street Pastors** are people who are trained to patrol the streets in urban areas. They help vulnerable people by providing a reassuring presence on the street.

The importance of helping in the local community

- Jesus taught that **Christians should help others by showing agape love** towards them. For example, in the parable of the Sheep and the Goats, Jesus teaches Christians they should give practical help to people in need (see page 20).
- Two examples of Christian organisations that provide practical help to local communities are Street Pastors and Parish Nursing Ministries UK.

> ❝Faith by itself, if it is not accompanied by action, is dead.❞
>
> *James 2:17* [NIV]

TIP
You could use this quote in your exam to show that Christians believe it is very important to take practical action to help others.

Street Pastors and Parish Nursing Ministries UK

Street Pastors	Parish Nursing Ministries UK
• An initiative started in London in 2003, by the Christian charity the Ascension Trust. • Adult volunteers are trained to patrol the streets in urban areas. • The main aim originally was to challenge gang culture and knife crime in London. • The focus then widened to responding to drunkenness, anti-social behaviour and fear of crime. • Street Pastors work closely with police and local councils. • They listen to people's problems, advise on where they might get help, and discourage anti-social behaviour. • A similar group called School Pastors was set up in 2011 to discourage illegal drug use, bullying and anti-social behaviour in schools.	• This Christian charity supports whole-person healthcare through the local church. • They provide churches with registered parish nurses, who promote well-being in body, mind and spirit among the local community. • The nurses help to provide early diagnosis of health problems. • They train and coordinate volunteers to help combat loneliness or provide support during times of crisis. • They give additional help to the NHS. • They encourage people to exercise and have a good diet. • They focus on the whole person, including listening to people and praying with them if asked. They also direct people to specific services if needed.

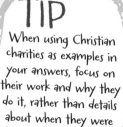
TIP
When using Christian charities as examples in your answers, focus on their work and why they do it, rather than details about when they were founded and by whom.

APPLY

(A) Explain **two** ways in which Street Pastors carry out their Christian duty.

Refer to Christian teaching in your answer. (AQA Specimen question paper, 2017)

(B) 'All Christians should do something practical to help their community, including praying for their neighbours.'

Develop two religious arguments in support of this statement, and **two** non-religious arguments against it.

RECAP

Essential information:

☐ A **mission** is a vocation or calling to spread the faith. The Church has a mission to tell non-believers that Jesus Christ, the Son of God, came into the world as its saviour.

☐ Christians spread the faith through **evangelism** (showing faith in Jesus by example or by telling others).

☐ They do this to fulfil Jesus' instructions to the disciples to spread his teachings (the **Great Commission**).

The Great Commission

> ❝Therefore go and make disciples of all nations, baptising them in the name of the Father and of the Son and of the Holy Spirit, and teaching them to obey everything I have commanded you. ❞
>
> *Matthew 28:19–20* [NIV]

TIP

You can use this quote in your exam to show what the Great Commission involves. Jesus instructs his disciples to baptise people and to spread his teachings.

- Jesus gave a Great Commission to his disciples to **spread the gospel** and **make disciples of all nations through baptism**.
- The **Holy Spirit** at Pentecost gave the disciples the gifts and courage needed to carry out the Great Commission.
- All Christians have a duty to spread the gospel and tell others of their faith, but some become **missionaries** or **evangelists** (people who promote Christianity, for example by going to foreign countries to preach or do charitable work).
- The aims of missionary work and evangelism are to **persuade people to accept Jesus as their Saviour**, and to extend the Church to all nations.

Alpha

- Alpha is an **example of evangelism in Britain**.
- It was started in London by an Anglican priest, with the aim of helping church members understand the basics of the Christian faith.
- The course is now used as an **introduction for those interested in learning about Christianity**, by different Christian denominations in Britain and abroad.
- The organisers describe it as 'an opportunity to explore the meaning of life' through talks and discussions.
- Courses are held in homes, workplaces, universities and prisons as well as in churches.

APPLY

 A Give **two** ways in which the Church tries to fulfil its mission.

 B **Unscramble the arguments** in the table below referring to the statement, 'Every Christian should be an evangelist.' Decide which arguments could be used to support the statement and which could be used against it.

Write a paragraph to explain whether you agree or disagree with the statement, having evaluated both sides of the argument.

1. If Christians don't help to spread the faith, it might die out.	4. Not every Christian should be an evangelist because some people are just too shy.
2. Some Christians live in countries where they are persecuted, so if they spoke in public about their faith they would be risking death or imprisonment.	5. All Christians have received the Great Commission from Jesus to preach to all nations.
3. Evangelism can happen in small ways, for example Christians can spread their faith to people they meet in everyday life or just give a good example of loving their neighbours.	6. Christians who go around evangelising can annoy people, so it does not help their cause.

RECAP

Essential information:

- [ ] Up to a third of the world's population claim to be Christian (including people who rarely attend church), and around 80,000 people become Christians each day.
- [ ] The Church expects new Christians to help spread the faith as part of their commitment to Jesus.
- [ ] Christ for all Nations is an example of a Christian organisation that promotes evangelism.

The growth of the Church

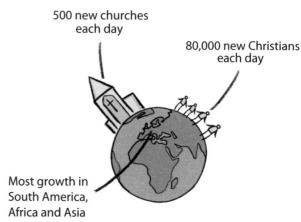

500 new churches each day

80,000 new Christians each day

Most growth in South America, Africa and Asia

- The Church is growing rapidly in South America, Africa and Asia, but not in the USA, Europe and the Middle East (where Christians have been persecuted).
- Worldwide around 80,000 people become Christians each day, and over 500 new churches are formed.
- The Church's mission is to make disciples, not just new believers. This means **new Christians are also expected to help spread the faith**.
- Evangelism should therefore be followed up by training new **converts** (people who decide to change their religious faith) in the way of following Jesus.
- Every Christian has a role in **encouraging fellow believers**. They might do this in the following ways.

advertising and using media (such as Facebook, Twitter or Premier Christian Radio)

sharing what God has done for them with others

Ways Christians can spread the faith

praying for others to accept God

inviting people to Christian meetings, fellowship meals and social events

Christ for all Nations

- Christ for all Nations is an example of a **Christian organisation promoting evangelism**. They do this by holding evangelistic meetings throughout the world, but particularly in Africa.
- They are led by the evangelists Richard Bonnke and Daniel Kolenda.
- Some of their large open-air rallies held in Africa have drawn crowds of up to 1.6 million people.
- It is claimed that many miracles of healing take place at the meetings.
- Christ for all Nations claims that 74 million people have filled in decision cards to follow Christ at their meetings.

APPLY

(A) Give **two** ways in which the Church gets its message to people.

(B) **Evaluate this argument** in response to the statement, 'Christians should just rely on evangelists for Church growth.' Explain your reasoning and suggest how you would improve the argument.

TIP

You will not be asked a specific question about Christ for all Nations in your exam, but being able to give examples of the work of Christian organisations or charities may be very helpful.

"Christians should not just rely on evangelists for Church growth because there are not that many specially trained evangelists to promote Christianity. People are more likely to be drawn to Christianity by the inspiration of someone they know, like a neighbour who is kind and considerate and demonstrates the love that Jesus taught."

RECAP

Essential information:

☐ The worldwide Church has a mission to restore people's relationship with God and with one another.

☐ The Church therefore plays an important role in **reconciliation** (restoring harmony after relationships have broken down), through initiatives to develop peace and understanding.

Working for reconciliation

- Christians believe humans were **reconciled to God** through Jesus' death and resurrection. This means Jesus' death and resurrection helped to **restore the relationship between God and humanity**, which had been broken by sin (see page 22).
- For Catholics, the **sacrament of Reconciliation** also helps to restore people's relationship with God.
- Matthew 5:23–24 teaches that Christians should be **reconciled to each other**.
- Reconciliation is therefore an **important part of the Church's work**. This might involve anything from trying to restore relationships between individual people, to working for peace between different religious groups or nations at conflict.

> **❝** For if, while we were God's enemies, we were reconciled to him through the death of his Son, how much more, having been reconciled, shall we be saved through his life! **❞**
>
> *Romans 5:10* [NIV]

TIP

You could use this quote in your exam to show that humanity's relationship with God was restored (or reconciled) through the death of Jesus.

Examples of organisations working for reconciliation

- The **Irish Churches Peace Project** brings Catholics and Protestants together in Northern Ireland.
- The project aims to develop peace and understanding between these two denominations.

- The **World Council of Churches** works for reconciliation between different Christian denominations and members of other faiths.
- For example, the Pilgrimage of Justice and Peace initiative supports inter-religious dialogue and cooperation.

- After the bombing of Coventry Cathedral in World War II, local Christians showed forgiveness to those responsible, and the cathedral became a world centre for peace and reconciliation.
- The cathedral is home to the **Community of the Cross of Nails**, which works with partners in other countries to bring about peace and harmony.

- The **Corrymeela Community** brings together people from different backgrounds, including people of different faiths or political leanings.
- They meet at a residential centre in Northern Ireland to build trust and explore ways of moving away from violence so they can work together constructively.

APPLY

(A) Give **two** examples of how the Church has helped to work towards reconciliation.

(B) 'Reconciliation to God is more important than reconciliation to other people.'

Develop this argument to support the statement by explaining in more detail, adding an example, or referring to a relevant religious teaching or quotation.

"Reconciliation to God is more important because God is the Supreme Being. God will judge us when we die and if we are not sorry for our sins we will not receive eternal life with God in heaven."

2.13 Christian persecution

Essential information:

- [ ] Christians have faced **persecution** (hostility and ill-treatment) from the beginning of the Church, and Christians are still persecuted worldwide today.

- [ ] For some Christians, persecution can have positive effects: it can strengthen their faith, allow them to share in Jesus' sufferings, and even inspire others to become Christian.

- [ ] The Church helps those who are persecuted through prayer, practical help and financial support, and by raising awareness of persecution and campaigning against it.

What is persecution?

- The International Society for Human Rights estimates 80% of all acts of religious discrimination today are aimed at Christians.
- This persecution happens around the world, but particularly in countries such as North Korea, Somalia, Iraq and Syria.
- It might involve:
    - being forced to pay extra tax
    - job discrimination
    - being forbidden to build churches
    - attacks on Christian homes, churches and families, including murder.

> **TIP**
> These examples of the kinds of persecution Christians face will be helpful if you need to give an explanation of persecution in your exam.

Some Christian Responses to persecution

Response	Supporting quote from scripture
• For some Christians, persecution can have a **positive effect**, as it strengthens their faith and conviction. • It also allows them to share in the suffering of Jesus.	"I want to know Christ – yes, to know the power of his resurrection and participation in his sufferings" (*Philippians 3:10*) This quote shows that one way Christians can get to know Jesus is by sharing in his suffering.
• The Church believes it is important to **act against persecution**, by supporting persecuted Christians wherever possible and campaigning on their behalf.	"If one part suffers, every part suffers with it" (*1 Corinthians 12:26*) This quote refers to the Church. It shows that helping individual Christians also helps the whole Church.
• Christians are **encouraged to show love and forgiveness** towards their persecutors.	"Do not be overcome by evil, but overcome evil with good" (*Romans 12:21*) This quote shows that Christians should respond to evil with love.

Some ways the Church has helped persecuted Christians

- Christians have smuggled Bibles into the USSR (Russia) to strengthen and give comfort to persecuted Christians.
- The Barnabas Fund sends money to support people persecuted for their faith.
- Christian Solidarity Worldwide campaigns for religious freedom for all.

A Give **two** ways in which Christians support those in countries where it is forbidden to follow Jesus.

B **Develop** one religious argument and one non-religious argument in response to the statement, 'It is not possible to "rejoice and be glad" if you are suffering persecution.'

> **TIP**
> 'Develop' means you need to add some detail to your argument, for example by explaining it more fully and giving examples.

2.14 The Church's response to world poverty

Essential information:

☐ Christian charities follow the example and teaching of Jesus in working to relieve poverty.

☐ Christians believe they should show Jesus to the world through helping the disadvantaged.

☐ Three Christian charities that help the poor are Christian Aid, Tearfund and CAFOD.

Helping those in poverty

Christians try to help those living in poverty because Jesus taught that this was important. For example:

- Jesus once told a rich man to sell everything and give to the poor (Mark 10:21).
- The parable of the Rich Man and Lazarus tells of a rich man who ends up in hell for ignoring a beggar.
- The parable of the Good Samaritan teaches the importance of helping all people.
- Jesus helped outcasts such as lepers, tax collector and sinners.

> **❝** If anyone has material possessions and sees a brother or sister in need but has no pity on them, how can the love of God be in that person? Dear children, let us not love with words or speech but with actions and in truth. **❞**   *1 John 3:17–18* [NIV]

> **TIP**
> You only need to know about one of these organisations for your exam.

Three Christian charities that help those in poverty are Christian Aid, Tearfund and CAFOD (Catholic Agency for Overseas Development). These charities:

Charity	Examples of their work
Christian Aid	• Supports projects to encourage sustainable development. • Provides emergency relief, such as food, water, shelter and sanitation. • Campaigns to end poverty alongside organisations such as the Fairtrade Foundation, Trade Justice and Stop Climate Chaos.
Tearfund	• Works with over 90,000 churches worldwide to help lift people out of poverty. • Supplies emergency aid after natural disasters and conflict. • Provides long-term aid to help communities become more self-reliant, such as education or new farming equipment. • Supported by donations, fundraising events and prayer from churches in the UK.
CAFOD	• Works with local organisations to train, supply and support communities to work their own way out of poverty. • Gives short-term aid such as food, water and shelter during conflicts and disasters. • Lobbies UK government and global organisations for decisions that respect the poorest. • Encourages Catholic schools and parishes to pray, give money and campaign for justice.

A Here are two ways in which a worldwide Christian relief organisation carries out its mission overseas. **Develop one of the points** by adding more detail and by referring to a relevant religious teaching or quotation.

> **TIP**
> Emergency aid gives help such as food, water and temporary shelter to people immediately after a disaster. In contrast, long-term aid tries to help people to become more self-sufficient over a longer period of time.

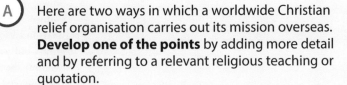

"One way that Christian Aid carries out its mission overseas is to provide emergency relief when there is a disaster."

"Another way they help is by setting up longer-term programmes that encourage sustainable development."

B **Write a paragraph** either supporting or against the statement, 'Religious charities should just concentrate on emergency aid.' Include a Christian teaching in your answer.

2 Exam practice

Test the 1 mark question

1. Which **one** of the following is a type of worship that follows a set pattern?

   [A] Informal worship
   [B] Private worship
   [C] Non-liturgical worship
   [D] Liturgical worship
   [1 mark]

2. Which **one** of the following is the festival that celebrates the incarnation of Jesus?

   [A] Easter
   [B] Good Friday
   [C] Christmas
   [D] Lent
   [1 mark]

Test the 2 mark question

3. Give **two** ways in which the Church responds to world poverty. **[2 marks]**

   1) _____

   2) _____

4. Give **two** reasons why prayer is important to Christians. **[2 marks]**

   1) _____

   2) _____

Test the 4 mark question

5. Explain **two** contrasting ways in which Christians worship. **[4 marks]**

● **Explain one way.**	Some Christians worship with other people in church on Sunday by going to a service called Holy Communion.
● Develop your explanation with more detail/an example/ reference to a religious teaching or quotation.	During the liturgy, they receive bread and wine that they believe is the body and blood of Jesus.
● **Explain a second contrasting way.**	Other Christians prefer informal worship, sometimes meeting in someone's home.
● Develop your explanation with more detail/an example/ reference to a religious teaching or quotation.	These Christians share their faith by reading and discussing a passage from scripture and praying together in their own words.

TIP
In this answer formal worship is contrasted with informal worship, but you could also contrast public worship with private worship or liturgical worship with charismatic worship.

6. Explain **two** contrasting ways in which Christians practise baptism. **[4 marks]**

● **Explain one way.**	
● Develop your explanation with more detail/an example/ reference to a religious teaching or quotation.	
● **Explain a second contrasting way.**	
● Develop your explanation with more detail/an example/ reference to a religious teaching or quotation.	

TIP
The question asks for different 'ways' in which Christians practise baptism, not different beliefs about baptism. The clearest contrast is between believers' baptism and infant baptism, but you should focus your answer on the way each of these is carried out, not what people believe about them.

7. Explain **two** contrasting interpretations of the meaning of Holy Communion. **[4 marks]**

2 Exam practice

Test the 5 mark question

8 Explain **two** ways that Christian charities help the poor in less economically developed countries.
Refer to sacred writings or another source of Christian belief and teaching in your answer. **[5 marks]**

● **Explain one way.**	One way that Christian charities help the poor in less economically developed countries is by providing emergency aid when there has been a natural disaster, like an earthquake or famine.
● Develop your explanation with more detail/an example.	For example, Tearfund, a Christian charity, was set up originally to provide emergency aid in response to the famine in Biafra, Nigeria, where it sent emergency food and clothing to refugees fleeing the famine-struck country.
● **Explain a second way.**	A second way that Christian charities help is by providing long-term aid that helps countries become self-sufficient or less dependent on aid.
● Develop your explanation with more detail/an example.	CAFOD, for example, works on development projects to give people access to education, healthcare, and clean water.
● Add a reference to sacred writings or another source of Christian belief and teaching. If you prefer, you can add this reference to your first belief instead.	These charities are inspired by Christian teachings such as the parable of the Rich Man and Lazarus, where Jesus taught that rich people who ignore the needs of the poor will be punished by God.

TIP
Here the student has used a parable from the bible. Another 'source of Christian belief and teaching' could be official statements or documents by leaders of the Church.

9 Explain **two** reasons why Christians practise evangelism.
Refer to sacred writings or another source of Christian belief and teaching in your answer. **[5 marks]**

● **Explain one reason.**	
● Develop your explanation with more detail/an example.	
● **Explain a second reason.**	
● Develop your explanation with more detail/an example.	
● Add a reference to sacred writings or another source of Christian belief and teaching. If you prefer, you can add this reference to your first teaching instead.	

TIP
It is helpful to start by explaining the meaning of 'evangelism' before explaining why Christians practise it.

10 Explain **two** ways that Christians may work for reconciliation.
Refer to sacred writings or another source of Christian belief and teaching in your answer. **[5 marks]**

2 Exam practice

Test the 12 mark question

11 'The most important duty of the Church is to help people in need.'

Evaluate this statement. In your answer you should:

- refer to Christian teaching
- give reasoned arguments to support this statement
- give reasoned arguments to support a different point of view
- reach a justified conclusion.

[12 marks]

REASONED ARGUMENTS IN SUPPORT OF THE STATEMENT ● **Explain why some people would agree with the statement.** ● Develop your explanation with more detail and examples. ● Refer to religious teaching. Use a quote or paraphrase or refer to a religious authority. ● **Evaluate the arguments.** Is this a good argument or not? Explain why you think this.	'The Church' in this statement clearly stands for the Christian believers and not the actual building. So what does the Bible say about the duty of Christians? Jesus taught his followers that helping those in need is extremely important and he showed he believed that by the way he acted. If he saw a person suffering from an illness he healed them. He touched lepers in order that they might be cured, even though it was something other people would not do because it was against the law and they feared catching leprosy. He gave sight to the blind, healed the crippled and even cast out evil spirits that were tormenting a naked madman. Jesus did this because he had compassion and pity on those he saw were in need. Jesus also showed in his teaching that Christians should help people in need. In the parable of the Good Samaritan it is the traveller who showed pity on the wounded man and helped him that is the hero of the story. Furthermore Jesus warns that those who do not help will face the anger of God on judgement day in the parable of the Sheep and the Goats. The sheep represented the people who helped and were given the reward of eternal life, but the goats did not and were thrown out of God's presence. So you could argue that it is the most important duty of the Church to help people who are in need.
REASONED ARGUMENTS SUPPORTING A DIFFERENT VIEW ● **Explain why some people would support a different view.** ● Develop your explanation with more detail and examples. ● Refer to religious teaching. Use a quote or paraphrase or refer to a religious authority. ● **Evaluate the arguments.** Is this a good argument or not? Explain why you think this.	On the other hand, Jesus summed up the duty for Christians and the Church in two commandments. He said that the first, most important commandment is to love God. The second is to love our neighbour as ourselves. If that is the case, then the most important duty of the Church (Christians) is to love and worship God, and this is more important than helping those in need.
CONCLUSION ● **Give a justified conclusion.** ● Include your own opinion together with your own reasoning. ● **Include evaluation.** Explain why you think one viewpoint is stronger than the other or why they are equally strong. ● Do not just repeat arguments you have already used without explaining how they apply to your reasoned opinion/conclusion.	In conclusion I would say that the statement is wrong and I would argue that the most important duty is to love God. The only way the Church can show love of God is by loving human beings who need help. So that is also important, but not the most important duty. It merely follows on from the most important duty.

TIP
The student has developed this argument by referring to the Bible. Although there are no direct quotations, the answer shows excellent knowledge of Jesus' actions and teaching and uses these to support the statement.

TIP
This argument could be developed further for more marks. For example, it could go into more detail about other important duties of the Church (such as preaching the gospel or administering the sacraments), and explain why these are equally or more important than helping people in need.

44

12 'The best way for Christians to grow closer to God is to go on a pilgrimage.'

Evaluate this statement. In your answer you should:

- refer to Christian teaching
- give reasoned arguments to support this statement
- give reasoned arguments to support a different point of view
- reach a justified conclusion.

TIP
Look for the key words in questions. Here it is 'best'. The answer should focus on whether or not a pilgrimage is the <u>best</u> way for Christians to grow closer to God or whether there are other ways that might be better.

[12 marks]

REASONED ARGUMENTS IN SUPPORT OF THE STATEMENT ● **Explain why some people would agree with the statement.** ● Develop your explanation with more detail and examples. ● Refer to religious teaching. Use a quote or paraphrase or refer to a religious authority. ● **Evaluate the arguments.** Is this a good argument or not? Explain why you think this.	
REASONED ARGUMENTS SUPPORTING A DIFFERENT VIEW ● **Explain why some people would support a different view.** ● Develop your explanation with more detail and examples. ● Refer to religious teaching. Use a quote or paraphrase or refer to a religious authority. ● **Evaluate the arguments.** Is this a good argument or not? Explain why you think this.	
CONCLUSION ● **Give a justified conclusion.** ● Include your own opinion together with your own reasoning. ● **Include evaluation.** Explain why you think one viewpoint is stronger than the other or why they are equally strong. ● Do not just repeat arguments you have already used without explaining how they apply to your reasoned opinion/conclusion.	

13 'A Christian's most important duty is to tell others about their faith.'

Evaluate this statement. In your answer you should:

- refer to Christian teaching
- give reasoned arguments to support this statement
- give reasoned arguments to support a different point of view
- reach a justified conclusion.

TIP
'To tell others about their faith' is the meaning of <u>evangelism</u>, which is part of a Christian's <u>mission</u>. Try to use these terms in your answer to show the depth of your understanding about this topic.

[12 marks]

Check your answers using the mark scheme on pages 162–163. How did you do?
To feel more secure in the content you need to remember, re-read pages 28–41.
To remind yourself of what the examiner is looking for, go to pages 6–11.

3.1 The birth of the Buddha and his life of luxury

RECAP

Essential information:

- [ ] The Buddha was born near the border of India and Nepal some 2500 years ago.
- [ ] Stories of his life combine facts with legends to express spiritual truths.
- [ ] He was born into a privileged life.

The Buddha's birth

- **Buddhism** is a religion founded around 2500 years ago by Siddhartha Gautama.
- Siddhartha was born around 500 BCE in southern Nepal. His parents were King Suddhodana and Queen Maya.
- After Siddhartha was enlightened he became known as the **Buddha**, which is a title meaning 'awakened one' or 'enlightened one'.
- There are many stories of Siddhartha's life, recording different events or details. These include legendary or miraculous events which communicate spiritual truths.

TIP

Use pictures to create a narrative of key events in the Buddha's life, to help you remember them.

The following traditional story is commonly told about Siddhartha's birth:

Queen Maya dreamed a white elephant came down from heaven and told her she would give birth to a holy child.	She gave birth to Siddhartha in the Lumbini Gardens, where she had stopped to rest on the way to her parents' house.	According to legend, Siddhartha: • could immediately walk and talk • walked seven steps and lotus flowers appeared under his feet • declared that he would not be reborn.	Shortly after his birth, a prophecy was made that Siddhartha would become a great king or a holy man.

Siddhartha's life of luxury

- Queen Maya died seven days after the birth of Siddhartha.
- King Suddhodana wanted to protect Siddhartha from hardship. Siddhartha grew up in a palace surrounded by luxury, and his father prepared him to become a king.
- The *Anguttara Nikaya* describes how he was 'delicately nurtured': he was entertained by female dancers, there were lotus ponds of many colours, he was always protected by a sunshade, and he had three mansions (one each for the winter, summer, and rainy seasons).

APPLY

(A) Give **two** ways in which Siddhartha lived a life of luxury. **Refer to sacred writings** in your answer.

(B) Read the following response to the statement, 'Stories of Siddhartha's early life cannot be accepted as being true.' **Explain how this answer could be improved.**

"We cannot believe the Buddha could immediately walk and talk when he was born, or that he took seven steps and lotuses popped up to cushion his feet. These stories are just made up to make the Buddha seem more impressive. There are many different stories that tell of the Buddha's life and they all have different details, which proves they can't all be true."

3.2 The four sights

Essential information:

- [ ] **The four sights** (old age, illness, death, and a holy man) inspired Siddhartha to renounce his life of luxury.

- [ ] The four sights can be seen as spiritual insights into the nature of suffering and the spiritual path.

- [ ] The four sights can be divided into two sections: the first three show a deepening awareness of the problem of suffering, while the fourth shows the solution.

What are the four sights?

- As he got older, Siddhartha grew more curious about life outside the palace walls.
- One day he decided to leave the palace grounds and travel with Channa, his attendant and chariot driver, to the nearby city.
- This story is found in *Jataka 75* (the **Jakata** tales are popular stories about the lives of the Buddha).
- Siddhartha encountered four sights while he was outside the palace:

Old age	Illness
Siddhartha saw a frail old man and realised that everyone will age.	Siddhartha saw someone lying in the road in agony and realised that illness is a reality of life. 

Death	A holy man
Siddhartha saw a dead man being carried through the streets in a funeral procession and realised that everyone will die. 	Siddhartha wanted answers to the problems of old age, illness and death. He saw a holy man walking through the streets with a peaceful expression. This inspired Siddhartha to believe that a spiritual answer to suffering was possible.

Leaving the palace

- Siddhartha realised he wouldn't find answers to the problem of suffering by living his life of luxury. Leaving the palace, he abandoned his horse, cut off his hair, and gave back his jewellery and comfortable clothes.
- Siddhartha left behind his newborn son and wife to pursue spiritual enlightenment.
- The four sights resulted in Siddhartha's renunciation. Renunciation means letting go and is an important aspect of the Buddhist life.

> **TIP**
> The first three sights communicate painful aspects of human life. They express the idea of dukkha or suffering. See page 52 to link this story with the idea of dukkha.

(A) Explain the importance of **two** of the four sights.

(B) 'Seeing the four sights was the most important event in the Buddha's life.'

Evaluate this statement using **two** arguments to support the statement and **two** arguments to support a different point of view.

3.3 The Buddha's ascetic life

Essential information:

- [ ] Siddhartha lived as an ascetic for six years to seek the solution to the problem of suffering.
- [ ] He concluded that asceticism by itself was not the path to spiritual wisdom and so stopped following ascetic practices.
- [ ] He began to think in terms of a 'middle way' between the extremes of indulgence and self-denial.

Living as an ascetic

Ascetics live a simple and strict lifestyle with few pleasures or possessions. They believe extreme self-discipline and self-denial can lead to spiritual wisdom.

Siddhartha was impressed by the sense of peace he felt coming from the holy man (who was an ascetic) before he left the palace. This inspired him to follow ascetic practices for six years to try to overcome the problem of suffering. He practised:

- living in dangerous and hostile forests which were too hot in the day and freezing at night
- sleeping on a bed of thorns
- eating so little that he looked like a skeleton.

Siddhartha also learnt meditation under the guidance of various masters. **Meditation** is the practice of calming and focusing the mind, and reflecting deeply on specific teachings to penetrate their true meaning.

> 66 When the Great Being was practising severe austerities for six years **it was to him like a time of intertwining the sky with knots.** 99
> *The Jataka, vol. 1, p. 67*

TIP
You could use this quote in your exam to show that for Siddhartha, asceticism did not provide the solution to suffering.

Turning away from asceticism

- As a result of his ascetic practices, Siddhartha became very thin and weak, and could not meditate effectively.
- He learnt discipline and willpower, but did not find the answer to the problem of suffering.
- He decided finally to reject asceticism as ineffective.
- He accepted rice and milk from a cowgirl and restored his health and strength.
- The *Jataka* describes how he then returned to the life of collecting alms from villagers.

Spiritual understanding

- Siddhartha had previously realised that a life of luxury was not the path towards spiritual wisdom.
- He now realised that suffering through self-denial was not the path either.
- This inspired him to follow a middle way between the two extremes.

> 66 Realising the practice of such austerities was not the path to Enlightenment he went about gathering alms in villages and townships. 99
> *The Jataka, vol. 1, p. 67*

(A) Give **two** ways in which Siddhartha practised asceticism.

(B) Here are some arguments that could be used to evaluate the statement, 'Siddhartha's asceticism was a necessary part of his path to enlightenment.' Sort them into arguments in support of this statement, and arguments in support of different views. **Write your own justified conclusion.**

1. Asceticism taught Siddhartha self-discipline	4. Asceticism was a waste of time because it did not provide an answer to suffering
2. He became too weak to meditate	5. Through asceticism Siddhartha learnt a middle way
3. He confronted his fears	6. He learnt various meditation techniques

RECAP

Essential information:

☐ After rejecting asceticism, Siddhartha thought meditation might help him to gain **enlightenment** (spiritual wisdom that arises from understanding the true nature of reality).

☐ Siddhartha meditated under a peepul tree (a kind of fig tree). Here he was tempted by **Mara** (a demon that represents spiritual obstacles, particularly temptation), who tried to prevent him from reaching enlightenment.

☐ His enlightenment took place during **the three watches of the night**, which refer to the three realisations that Siddhartha made in order to achieve enlightenment.

Siddhartha's meditation

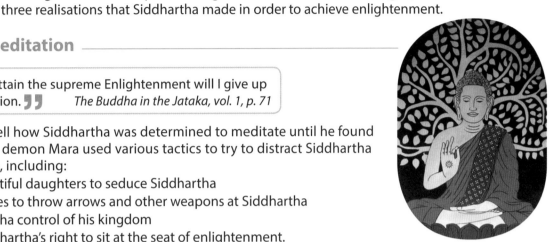

> 66 [...] not until I attain the supreme Enlightenment will I give up this seat of meditation. 99 *The Buddha in the Jataka, vol. 1, p. 71*

Traditional stories tell how Siddhartha was determined to meditate until he found enlightenment. The demon Mara used various tactics to try to distract Siddhartha from his meditation, including:

- sending his beautiful daughters to seduce Siddhartha
- sending his armies to throw arrows and other weapons at Siddhartha
- offering Siddhartha control of his kingdom
- questioning Siddhartha's right to sit at the seat of enlightenment.

In response, Siddhartha stayed focused on his meditation:

- He was not swayed by the charms of Mara's daughters but continued meditating.
- The arrows and other weapons turned to lotus flowers before reaching him.
- He touched and called on the earth to witness his right to sit at the seat of enlightenment. The earth shook to acknowledge his right.

TIP

The stories about Mara's temptations show that Siddhartha used his discipline to overcome negative emotions such as fear, lust and doubt to remain focused on his meditation.

The enlightenment

According to legend, Siddhartha's enlightenment took place during three parts (or 'watches') of the night:

First watch	Second watch	Third watch
• Siddhartha gained knowledge of all his previous lives.	• He understood the repetitive cycle of birth, death, and rebirth. • He understood how beings are reborn according to their kamma or actions (see page 75). • He understood that nothing has an unchanging essence (anatta) (see page 54).	• He understood that beings suffer because of desire and attachment (see page 57). • He understood that suffering can be overcome through the path to enlightenment (see page 59).

After he became enlightened, Siddhartha:

- became known as the Buddha (the enlightened or awakened one)
- taught his spiritual wisdom to **the five ascetics**, who became his first disciples
- asked his followers to choose a middle way between the two extremes of luxury and asceticism.

TIP

Some questions in the exam will require you to combine your knowledge from different topics. Here you could refer to material from other sections to fill out your picture of enlightenment.

APPLY

Ⓐ Give **two** ways in which Mara tried to distract Siddhartha from enlightenment.

Ⓑ 'The Buddha's enlightenment can be best described as a state of knowledge.'

Develop one argument to support this statement and one argument against it. Then **write a conclusion** where you decide whether you agree with the statement or not and explain your reasons why.

3.5 The Dhamma

Essential information:

☐ **Dhamma** (or Dharma) refers to the truth the Buddha realised when he became enlightened, and to the path of training he recommended.

☐ The Dhamma is one of the three refuges, which are the central values in a Buddhist's life.

☐ The Dhamma is important to Buddhists as they believe by following it they will reduce their own suffering and the suffering of others.

What is the Dhamma?

Dhamma generally refers to **the Buddha's teachings,** but it also has the following meanings:

The 'truth' about the nature of existence, as understood by the Buddha when he became enlightened.	The path of training the Buddha recommended for anyone who wants to get closer to enlightenment.	A universal 'law' that governs how reality works, i.e. the way that things are.

In his book *Old Path White Clouds*, the monk Thich Nhat Hanh tells how the Buddha thought of his teachings as something to be practised but not to be worshipped or held on to. In this sense his teachings are like a raft used to cross the river: it is necessary for crossing the river itself (or for reaching enlightenment), but a person should not become so attached to the raft that they cannot leave it behind once they reach the other shore.

The Buddha described his insights into reality as the 'truth', but still encouraged his followers to test and question his teachings themselves.

The importance of the Dhamma

- There are three refuges (or jewels) in Buddhism: the Buddha, the Dhamma, and the Sangha (the Buddhist community).
- For a Buddhist, the three jewels are the **central values** in their life. A Buddhist could be defined as someone who goes for refuge to the three jewels. This means trusting the three jewels as **sources of relief from suffering**.
- In Buddhist rituals it is common to recite the three refuges. They are also recited in the ceremony where a person becomes a Buddhist.

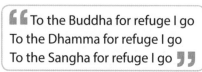
❝ To the Buddha for refuge I go
To the Dhamma for refuge I go
To the Sangha for refuge I go ❞

TIP
A Buddhist might use these words when reciting the three refuges. You could use this quote in your exam to show that the Dhamma is important to Buddhists because it is a 'refuge' from suffering.

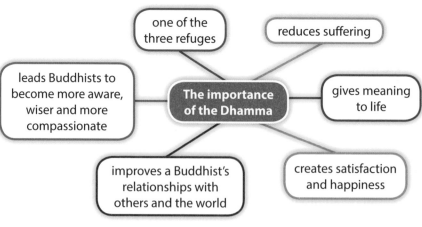

one of the three refuges

reduces suffering

leads Buddhists to become more aware, wiser and more compassionate

The importance of the Dhamma

gives meaning to life

improves a Buddhist's relationships with others and the world

creates satisfaction and happiness

A Give **two** ways in which Buddhists understand the term 'Dhamma'.

B **Evaluate** this argument in response to the statement, 'The Dhamma is the most important of the three refuges.'

"The Dhamma is the most important refuge because it is the raft or the means to enlightenment, which is the goal of Buddhism. In addition, it does not depend on the Buddha but can be discovered by anyone at any time. By practising the Dhamma, Buddhists gain meaning, purpose and happiness in their lives."

3.6 The concept of dependent arising

RECAP

Essential information:

☐ **Dependent arising** is the idea that everything arises in dependence upon conditions.

☐ Dependent arising is illustrated in the Tibetan Wheel of Life and other Buddhist teachings.

☐ It expresses the Buddhist view or vision of the nature of reality.

What it dependent arising?

- Dependent arising is the idea that **everything depends on supporting conditions**: nothing is independent.
- Dependent arising also means that everything is in a **constant process of change**, because everything is dependent on conditions which are themselves continually changing.

> ❝ All events and incidents in life are so intimately linked with the fate of others that a single person on his or her own cannot even begin to act. ❞
> *Tenzin Gyatso (the Dalai Lama)*

Example 1	Example 2	Example 3
• A **tree** depends on soil, rain and sunshine to survive. • These conditions change as the weather changes. 	• A **wave** depends on how strong the wind is, which is always changing. ❝ [A wave] is something made temporarily possible by wind and water, and […] is dependent on a set of constantly changing circumstances […] **every wave is related to every other wave.** ❞ *Sogyal Rinpoche*	• **Kamma** is an example of dependent arising that shows how someone's happiness and suffering depend on conditions, especially their previous actions (see page 75). • The type of world a person is born into in their next life (for instance, human, animal or heavenly being) depends on their kamma.

The Tibetan Wheel of Life

- **The Tibetan Wheel of life** is an image that illustrates dependent arising as applied to the birth, death and rebirth of beings (**samsara**).
- The outer wheel shows 12 links or stages (**nidanas**). These illustrate how human beings are subject to birth, death and rebirth.
- This process of birth, death and rebirth continues for many lifetimes until the cycle is broken by following the Buddhist path.
- When the cycle is broken (particularly by breaking free from the habit of craving – see page 57), this allows the possibility of **nibbana** (liberation and a state of complete enlightenment, happiness and peace).

APPLY

Ⓐ Give **two** examples which show dependent arising.

Ⓑ **Develop** this argument to support the statement, 'Dependent arising is the essence of the Buddha's teaching.'

"Dependent arising is very important as it is what the Buddha understood in his enlightenment, and it underpins all other Buddhist teachings."

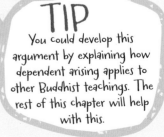

TIP
You could develop this argument by explaining how dependent arising applies to other Buddhist teachings. The rest of this chapter will help with this.

3.7 The three marks of existence: dukkha

Essential information:

☐ Buddhism draws attention to three aspects of experience: suffering (dukkha), impermanence (anicca), and having no permanent, fixed self or soul (anatta). These are **the three marks of existence**.

☐ **Dukkha** means suffering, dissatisfaction or unsatisfactoriness.

☐ Buddhism teaches that dukkha is an inevitable part of life, but can be overcome by attaining enlightenment.

What is dukkha?

- Buddhism teaches that suffering is an **inevitable part of life**.
- The main reason why the Buddha left his life of luxury in the palace was to discover an answer to the problem of suffering.
- Buddhists try to reduce suffering through following the Buddha's teachings. They believe that when they finally achieve enlightenment they will no longer suffer.
- The Buddha taught that there are **seven states of suffering**, of which four are physical and three are mental:

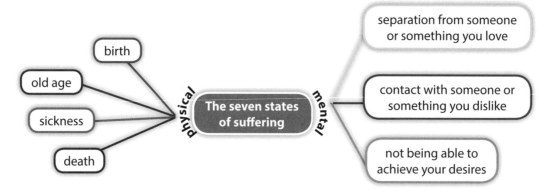

birth · old age · sickness · death — physical

The seven states of suffering

mental — separation from someone or something you love · contact with someone or something you dislike · not being able to achieve your desires

> " […] what I teach is suffering and the cessation of suffering. " *The Buddha in the Majjhima Nikaya, vol. 1, p. 140*

Different types of suffering

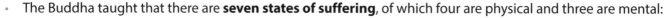

As well as the seven states of suffering, the Buddha also talked about three different kinds of suffering:

Type of suffering	Meaning	Examples
Ordinary suffering (dukkha-dukkhata)	Physical and mental pain	Breaking a leg, missing someone, being upset at failing an exam.
Suffering because of change (viparinama-dukkha)	Caused by losing something good	Getting older, moving to a new city, the weather turning bad.
Suffering because of attachment (samkhara-dukkha)	Dissatisfaction with life as a result of craving and attachment	Trying to hold on to things a person is attached to. Always present as a dissatisfaction with life; feeling unhappy for no reason.

(A) Give **one** example of ordinary suffering and **one** example of suffering because of change.

(B) **Develop** the following argument to oppose the statement, 'Emphasising suffering makes Buddhism seem pessimistic.'

"While Buddhism emphasises the inevitability of suffering, the aim is not to cause depression but to help people wake up and see that they and others are suffering."

TIP
To develop this argument you could explain why Buddhists believe it is important to accept suffering as a fact of life (see page 56). You could also explain how Buddhists aim to reduce suffering and eventually overcome it altogether (see page 59).

3.8 The three marks of existence: anicca

Essential information:

☐ **Anicca** means impermanence. It refers to the idea that everything constantly changes.

☐ Buddhism teaches that suffering arises when people resist change because they are too attached to things.

☐ Awareness of anicca leads to the letting go of attachment and so lessens suffering.

What is anicca?

Anicca affects the world in three different ways:

What is affected	Example
Living things	A tree sprouts from a seed, grows, and eventually dies
Non-living things	An iron nail will rust if left out in the rain
People's minds	A person's thoughts and feelings change throughout their lives

The relationship between anicca and dukkha

Buddhism teaches that when people expect things to remain unchanged, they become attached to them. Therefore when things do change (anicca), people experience suffering (dukkha) as a result of their attachment. For example:

Desire: New mobile phone → **Action:** Purchase a phone thinking it will bring happiness → **Consequence:** Temporary happiness → **Impermanence:** Drop mobile phone in the toilet by accident → **Result:** Suffering

Awareness of impermanence helps to overcome attachment (and therefore reduces suffering). For example:

Desire: New mobile phone → **Reflection:** Mobile phones are subject to change and may break → **Consequence:** Purchase with awareness of impermanence → **Impermanence:** Drop mobile phone in the toilet by accident → **Result:** Disappointment that is soon overcome due to awareness of impermanence

The story of Kisa Gotami teaches about suffering because of anicca. This is a traditional Buddhist story that can be found in the *Therigatha*. The main events in the story are as follows:

- Kisa Gotami's child died at a young age, and she went out of her mind with sorrow.
- The Buddha told her she should visit all the houses in the village and ask for a mustard seed from any house in which no one had died.
- She could not find a house where no one had died.
- Eventually she realised that death is inescapable and buried her child.

APPLY

Ⓐ Explain **two** Buddhist teachings about impermanence. **Refer to scripture or sacred writings** in your answer.

Ⓑ Here is an argument to support the statement, 'Impermanence causes suffering.' **Write an argument** to support another view.

"Impermanence causes suffering because everything changes and, because of our attachment to things, we don't want that to happen. We cling on to things and so, when they change, we suffer. For instance, I love my mobile phone and if it were to break I would suffer a lot."

TIP
When Kisa Gotami realised that death (a result of anicca) is something that everyone has to experience, her suffering became more bearable. You could use this story in your exam as an example of how an awareness of impermanence helps to reduce suffering.

3.9 The three marks of existence: anatta

Essential information:

☐ **Anatta** is the idea that people do not have a fixed self or soul. This means there is no unchanging essence to the human being that is permanent or eternal.

☐ The Buddha taught that a person is made up of five aspects, called **the five aggregates** (skandhas). These show how there is no unchanging self.

What is anatta?

The Buddha taught that there is no fixed part of a person that does not change. This idea of anatta is illustrated in the story of Nagasena and the chariot:

- One day a monk called Nagasena arrived at the court of King Milinda.
- The king asked Nagasena what his name was.
- Nagasena answered but said there was no person behind the name.
- The king was confused and asked who then was standing before him.
- Nagasena answered using the analogy of the chariot:
  - A chariot is made up from a number of different parts.
  - The term 'chariot' is a name used to refer to all of these parts.
  - There is no chariot independent of its parts.
  - Likewise, a person exists but only because of the parts they are made up from.
  - There is no separate 'self' that is independent to these parts.

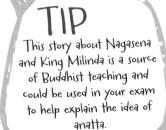

TIP
This story about Nagasena and King Milinda is a source of Buddhist teaching and could be used in your exam to help explain the idea of anatta.

The five aggregates

Buddhists divide the 'self' into five parts (the five aggregates or skandhas) to show there is no unchanging essence or core to a person. The Buddha taught that as these parts are constantly changing, the 'self' is also constantly changing.

Aggregate	Meaning	Example
Form	Our bodies	My knee
Sensation	Our feelings	My knee hurts
Perception	Our ways of interpreting and understanding things	My knee hurts because I bashed it against the door
Mental formations	Our thoughts	I want my knee to stop hurting; I don't like it
Consciousness	Our general awareness of things	Awareness of my knee

TIP
The five aggregates are discussed in more detail on page 60.

The five aggregates are discussed in more detail on page 60.

APPLY

Ⓐ Explain **two** of the five aggregates.

Ⓑ **Evaluate** this argument to support the statement, 'Anatta shows that nothing has a fixed self.'

"Anatta means that nothing really exists because we don't see things properly. We think we do but really we don't. Everything is just in our mind and not really there. We are kind of making it all up. Buddhism talks about five things that show this and one of them is the body, which doesn't really exist either. There was a monk who talked to a king about this."

3.10 An introduction to the Four Noble Truths

RECAP

Essential information:

☐ **The Four Noble Truths** are the four truths the Buddha taught about suffering. They explain why people suffer and how they can overcome it.

☐ The Four Noble Truths are part of the Dhamma (see page 50), and said to be the Buddha's first teaching after his enlightenment.

☐ Full understanding of the Four Noble Truths leads to enlightenment for Theravada Buddhists.

What are the Four Noble Truths?

The Four Noble Truths were discovered by the Buddha while he was meditating under the peepul tree (see page 49). The Four Noble Truths are:

TIP
The Four Noble Truths apply the concept of dependent arising (see page 51) to the experience of suffering. They show how suffering arises in dependence on conditions and how suffering can end.

1. There is suffering **dukkha**

2. Suffering has a cause **samudaya**

3. Suffering can come to an end **nirodha**

4. There is a means to bring suffering to an end **magga**

The Four Noble Truths are sometimes explained using the idea of illness, where the Buddha is compared to a doctor:

| A doctor establishes that you have an **illness** (the first noble truth) | → | He finds the **cause** of the illness (the second noble truth) | → | He tells you there is a **cure** for the illness (the third noble truth) | → | Undergoing the **treatment** makes you feel better (the fourth noble truth) |

> ❝The truth of suffering is like a disease, the truth of origin is like the cause of the disease, the truth of cessation is like the cure of the disease, and the truth of the path is like the medicine.❞ *The Visuddhimagga, p. 512*

suffering / the Buddha / 8 fold path / medicine

- Buddhists aim to come to understand the Four Noble Truths through study, reflection, meditation and other practices.
- For Theravada Buddhists (see page 60), understanding the Four Noble Truths leads to enlightenment.
- In Mahayana Buddhism (see page 61), other teachings such as the development of compassion are also very important in addition to understanding the Four Noble Truths.

TIP
The 'cure' to overcome suffering is the Eightfold Path – see page 59.

APPLY

A **Explain** how the Four Noble Truths can be compared to the idea of a doctor treating an illness.

B Here are some arguments that could be used to evaluate the statement, 'The Four Noble Truths are the most important Buddhist teaching.' Sort them into arguments in support of the statement, and arguments in support of different views. **Write your own justified conclusion.**

1. The Buddha taught the Four Noble Truths in his first sermon	5. They seem rather pessimistic
2. Compassion is also important for enlightenment	6. Dependent arising is the most important teaching
3. Understanding the Four Noble Truths leads to nibbana	7. The Eightfold Path is the way to enlightenment
4. The Four Noble Truths don't include anatta	8. The second noble truth shows why we suffer

RECAP

Essential information:

☐ The first noble truth is that suffering (dukkha) exists and it is something everyone experiences.

☐ Buddhism teaches that accepting suffering is a part of life is the first step to overcoming it.

How do we respond to suffering?

Buddhism teaches the following about suffering and how to respond to it:

- Suffering is universal – it affects everyone at some point in their lives.
- So suffering is a problem that everyone needs to overcome.

- There are also many different types of happiness and pleasures that everyone can experience.
- But even though these are real they are also impermanent.

- For example, Megan feels sad because she was made fun of at school.
- She goes to the cinema to cheer herself up.
- But the happiness is only temporary, and afterwards she remembers what happened and feels sad again.

- It is easier to accept suffering is a part of life by trying not to personalise it.
- Instead of thinking, 'Why must I suffer?', a person should just recognise that there is suffering.

> ❝The insight is simply […] that there is this suffering without making it personal. ❞
> *Ajahn Sumedho*

- Part of dealing effectively with suffering is recognising that it is a part of life, instead of trying to run away from it.
- This is the first noble truth.

- Because happiness and pleasures are only temporary distractions, they cannot ultimately solve the problem of suffering.

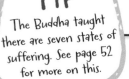
TIP
The Buddha taught there are seven states of suffering. See page 52 for more on this.

Suffering and happiness

- Some people think that to focus on suffering is pessimistic.
- Buddhists would say the Buddha's teachings are not pessimistic but realistic, as suffering affects everyone at some point in their lives.
- Buddhism also teaches that suffering *does* have an end, which can be reached by following the Buddhist path.
- Buddhists feel that reflecting on suffering helps people to understand what it truly important and to connect with others.

APPLY

Ⓐ Give **two** ways in which beliefs about dukkha influence Buddhists today.

Ⓑ **Prepare an essay plan** that includes arguments to support and oppose the statement, 'Seeking pleasure is not the solution to suffering.' In your plan include:

- arguments to support this statement
- arguments to support a different point of view
- reference to Buddhist teachings
- a justified conclusion.

TIP
Writing a series of bullet points is one way to create an essay plan.

RECAP

Essential information:

☐ The second noble truth explains why people suffer. It teaches that one of the main causes of suffering is **tanha** (craving).

☐ **The three poisons** of greed, hatred and ignorance keep people trapped in the cycle of samsara and prevent them from overcoming suffering.

☐ Buddhism teaches that understanding why people suffer is important if suffering is to be reduced.

The concept of tanha

Tanha means craving (wanting or desiring something). The Buddha taught there are three main types of craving:

1. Sensory craving	**2. Craving for being**	**3. Craving for non-being**
• Craving things that please the senses	• Wanting to become something you are not	• Wanting to stop experiencing something
• E.g. craving pleasant smells or tasty foods	• E.g. craving to become smart, attractive or successful	• E.g. not wanting to feel pain or embarrassment

- Buddhism teaches that people suffer because they become attached to things they like.
- But the things they like are impermanent, so will change or disappear.
- As a result, attachment leads to suffering.
- The temporary pleasures that people crave cannot last or make them feel permanently happy.

> 66 Now this [...] is the noble truth of the origin of suffering: **it is this craving which leads to renewed existence** [...] craving for sensual pleasures, craving for existence, craving for extermination. 99
> *The Buddha in the Samyutta Nikaya, vol. 5, p. 421*

Suffering and the three poisons

Buddhism teaches that people are driven by the three poisons:

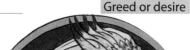

- **greed or desire** (represented by a cockerel)
- **hatred or anger** (represented by a snake)
- **ignorance** (represented by a pig).

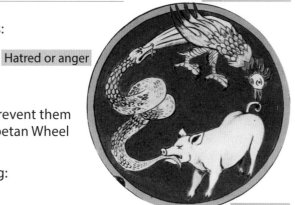

Greed or desire

Hatred or anger

Ignorance

These three poisons trap people in the cycle of samsara and prevent them from achieving enlightenment. They sit in the centre of the Tibetan Wheel of Life and keep it turning.

The Buddha taught that the three poisons are linked to craving:

- Craving **leads to greed and hatred**.
- Craving is also **rooted in ignorance**. Ignorance is not simply a lack of general knowledge, but a deeper ignorance about the world and the nature of reality. It is a kind of deliberately ignoring the truth of the way things are.
- Because people do not wake up to the truth of things (the three marks of existence), they continue spinning round the Wheel of Life and continue to suffer.

TIP

The Tibetan Wheel of Life is an image that symbolises the repeating cycle of birth, life, death and rebirth. See page 51 for more on this.

APPLY

Ⓐ Give **two** ways in which beliefs about craving influence Buddhists today.

Ⓑ 'Buddhism teaches that all desire leads to suffering.'

Using bullet points, **prepare some notes** to oppose this statement.

RECAP

Essential information:

☐ The third noble truth is that there is an end to suffering, which anyone is capable of achieving.

☐ The third noble truth teaches that suffering can be ended by overcoming craving and ignorance.

☐ When a person overcomes suffering they become enlightened and reach **nibbana**, which is a state of complete freedom, happiness and peace.

Overcoming craving and ignorance

The third noble truth teaches that a person can end their suffering through their own actions and efforts. This is important for Buddhists because it means it is possible for anyone to overcome suffering and achieve happiness.

The third noble truth teaches that suffering can be ended by **overcoming craving and ignorance**:

- People suffer because of their **craving and attachment** to things that are impermanent.
- This doesn't mean people should just avoid the things they enjoy.
- Instead they should enjoy things but recognise they can't last, and be ready to let go of them.
- **Ignorance** makes people think that impermanent pleasures are sources of complete fulfilment.
- But by **overcoming this ignorance** – by realising that temporary pleasures cannot bring true happiness – people can **overcome their craving** for these pleasures.
- This helps them to end their suffering.

> ❝ […] the noble truth of the cessation of suffering […] is the remainderless **fading away and cessation of that same craving**. ❞
> *The Buddha in the Samyutta Nikaya, vol. 5, p. 421*

Interpretations of nibbana or enlightenment

- Nibbana literally means 'extinction'. It refers to the **extinction of the three poisons** (or three fires) of greed, hatred and ignorance.
- Nibbana also refers to a **state of complete liberation, peace and happiness**. This is reached when a person becomes enlightened.
- Another word for enlightenment is 'bodhi', which means 'awakening' – like waking up from a sleep. It also refers to a state of knowing.
- A Buddha is someone who has **woken up to the truth of existence**. Through becoming enlightened, they have achieved the characteristics shown in the diagram on the right.

is completely free of the three poisons

understands and lives in harmony with the four noble truths

knows the truth about the nature of existence

naturally behaves according to the five moral precepts

knows exactly what causes suffering

APPLY

(A) Which Buddhist word means extinction and refers to enlightenment?

(B) 'Non-attachment means not caring about anything.'

Evaluate the following argument. Then note down the arguments you would use to oppose this point of view.

"Buddhism says desire is bad because it leads to suffering. For instance, if I eat an ice cream, I suffer. So you have to stop liking things which means not to be attached. Then you don't suffer and reach nibbana."

> **TIP**
> Try to learn the key Buddhist terms (such as 'enlightenment' and 'nibbana') so you can use them in your answers to demonstrate your knowledge.

> **TIP**
> Remember that while most Buddhists believe the Buddha knew the truth about the nature of existence, they do not believe he gained knowledge of <u>everything</u> when he became enlightened. This would imply he was omniscient and had supernatural powers, which most Buddhists do not think is true.

RECAP

Essential information:

☐ The fourth noble truth is a series of practices that Buddhists can follow to overcome suffering.

☐ This is known as the middle path or middle way, as the Buddha taught that people should lead a moderate life between the two extremes of luxury and asceticism.

☐ The path consists of eight practices (the Eightfold Path) that are sometimes grouped into three sections (the threefold way).

The Eightfold Path and the threefold way

• **The Eightfold Path** consists of eight aspects that Buddhists practise and live by in order to achieve enlightenment.
• The Eightfold Path is sometimes split into three different sections (ethics, meditation and wisdom), which make up **the threefold way**.
• The Eightfold Path can be understood as a range of practices that can all be developed at the same time, as they are all interlinked and reinforce each other.

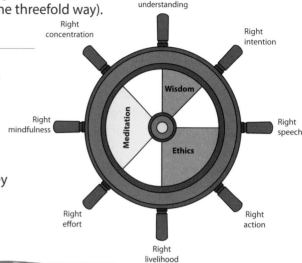

> ❝ But if any one goes to the Buddha, the Doctrine and the Order as a refuge, he perceives with proper knowledge the four noble truths: Suffering, the arising of suffering, and the overcoming of suffering, and the noble eightfold path leading to the cessation of suffering. ❞
> *The Buddha in the Dhammapada, verses 190–191*

TIP
Make sure you understand this quote. It refers to the three refuges (see page 50) and the Four Noble Truths (see pages 55–59). It essentially says that if someone follows the three refuges (including the Buddha's teachings), they will come to understand the Four Noble Truths. This will end their suffering.

Section of the threefold way	Aspect of the Eightfold Path	Explanation
Ethics (sila) Emphasises the importance of having good morals and behaviour, and living in an ethical way.	Right speech	Speaking truthfully, helpfully and kindly. Avoiding lying and gossiping about others.
	Right action	Practising the five moral precepts (especially not causing harm to others).
	Right livelihood	Earning a living in a way that does not harm others (e.g. not doing work that exploits people or harms animals).
Meditation (samadhi) Emphasises the importance of meditating effectively in order to develop wisdom.	Right effort	Putting effort into developing and sustaining skilful mental states.
	Right mindfulness	Developing awareness of yourself and the world around you.
	Right concentration	Developing the concentration and focus that is required to meditate effectively.
Wisdom (panna) Emphasises the importance of overcoming ignorance in order to achieve enlightenment.	Right understanding	Developing a clear understanding of the Buddha's teachings, especially the Four Noble Truths.
	Right intention	Following the Eightfold Path with the correct intention and a sincere attitude.

APPLY

(A) Two elements of the threefold way are meditation and wisdom.

Referring to Buddhist teaching, **explain** how these can be linked to the Eightfold Path.

(B) 'The Eightfold Path is the most important of the Four Noble Truths.'

Prepare **one** developed argument either for or against this statement.

TIP
Remember that a developed argument includes a statement or opinion, and some further explanation or examples to support that opinion.

RECAP

Essential information:

☐ **Theravada Buddhism** is one of the oldest schools of Buddhism, practised mainly in southern Asia.

☐ Theravada Buddhism teaches that the human personality is made up of five parts or aggregates: form, sensation, perception, mental formations and consciousness.

Theravada Buddhism

Some of the main characteristics of Theravada Buddhism include the following:

- Ordination in the monastic community is emphasised.
- Full ordination is primarily reserved for men (see page 145).
- The Buddha is a focus of worship and is seen as the teacher and guide, but is not considered to be a god.
- The goal is to achieve enlightenment and reach nibbana.
- Some Theravada Buddhists believe that good fortune (or merit) may be transferred to others. This practice is emphasised when someone has died (see page 73).

The human personality in Theravada Buddhism

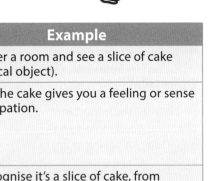

- Theravada Buddhism teaches that people are made up of five parts, called **the five aggregates**.
- These interact with each other to make up a person's identity and personality.
- The purpose of thinking about a person in this way is to help understand that nothing has a fixed, unchanging nature (see page 54).
- These categories also aid understanding of the processes of sense perception, craving, and how people form habits.

Aggregate	Explanation	Example
Form	• A person's body, or **objects in the world** (including other people).	You enter a room and see a slice of cake (a physical object).
Sensation	• The **feelings or sensations** that occur when people come into contact with things. • Can be physical (e.g. a sensation of pain after tripping over) or emotional (e.g. feeling joy after seeing a friend).	Seeing the cake gives you a feeling or sense of anticipation.
Perception	• How people **recognise (or perceive) what things are**, based on their previous experiences.	You recognise it's a slice of cake, from having seen other slices of cake in the past.
Mental formations	• **Thoughts and opinions** – how a person responds mentally to the things they experience. • Includes likes and dislikes, and a person's attitude towards different things.	You form an opinion about whether or not you want to eat the cake.
Consciousness	• A person's **general awareness** of the world around them.	Your underlying awareness of all of the above processes.

APPLY

A Using examples, **explain** the differences between 'sensation' and 'mental formations'.

B 'The idea that people consist of five aggregates is the most useful Buddhist teaching to help explain the concept of anatta.'

Develop one argument to support this statement and one argument to support a different point of view.

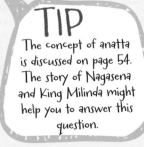

TIP

The concept of anatta is discussed on page 54. The story of Nagasena and King Milinda might help you to answer this question.

3.16 Mahayana Buddhism

Essential information:

- [ ] **Mahayana Buddhism** is a term used to describe a number of different Buddhist traditions that share some overlapping characteristics. It includes Pure Land Buddhism, Zen Buddhism and Tibetan Buddhism.

- [ ] Mahayana Buddhism emphasises the teaching of **sunyata** (emptiness): the idea that nothing has a separate, independent 'self' or 'soul'.

- [ ] **Buddha-nature** is also important in some Mahayana traditions. This is the idea that everyone has the essence of the Buddha inside them.

Sunyata

- Sunyata (emptiness) is an important concept in Mahayana Buddhism.
- It is a restatement of anatta (see page 54), but applies to all things rather than just human beings.
- It teaches that **nothing has a fixed, independent, unchanging nature**. Everything exists in relation to, or because of, other things.
- For Buddhists, realising that everything depends on everything else can lead to trust, compassion and selflessness.

Example: the empty laptop

- A laptop does not have a 'soul' – a separate, independent bit that forms the essence of the laptop.
- Instead, the word 'laptop' is just a name given to a collection of parts.
- These parts all rely on each other in order for the laptop to function.
- The laptop is impermanent: one of the parts will eventually break down and, because the other parts rely on it to function properly, the laptop will stop working.
- The laptop has the nature of sunyata (empty of independent existence).

Buddha-nature and attaining Buddhahood

Buddha-nature is an important concept in some Mahayana traditions. It refers to the following teaching:

Everyone has the essence (or nature) of a Buddha already inside them.	A person's Buddha-nature is hidden by desires, attachments, ignorance and negative thoughts.	When a person truly comes to understand the Buddha's teachings, they experience their inner Buddha-nature.

The *Uttaratantra Shastra* uses the following metaphor: Buddha-nature is like honey surrounded by a swarm of bees. The honey is sweet and tasty, but as long as it is surrounded by bees it isn't possible to eat it, even though it's been there all the time. The only way to experience the honey is to get rid of the bees.

Mahayana Buddhists aim to achieve **Buddhahood**: to become Buddhas (enlightened beings). They believe everyone has the potential to do this became of their inherent Buddha-nature.

A Which term in Mahayana Buddhism refers to the potential of all people to become Buddhas?

B 'Sunyata is a different idea from anatta.'

Develop one argument to oppose this statement.

3.17 The Arhat and the Bodhisattva

Essential information:

☐ Theravada and Mahayana Buddhism have different ideas of the ideal Buddhist.

☐ A Theravada Buddhist aims to become an Arhat by following the Eightfold Path.

☐ A Mahayana Buddhist aims to become a Bodhisattva by developing six spiritual qualities (the six perfections).

Becoming an Arhat

- An **Arhat** is a 'perfected person' who has overcome the main sources of suffering – the three poisons – to become enlightened.
- When someone becomes an Arhat, they are **no longer reborn when they die**.
- They become free from the cycle of birth, death and rebirth (samsara) to reach nibbana.
- This goal is achieved by **following and fulfilling the Eightfold Path** (see page 59).
- It is said that many of the Buddha's disciples became Arhats.

Becoming a Bodhisattva

- A **Bodhisattva** sees their own enlightenment as being bound up with the enlightenment of all beings.
- Out of compassion, after they achieve enlightenment, they **choose to remain in the cycle of samsara** to help others achieve enlightenment too.
- Bodhisattvas combine **being compassionate with being wise**. They believe the original emphasis of the Buddha's teachings was to 'go forth for the welfare of the many'.

> ❝ However innumerable sentient beings are; **I vow to save them.** ❞ *A Bodhisattva vow*

A person becomes a Bodhisattva by practising the six perfections:

Attribute	Aim
Generosity	To be charitable and generous in all that is done
Morality	To live ethically by following the moral precepts
Patience	To practise being patient in all things
Energy	To cultivate the energy and perseverance needed to keep going
Meditation	To develop concentration and awareness
Wisdom	To obtain wisdom and understanding

TIP
The six perfections are discussed in more detail on page 79.

Mahayana Buddhists believe there are **earthly and transcendent Bodhisattvas**:

- Earthly Bodhisattvas continue to be reborn into the world, to live on earth and help others.
- Transcendent Bodhisattvas are purely spiritual beings beyond time and space. They may appear in different forms in the world, to help others and lead beings to enlightenment. Mahayana Buddhists may pray to these Bodhisattvas in times of need.

APPLY

Ⓐ Explain **two** differences between an Arhat and a Bodhisattva. **Refer to Buddhist teachings** in your answer.

Ⓑ **Prepare an essay plan** to evaluate the statement, 'Becoming a Bodhisattva is harder than becoming an Arhat.' In your plan include:

- arguments to support this statement
- arguments to support a different point of view
- reference to Buddhist teachings
- a justified conclusion.

TIP
Your conclusion should say whether or not you agree with the statement and why. (It's possible you may partly agree with the statement, in which case you can say this and explain why.)

3.18 Pure Land Buddhism

Essential information:

- [ ] **Pure Land Buddhism** is a tradition within Mahayana Buddhism. It is based on faith in **Amitabha Buddha** and his paradise.

- [ ] Pure Land Buddhists hope to be reborn and gain enlightenment in the Pure Land.

- [ ] The main practice in Pure Land Buddhism is the recitation of Amitabha's name.

Amitabha Buddha and the Pure Land

- Pure Land Buddhism is one of the main forms of Buddhism in Japan today.
- It is based on faith in Amitabha Buddha, who is believed to have created a paradise or pure land called **Sukhavati** when he became enlightened.
- Pure Land Buddhists hope to be reborn into this world, in which it is considered to be easier to achieve enlightenment.

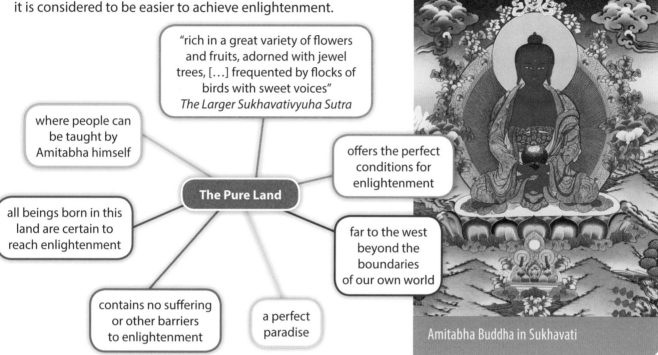

"rich in a great variety of flowers and fruits, adorned with jewel trees, [...] frequented by flocks of birds with sweet voices"
The Larger Sukhavativyuha Sutra

where people can be taught by Amitabha himself

offers the perfect conditions for enlightenment

The Pure Land

all beings born in this land are certain to reach enlightenment

far to the west beyond the boundaries of our own world

contains no suffering or other barriers to enlightenment

a perfect paradise

Amitabha Buddha in Sukhavati

How to reach the Pure Land

- T'an-luan (the founder of Pure Land Buddhism in China) recommended five practices: reciting scriptures, meditating on Amitabha and his paradise, worshipping Amitabha, chanting his name, and making praises and offerings to him.
- As Pure Land Buddhism developed, the most important practice became reciting Amitabha's name.

Pure Land Buddhism contrasts with Theravada Buddhism in the following ways:

Pure Land Buddhism	Theravada Buddhism
Faith in Amitabha is the focus of practice, and more important than a person's actions and behaviour.	A person can only gain enlightenment through their actions and behaviour (e.g. by following the Eightfold Path).
Amitabha will help people to be reborn in the Pure Land.	People cannot rely on any outside help to achieve enlightenment.

Pure Land Buddhism offers a simple practice (the recitation of Amitabha's name), and the promise of receiving Amitabha's help to reach enlightenment. This has helped the tradition to gain a popular following.

(A) Referring to a relevant scripture, give **two** characteristics of Amitabha's Pure Land.

(B) 'Pure Land Buddhism offers an easy way to gain enlightenment.'
Write a developed argument to support this statement.

3 Exam practice

Test the 1 mark question

1 Which **one** of the following is **not** one of the Four Noble Truths?

| A | Suffering exists | B | Suffering can be overcome |

| C | Not everyone suffers | D | Following the Eightfold Path can end suffering | **[1 mark]**

2 Which **one** of the following is one of the three marks of existence?

| A | Anicca | B | Metta | C | Peace | D | Sunyata | **[1 mark]**

Test the 2 mark question

3 Give **two** of the six perfections. **[2 marks]**

1) _____

2) _____

4 Give **two** reasons why Siddhartha decided to turn away from asceticism. **[2 marks]**

1) _____

2) _____

Test the 4 mark question

5 Explain **two** ways in which belief in the Buddha's enlightenment influences Buddhists today. **[4 marks]**

● **Explain one way.**	One way is that it makes Buddhists believe they can also achieve enlightenment.
● Develop your explanation with more detail/an example/ reference to a religious teaching or quotation.	So they will put more effort into Buddhist practices, such as following the Eightfold Path or five moral precepts.
● **Explain a second way.**	A second way is that it makes Buddhists more respectful of the Dhamma (the Buddha's teachings).
● Develop your explanation with more detail/an example/ reference to a religious teaching or quotation.	For example, Buddhists respect the Dhamma as one of the three refuges, which are the three central values to a Buddhist's life.

TIP

If a question asks you about how a belief influences people today, you need to make sure your answer focuses on how people today are affected. For example, how does their approach to the religion or practice of it change as a result?

6 Explain **two** ways in which learning about the four sights influences Buddhists today. **[4 marks]**

● **Explain one way.**	
● Develop your explanation with more detail/an example/ reference to a religious teaching or quotation.	
● **Explain a second way.**	
● Develop your explanation with more detail/an example/ reference to a religious teaching or quotation.	

7 Explain **two** differences between an Arhat and a Bodhisattva. **[4 marks]**

3 Exam practice

Test the 5 mark question

8   Explain **two** Buddhist beliefs about the third noble truth.

Refer to sacred writings or another source of Buddhist belief and teaching in your answer.   **[5 marks]**

● **Explain one belief.**	*The third noble truth is the end of suffering. It teaches that suffering can be ended by overcoming craving.*
● Develop your explanation with more detail/an example.	*Buddhism teaches that if people become less attached to things, they suffer less when those things change or disappear (as a result of impermanence).*
● **Explain a second belief.**	*The third noble truth teaches that the end of suffering is nibbana or enlightenment.*
● Develop your explanation with more detail/an example.	*Nibbana means 'extinction', and it refers to the extinction of the three poisons: greed, hatred and ignorance.*
● Add a reference to sacred writings or another source of Buddhist belief. If you prefer, you can add this reference to your first belief instead.	*In the Samyutta Nikaya, the Buddha says that the third noble truth is the 'fading away and cessation of that same craving'.*

TIP

'Another source of Buddhist belief and teaching' could be the words of Buddhist leaders and teachers, such as the Dalai Lama or Thich Nhat Hanh.

9   Explain **two** realisations the Buddha made during the three watches of the night, when he became enlightened.

Refer to sacred writings or another source of Buddhist belief and teaching in your answer.   **[5 marks]**

● **Explain one realisation.**	
● Develop your explanation with more detail/an example.	
● **Explain a second realisation.**	
● Develop your explanation with more detail/an example.	
● Add a reference to sacred writings or another source of Buddhist belief. If you prefer, you can add this reference to your first realisation instead.	

10   Explain **two** Mahayana teachings.

Refer to sacred writings or another source of Buddhist belief and teaching in your answer.   **[5 marks]**

3 Exam practice

Test the 12 mark question

11 'The stories of the Buddha's birth have no relevance for Buddhists today.'
    Evaluate this statement. In your answer you should:

    - refer to Buddhist teaching
    - give reasoned arguments to support this statement
    - give reasoned arguments to support a different point of view
    - reach a justified conclusion.

[12 marks]

Plus SPaG 3 mark

REASONED ARGUMENTS IN SUPPORT OF THE STATEMENT ● **Explain why some people would agree with the statement.** ● Develop your explanation with more detail and examples. ● Refer to religious teaching. Use a quote or paraphrase or a religious authority. ● **Evaluate the arguments.** Is this a good argument or not? Explain why you think this.	Some Buddhists might argue that stories about the Buddha's birth have no relevance because they are not believable. For example, the stories say that as soon as the Buddha was born, he could walk and talk. Also that he walked seven steps and lotus flowers bloomed beneath his feet. For modern Buddhists today who don't believe in miracles, it might be hard to see any point to these stories. Buddhists might also say that stories about the Buddha's birth are much less relevant than stories about his enlightenment and teachings. These stories might actually help Buddhists to become closer to their own enlightenment, whereas stories about the Buddha's birth don't really help them to follow the Buddha's teachings. They are more like fairy stories than a guide to practice.
REASONED ARGUMENTS SUPPORTING A DIFFERENT VIEW ● **Explain why some people would support a different view.** ● Develop your explanation with more detail and examples. ● Refer to religious teaching. Use a quote or paraphrase or a religious authority. ● **Evaluate the arguments.** Is this a good argument or not? Explain why you think this.	Other Buddhists might argue that the stories about the Buddha's birth symbolise how special he was, and help to show that he is worth following as a teacher. The stories also help to give context to the Buddha's life and teachings. For example, the stories show that the Buddha was born into a royal family and a life of luxury. This helps to explain why the Buddha later rejected a life of luxury for a life of asceticism, and then he also rejected that to teach a middle way between the two extremes. This middle way wouldn't have been developed without first being born into a royal family. So the stories help to make sense of the Buddha's teachings.
CONCLUSION ● **Give a justified conclusion.** ● Include your own opinion together with your own reasoning. ● **Include evaluation.** Explain why you think one viewpoint is stronger than the other or why they are equally strong. ● Do not just repeat arguments you have already used without explaining how they apply to your reasoned opinion/conclusion.	The stories about the Buddha's birth may be hard to believe, but they do not have to be taken literally. They can still express spiritual truths. I think many Buddhists might say there are more relevant stories – such as stories about the Buddha's enlightenment and teachings – but it is not true the stories have no relevance. They show how special the Buddha was, and they help to give context to the Buddha's teachings.

TIP

Including specific examples will help to support your arguments in the 12-mark question. Here, the student has given specific stories about the Buddha's birth. These help to support the argument that the stories are not believable.

12 'Achieving enlightenment is not that difficult.'

Evaluate this statement. In your answer you should:

- refer to Buddhist teaching
- give reasoned arguments to support this statement
- give reasoned arguments to support a different point of view
- reach a justified conclusion.

[12 marks]
Plus SPaG 3 marks

REASONED ARGUMENTS IN SUPPORT OF THE STATEMENT	
● **Explain why some people would agree with the statement.**	
● Develop your explanation with more detail and examples.	
● Refer to religious teaching. Use a quote or paraphrase or a religious authority.	
● **Evaluate the arguments.** Is this a good argument or not? Explain why you think this.	
REASONED ARGUMENTS SUPPORTING A DIFFERENT VIEW	
● **Explain why some people would support a different view.**	
● Develop your explanation with more detail and examples.	
● Refer to religious teaching. Use a quote or paraphrase or a religious authority.	
● **Evaluate the arguments.** Is this a good argument or not? Explain why you think this.	
CONCLUSION	
● **Give a justified conclusion.**	
● Include your own opinion together with your own reasoning.	
● **Include evaluation.** Explain why you think one viewpoint is stronger than the other or why they are equally strong.	
● Do not just repeat arguments you have already used without explaining how they apply to your reasoned opinion/conclusion.	

TIP

In your answer to this question, consider what different Buddhist traditions teach about how to achieve enlightenment. For example, you could compare Theravada Buddhism with Pure Land Buddhism. Do some of the different 'paths' to enlightenment seem easier than others?

13 'Buddhism teaches that in order to achieve enlightenment, it is most important to overcome ignorance.'

Evaluate this statement. In your answer you should:

- refer to Buddhist teaching
- give reasoned arguments to support this statement
- give reasoned arguments to support a different point of view
- reach a justified conclusion.

[12 marks]
Plus SPaG 3 marks

Check your answers using the mark scheme on page 163. How did you do?
To feel more secure in the content you need to remember, re-read pages 46–63.
To remind yourself of what the examiner is looking for, go to pages 6–11.

4.1 Places of worship

RECAP

Essential information:

☐ A **temple** is a place where Buddhists come together to practise. It is often at the heart of a Buddhist community.

☐ A **shrine** is an area with a statue or image of a Buddha or Bodhisattva. It provides a focal point for meditation and devotion.

☐ A **monastery** (**vihara**, or **gompa** in Tibet) is a place where a community of Buddhist monks or nuns lives.

Temples

A temple is an important centre of religious life where Buddhists can study, meditate and practise together. A temple may consist of just one building or several different buildings. Typically there is:

- A **main hall**, where Buddhists practise together. This usually contains a statue of the Buddha (a **Buddha rupa**). Mahayana temples may also include statues of Bodhisattvas.
- A **meditation hall**, which is a quiet space where Buddhists can meditate.
- A **study hall** for meetings and lectures.
- A **shrine** or shrines dedicated to the Buddha (or in Mahayana temples to a Bodhisattva).
- A **stupa** or pagoda, which is a tiered tower or mound-like structure that sometimes contains the remains or relics of an important Buddhist.

Labels on the stupa: Space/Wisdom, Air, Fire, Water, Earth

> **TIP**
> A stupa often functions as a type of shrine. It is common to walk in a clockwise direction around a stupa as a form of worship, often chanting a mantra (see page 69).

Stupas are usually designed to symbolise the five elements: earth, water, fire, air and space. Different segments of the building represent different elements, as shown here.

Shrines

- Shrines can be found in a temple, monastery or in the home.
- They provide a focal point for Buddhists to meditate and express devotion.
- Buddhists make offerings at shrines to show gratitude for the Buddha's teachings.
- Offerings can act as reminders of the Buddha's teachings, as shown in this table.

Light		Symbolises the Buddha, wisdom and enlightenment – which drive away the darkness of ignorance.
Flowers		As flowers wilt and decay, they remind Buddhists that all things are impermanent.
Incense		Symbolises purity, reminding Buddhists of the importance of practising pure thoughts, speech and behaviour.

Monasteries

- A monastery is a place where Buddhist monks or nuns live a simple, disciplined life of study, meditation, devotion and companionship.
- Some monasteries house large numbers of monks (especially in Tibet) and may be like small villages, while others consist of just one building.
- A stupa is often an important part of a monastery.

APPLY

A Give **two** examples of buildings or areas that you might find in a Buddhist temple, and explain what their function is.

B 'The best way for Buddhists to worship is in a monastery.'

Develop one argument for and one argument against this statement.

4.2 How Buddhists worship

RECAP

Essential information:

☐ Worship (**puja**) expresses gratitude and respect for the Buddha and his teachings.

☐ **Chanting** is a type of worship that involves reciting from the Buddhist scriptures.

☐ Buddhists may chant **mantras**: short sequences of sacred syllables.

Buddhist worship

The Buddha is usually the focus of worship (although other Buddhas or Bodhisattvas may also be worshipped). Worship helps Buddhists to:

- express their gratitude towards the Buddha and acceptance of his teachings
- deepen their understanding of the Buddha's teachings
- move closer to the Buddha and what he symbolises.

Worship may involve different activities, as shown in the diagram to the right.

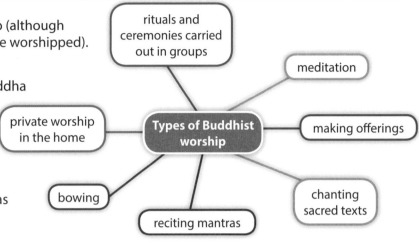

Chanting

- In the early days of Buddhism, sacred texts were remembered and taught orally – they were not written down. Chanting was used to **memorise and pass on teachings and texts**.
- Chanting is a **devotional practice** that is thought to increase receptivity towards the Buddha and his teachings.
- It also helps to **calm and focus the mind**, to increase concentration.
- Examples might include chanting the three refuges, the five moral precepts, or the Bodhisattva vows.

Mantras

- A mantra is a sequence of sacred syllables that is chanted out loud or silently in the mind, over and over again.
- Mantras help to **concentrate the mind** and so function as a form of meditation.
- Some Buddhists believe mantras have **magical powers**.
- They are often associated with the **spiritual qualities of a Buddha or Bodhisattva**.
- For example, *om mani padme hum* is a common mantra used by Tibetan Buddhists. It is associated with the Bodhisattva Avalokiteshvara, who represents compassion. Chanting this mantra helps Buddhists connect with the quality of compassion.

A mantra may be recited up to hundreds or thousands of times using a **mala** (a string of prayer beads) to help count the number of recitations

APPLY

(A) Explain **two** ways in which Buddhists worship.

(B) 'Worshipping the Buddha is wrong because it is treating him like a God.'

Evaluate this argument in response to the statement.

"The Buddha is not supposed to be God and so when Buddhists worship the Buddha they are treating him like God. For this reason, Buddhists should not worship the Buddha, only recognise that he is an important human being and guide towards enlightenment."

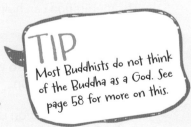

TIP
Most Buddhists do not think of the Buddha as a God. See page 58 for more on this.

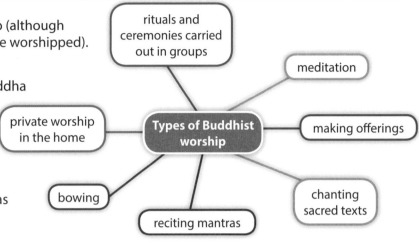
(diagram text: Types of Buddhist worship; rituals and ceremonies carried out in groups; meditation; making offerings; chanting sacred texts; reciting mantras; bowing; private worship in the home)

RECAP

Essential information:

☐ **Meditation** is a practice of calming and focusing the mind, and reflecting deeply on specific teachings to develop an insight into the nature of reality.

☐ **Samatha meditation** is a type of meditation that involves calming the mind and developing deeper concentration. It is important in Theravada Buddhism as preparation for vipassana meditation.

☐ **Mindfulness of breathing** is a popular technique in samatha meditation. It requires the meditator to become more aware of their breathing and to focus their attention on it.

The practice of meditation

- Meditation is a spiritual exercise that calms the mind and body, and leads to the development of insight into the nature of existence. It is an important practice in most Buddhist traditions.

> 〝 Even the gods envy those awakened and mindful ones who are intent on meditation. 〟
> *The Buddha in the Dhammapada, verse 181*

- There is a range of meditation techniques that help Buddhists to develop samatha (calm) and vipassana (insight).
- Meditating often begins with mindfulness of the body and breath.
- Buddhists may use a variety of objects as a focus for concentration, such as certain character traits or emotions, the breathing process, an image, a candle flame or even a Buddha.

Mindfulness of breathing

In samatha meditation, the breath can be used to become more 'mindful'. Mindfulness is a quality of **attention and awareness**.

- The breath is used as a focus for attention, as well as how the body responds to each breath.
- The aim is to become aware of the details of breathing, and all the tiny movements it creates in the body.
- When someone finds their mind wandering as they meditate, they simply bring their attention back to their breathing.
- Little by little they become more able to concentrate and focus on their breath.
- This leads them to feel more present and aware.

Using kasinas in samatha meditation

- Instead of focusing on their breathing, a meditator could focus on other objects called kasinas.
- There are ten kasinas in total. They include elements such as earth, water and fire, and colours such as blue, red and yellow.
- For example, the meditator could focus on a bowl of water or a red circle placed in front of them.
- As with breathing, the object gives the meditator something to focus their attention on.

The purpose of samatha meditation

- Focusing on a single object helps to create a calm and tranquil mind.
- It also helps to develop concentration and focus.
- It acts as preparation for vipassana meditation (see the next page).
- Samatha meditation can help Buddhists to feel happier and more alive.

> 〝 Do not encumber your mind with useless thoughts [...] Remain in the simplicity of the present moment. 〟
> *Dilgo Khyentse Rinpoche*

APPLY

(A) Explain **two** ways in which Buddhists practise samatha meditation.

(B) 'Meditation is the most important Buddhist practice.'

Give a developed argument to support this statement. Then give a developed argument to support a different point of view.

TIP
Remember that meditation is not about emptying the mind or making the mind go blank. Instead, think of it as a method of calming, settling and focusing the mind.

RECAP

Essential information:

☐ **Vipassana meditation** is a type of meditation that involves developing understanding of the nature of reality. It is the second main type of meditation in Theravada Buddhism.

☐ **Zazen** is a type of meditation in Zen Buddhism that involves awareness of the present moment.

What is vipassana meditation?

Vipassana meditation is often called 'insight meditation', as the aim is to penetrate and gain insight into the true nature of reality. This usually consists of reflecting on the three marks of existence (see pages 52–54).

Similarities and differences between vipassana and samatha meditation include the following:

Samatha meditation	Vipassana meditation
Both use the same technique of **mindfulness**: concentrating and focusing on specific things in a calm and detached manner.	
• The meditator focuses on **one neutral, simple object or process**. • E.g. a blue triangle, a candle flame, or the process of breathing.	• The meditator may **change their focus between a range of different objects, emotions, experiences,** etc., including things that are more personal to them. • E.g. a feeling of annoyance, their own body, or the sound of rain falling.
• The aim of focusing on the object is to **develop concentration and calm**. • E.g. the meditator focuses on their breath to become calmer and more aware.	• The aim of focusing on the object is to **understand its true nature**, and how it is **characterised by the three marks of existence**. • E.g. the meditator contemplates how their breath shows characteristics of the three marks of existence.

The main aims of vipassana meditation are to:

• understand how all things are characterised by the three marks of existence
• develop greater wisdom and awareness about the world
• ultimately achieve enlightenment.

TIP
Zazen can be understood as a form of vipassana meditation.

Zazen

• Zazen means 'seated meditation'.
• It is practised in Zen Buddhism, which originated in Japan.
• It leads to a deeper understanding of the nature of existence.
• It generally begins with sitting, relaxing and a period of mindfulness of breathing.
• The meditator then sits with awareness of the present moment.
• Thoughts and experiences come and go, and the meditator returns again and again to the present moment.

Walking meditation

TIP
This quote shows how the technique of mindfulness can be applied to walking.

• Meditation is often practised sitting on the floor in a cross-legged posture.
• But it is also possible to meditate while walking, as part of samatha or vipassana meditation.
• This consists of walking slowly and combining the movement of the feet with the in and out of the breath.

> **❝**Your objective is to attain total alertness, heightened sensitivity and a full, unblocked experience of the motion of walking.**❞**
> *Henepola Gunarantana*

APPLY

(A) Two meditation practices are mindfulness of breathing and walking meditation. **Explain** how these practices could be used as part of vipassana meditation.

(B) **Prepare an essay plan** to evaluate the statement, 'The aim of meditation is to reach enlightenment.' In your plan include:

• arguments to support this statement
• arguments to support a different point of view
• reference to Buddhist teachings
• a justified conclusion.

TIP
Remember that a 'justified' conclusion means you need to give reasons in your conclusion for why you agree or disagree with the statement. You can use some of the arguments you have already written to help support your opinion.

RECAP

Essential information:

☐ **Visualisation** of Buddhas and Bodhisattvas is used in Mahayana Buddhism as part of meditation.

☐ Buddhists may use thangkas or mandalas to help visualise a Buddha or Bodhisattva.

☐ These practices allow Buddhists to connect with the spiritual qualities of a Buddha or Bodhisattva.

What is visualisation?

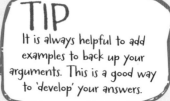

The Medicine Buddha

- The meditator visualises (imagines) an object in their mind.
- They may first use an image for inspiration and then afterwards visualise it.
- They try to imagine the object in great detail, examining all the qualities and characteristics of it.
- The object functions as a focus of concentration – the meditator will try to hold a detailed picture of the object in their mind for as long as possible.
- The object may also connect with spiritual qualities.

Deity visualisation

- When they meditate, Tibetan Buddhists will often visualise a deity (an enlightened being such as a Buddha or Bodhisattva, but not a god).
- The meditator focuses not just on the visual features of the deity, but also on its spiritual qualities. They may imagine themselves as that deity in order to absorb its spiritual qualities.
- Visualising themselves as a Buddha may help Buddhists to awaken their Buddha-nature.

Examples of Buddhas or Bodhisattvas that meditators might visualise include:

The Medicine Buddha	**Avalokiteshvara**	**Buddha Amitabha**
• The Buddha of healing. • Visualising this Buddha may reduce suffering and even promote healing powers.	• The Bodhisattva of compassion. • Visualising this Bodhisattva helps Buddhists to develop a sense of compassion.	• Pure Land Buddhists may visualise Buddha Amitabha in the hope he will help them to be reborn in the Pure Land (see page 63).

Using thangkas or mandalas in visualisation

Some Buddhists use thangkas or mandalas to help them visualise and call to mind a deity.

- A **thangka** is a detailed painting of a Buddha or Bodhisattva.
- A **mandala** is an intricate, colourful circle-shaped pattern. It is a sacred diagram that represents Buddhist principles or teachings. It may symbolise the universe, a Buddha or Bodhisattva, or a pure land or paradise.

In Tibetan monasteries, monks make mandalas out of brightly coloured sand. These are complicated and may take weeks to create. Once finished, they are brushed away to encourage the monks to focus on impermanence (see page 53).

APPLY

A Explain **two** ways in which Buddhists practise visualisation.

B **Develop** this argument to support the statement, 'Mahayana Buddhists visualise Buddhas to become enlightened.'

"In Mahayana Buddhism, the practice of deity visualisation is common. Through visualising the deity, the meditator hopes to appreciate and absorb their spiritual qualities. For example..."

TIP
It is always helpful to add examples to back up your arguments. This is a good way to 'develop' your answers.

4.6 Ceremonies and rituals associated with death and mourning

Essential information:

☐ Buddhist tradition teaches that when a Buddhist dies, their kammic energy leaves their body and is reborn in a new one.

☐ Death is not seen as an end but a transition between one life and the next.

☐ Funeral practices vary between different Buddhist traditions and countries.

Theravada funerals

- Little money is usually spent on funerals.
- Instead, family and friends may donate to a worthy cause and **transfer the merit** to the deceased. (The good kamma that is created by donating to a worthy cause is transferred to the dead person, to help them have a favourable rebirth – see page 75).
- Rituals that transfer merit to the deceased may be performed by family members or other mourners. For example, they may offer cloth to make new robes to a monastery on behalf of the dead person.

A Vietnamese Buddhist funeral procession

At the funeral itself, the following may happen:

- A shrine may display the deceased's portrait, along with an image of the Buddha and offerings to the Buddha.
- Monks often attend the funerals of lay people and perform rituals or give a sermon.
- The deceased may be cremated or buried, although cremation is traditional and more common.
- All mourners send good thoughts to the family and contemplate impermanence.

Funerals in Tibet

- **Sky burial** is a traditional funeral practice in Tibet. The body is left in a high place as a gift to the vultures.
- This tradition arose due to a lack of wood for cremation and problems with frozen ground for burial.
- However, it is now more common to burn the body.
- Revered teachers have always been cremated, and their remains placed in a stupa to become a site of worship (see page 68).
- Ceremonies involving prayers and offerings of yak-butter lamps may be made every seven days for 49 days after the death.

Funerals in Japan

- In Japanese Pure Land Buddhism, the coffin may be placed with the head pointing west, towards the direction of Sukhavati. Those assembled chant Amitabha's name as they process around the coffin (see page 63).
- It is common across all Japanese traditions for relatives to gather after the cremation and pick out the bones from the ashes, using chopsticks.
- As in Tibet, these remains may be kept for 49 days and prayers offered every seventh day.

APPLY

(A) Explain **two** ways that Buddhist beliefs influence funeral practices.

(B) 'The purpose of Buddhist funerals is to prepare the deceased for their next life.'

Write three linked sentences to support this statement.

TIP

Sentences can be linked together using words like 'therefore', 'in addition', or 'however'. Linking sentences together in a logical order will help to improve the clarity of your writing.

4.7 Wesak and Parinirvana Day

Essential information:

☐ **Festivals** allow Buddhists to celebrate important events in the history of Buddhism, while **retreats** provide an opportunity for intensive practice.

☐ **Wesak** is a Theravada festival that celebrates the Buddha's birth, enlightenment and passing away.

☐ **Parinirvana Day** is a Mahayana festival that commemorates the Buddha's passing away.

Buddhist festivals and retreats

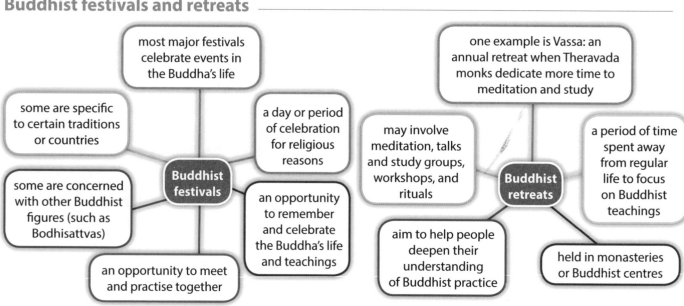

most major festivals celebrate events in the Buddha's life

some are specific to certain traditions or countries

a day or period of celebration for religious reasons

some are concerned with other Buddhist figures (such as Bodhisattvas)

Buddhist festivals

an opportunity to remember and celebrate the Buddha's life and teachings

an opportunity to meet and practise together

one example is Vassa: an annual retreat when Theravada monks dedicate more time to meditation and study

may involve meditation, talks and study groups, workshops, and rituals

Buddhist retreats

a period of time spent away from regular life to focus on Buddhist teachings

aim to help people deepen their understanding of Buddhist practice

held in monasteries or Buddhist centres

Wesak

Significance and meaning	• Commemorates three major events in the Buddha's life: his birth, enlightenment and passing away. • An opportunity to honour and remember the Buddha and his teachings. • Light is used during the festival to symbolise hope, enlightenment, and overcoming ignorance.
Celebrations	Celebrations vary from one country to the next, but Buddhists may: • light up their homes with candles, lamps or lanterns • make offerings to the Buddha and give gifts to the local monastery • attend the local temple or monastery to take part in worship and meditation, or listen to sermons on the Buddha's teachings and life • take part in ceremonies where caged animals are released as a symbol of liberation (in Singapore).

Parinirvana Day

Significance and meaning	• Celebrated during February to remember the Buddha's passing into parinirvana (the final state of nibbana). • A solemn occasion when Buddhists reflect on their own future death, and remember friends or relatives who have recently passed away. • The Buddhist teaching of impermanence (see page 53) is a focus for the day.
Celebrations	Buddhists may: • read and study the *Mahaparinirvana Sutra* (a Buddhist scripture that describes the Buddha's last days) • meditate and worship at home or with others in a temple or monastery • go on retreat to reflect and meditate, or go on pilgrimage: many Buddhists visit Kushinagar in India (which is where the Buddha is believed to have passed away).

A Explain **two** ways in which Buddhists celebrate festivals.

B 'Wesak is the celebration of the Buddhist belief in enlightenment.'

Write three linked sentences to oppose this statement.

TIP
Remember that how Buddhist festivals are observed changes from one country and tradition to the next.

RECAP

Essential information:

☐ **Kamma** is an ethical principle that explains how a person's actions lead to either happiness or suffering. It teaches that it is not just the action which is important but also the motivation behind it.

☐ Kamma is central to Buddhist ethics, as it motivates Buddhists to behave in a way that will increase their own and others' happiness.

The concept of kamma in Buddhism

- Kamma explains how the intentions behind a person's actions lead to happiness or suffering.
- The table below shows how different motives or qualities lead to good or bad actions, which in turn results in happiness or suffering.

Actions and their results		
Type of action	**Skilful** (good, ethical actions or behaviour)	**Unskilful** (bad, unethical actions or behaviour)
Motivated by	Generosity, compassion, understanding	Craving, hatred, ignorance
Results in	Happiness	Suffering

Kamma and rebirth

Buddhist tradition teaches that a person's actions in this life not only affect their happiness and suffering right now, but will also **affect their future lives.**

Depending on their kamma, they will be reborn into one of the six realms shown on the right.

By developing skilful mental states and actions, Buddhists can not only live a happier life but also lay the ground for a favourable rebirth. The hope is to be reborn into the human realm, which is said to be the best realm for reaching enlightenment.

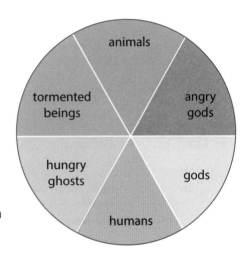

> **TIP**
> This quote shows the principle of kamma means a person cannot escape the consequences of their actions – which will affect not just their current life but also their future lives.

> 66 Not in the sky, not in the middle of the sea, not entering an opening in the mountains is there that place on earth where standing **one might be freed from evil action**. 99
>
> *Dhammapada, verse 127*

Buddhist ethics

- Kamma is central to Buddhist ethics. The fact that a person's own behaviour causes their happiness or suffering is a motivation to live in a more skilful way.
- Acting skilfully (ethically) reduces suffering for oneself and others, and enables progress on the path to enlightenment.
- Examples of skilful action might include helping the poor in the local community, acting compassionately towards others, and not harming life.

APPLY

(A) Give **two** of the motives that Buddhists believe characterise a skilful action.

(B) 'The principle of kamma encourages ethical behaviour.'

Referring to Buddhist teaching, **prepare one developed argument** to support this statement.

> **TIP**
> The five moral precepts help Buddhists to behave skilfully (see page 78).

4.9 Compassion (karuna)

Essential information:

☐ **Karuna** (compassion) is feeling concerned for the suffering of other people and wanting to relieve their suffering.

☐ Karuna is one of **the four sublime states** (the four qualities which the Buddha taught all Buddhists should develop).

☐ It is particularly important to Mahayana Buddhists, who view it as an essential quality for becoming a Bodhisattva.

What is karuna?

recognising that a person cannot be truly happy while others suffer

recognising when you are suffering and acting with compassion towards yourself

What is karuna?

feeling concern for the suffering of others, almost as if it were your own

wanting others to be free from suffering and trying to relieve it

> ❝I believe that at every level of society, the key to a happier and more successful world is the growth of compassion.❞
> *Tenzin Gyatso (the Dalai Lama)*

Green Tara is a Bodhisattva who represents compassion

The importance of karuna in Buddhism

Karuna is one of **the four sublime states**. These explain how Buddhists should act towards themselves and others. The four states are:

1. loving-kindness
2. compassion
3. sympathetic joy (being happy for others)
4. equanimity (staying stable and calm in the face of happiness and suffering)

Compassion is an important quality for all Buddhists to develop. In Mahayana Buddhism it is a crucial quality required to become a Bodhisattva.

ROKPA: an example of a charity motivated by compassion

'Rokpa' is a Tibetan word meaning 'help' or 'friend'. It is also the name of a charity set up in 1980 which is motivated by acting compassionately towards others.

ROKPA is involved in projects in Zimbabwe, Nepal and Tibet. The charity helps to run schools and provide education to thousands of children each year. It aims to help families out of poverty through better education, and also to teach children about the value of compassion. ROKPA believes that helping others is the way to bring about real and lasting change.

(A) Explain **two** ways in which beliefs about karuna influence Buddhists today.

(B) Here are some arguments that could be used to evaluate the statement, 'Wisdom is more important than compassion in Buddhism.' Sort them into arguments in support of the statement and arguments in support of different views. Use the arguments to **write a conclusion** where you explain why you agree or disagree with the statement.

1. On the night of his enlightenment, the Buddha came to understand the true nature of reality	5. Mahayana Buddhism emphasises compassion
2. The Buddha showed compassion by teaching others how to reach enlightenment	6. Enlightenment is understanding fully the three marks of existence
3. Amitabha created his pure land out of compassion for others	7. Buddhists practise the development of compassion
4. Theravada Buddhism speaks of enlightenment as a state of wisdom	8. Buddhist ethics encourages kindness to all beings and the rejection of violence

RECAP

Essential information:

- [ ] **Metta** (loving-kindness) is a desire for others to be happy.
- [ ] Metta can be developed through loving-kindness meditation. The meditator aims to develop an attitude of warmth and kindness towards all people, including themselves.
- [ ] Metta leads to happiness and peace.

What is metta?

- Buddhists aim to develop loving-kindness towards themselves and others.
- This **reduces the tendency to act out of negative emotions**, such as anger or greed.
- It makes a person **more caring** and more likely to love unconditionally (without expecting anything in return).
- This leads to a **feeling of peace** so there is no need for ill will or hostility.
- It helps Buddhists to **overcome suffering** and eventually achieve enlightenment.

What is metta?
- one of the four sublime states
- should be cultivated even towards people who act unskillfully
- a loving, kind, friendly attitude towards oneself and all beings
- does not depend on the goodness of others or expect anything in return

Metta and karuna are a little different from each other:

Metta	Karuna
• A general desire for other people to be happy. • An attitude of warmth and kindness that Buddhists try to feel towards all people. • E.g. when someone wants their friend to be happy.	• Arises when metta comes into contact with a specific person who is suffering. • E.g. when someone wants to help their friend after they have an accident.

> **"** Just as compassion is the wish that all sentient beings be free of suffering, loving-kindness is the wish that all may enjoy happiness. **"** *Tenzin Gyatso (the Dalai Lama)*

> **"** [...] one should cultivate an unbounded mind towards all beings, and **loving-kindness towards all the world. "**
> *The Sutta Nipata, verses 149–150*

Loving-kindness meditation

Loving-kindness meditation helps Buddhists to develop an attitude of metta. It often consists of five steps, which involve developing loving-kindness towards:

1. yourself → 2. a good friend → 3. a 'neutral' person (someone you come into contact with regularly but do not have strong feelings about) → 4. a 'difficult' person (someone you dislike) → 5. all four of these people, gradually followed by everyone else in the world

- The meditator might visualise or imagine one of these people looking happy.
- They might reflect on the positive qualities of the person and any acts of kindness they have done.

APPLY

(A) Give **two** ways in which metta is different from karuna.

(B) 'Metta should only be developed towards people we like.'

Referring to Buddhist scripture, **write a developed argument** to oppose this statement.

TIP
To answer this question you can use the quote on this page from the *Sutta Nipata*.

4.11 The five moral precepts

Essential information:

☐ **The five moral precepts** form a Buddhist ethical code. They are five principles that Buddhists try to follow to live ethically and morally.

☐ The first and most important precept is not to cause harm. The other precepts stem from this one.

☐ Buddhists practise the precepts voluntarily to improve their behaviour and purify their mind of greed, ignorance and hatred.

What are the five moral precepts?

1. To abstain from taking life	2. To abstain from taking what is not freely given	3. To abstain from misuse of the senses or sexual misconduct	4. To abstain from wrong speech	5. To abstain from intoxicants that cloud the mind

Buddhists aim not to harm or kill any living being. For this reason many Buddhists are vegetarian or vegan.	As well as not stealing, this means Buddhists aim to avoid manipulating or taking advantage of others.	Buddhists aim not to abuse or overindulge in sensual pleasures, or to use sex harmfully.	Buddhists aim not to lie or gossip about other people but to speak truthfully, kindly, helpfully and at the right time.	Not taking alcohol or drugs is important for Buddhists who have committed themselves to developing greater awareness.

> ❝Whoever destroys a living creature, and speaks untruth, takes what is not given in the world, and goes to another's wife, and whatever man applies himself to drinking liquor and intoxicants, that person digs up his own root here in this very world. ❞
>
> *The Buddha in the Dhammapada, verses 246–247*

Following the five moral precepts

- The five precepts are principles that Buddhists **practise voluntarily**. Buddhists do not believe in a god who will punish them if they do not follow the precepts.
- The precepts should be **applied sensitively**. Sometimes Buddhists have to balance one precept against another. For example, what if being truthful may lead to harm? It may sometimes be more ethical to lie, if this is motivated by genuine kindness.
- The precepts can be **practised on ever deepening levels**, especially at the level of the mind. For example, if a person wants to hurt someone this is still considered to be unskillful, even if they don't actually go ahead and hurt them.
- Applying the precepts **purifies the mind of greed, hatred and ignorance**, replacing these traits with wisdom and compassion.

> ❝We just keep on working, we are patient with ourselves, and on and on it goes [...] As our minds get clearer and clearer, it's not even a matter of breaking or maintaining the precepts; automatically they are maintained. ❞
>
> *Jan Chozen Bays*

(A) Explain **two** of the five moral precepts of Buddhism. **Refer to sacred writings** in your answer.

(B) **Prepare an essay plan** to evaluate the statement, 'It is always wrong to lie.' In your plan include:

- arguments to support this statement
- arguments to support a different point of view
- reference to Buddhist teachings
- a justified conclusion.

TIP
It would be easy to answer this question without referring to any religious teachings, but make sure you do. For example, you could refer to the fourth moral precept and discuss what it means to apply the precepts sensitively.

4.12 The six perfections

Essential information:

☐ **The six perfections** are six qualities or virtues that Mahayana Buddhists try to develop in order to become Bodhisattvas.

☐ The six perfections are generosity, morality, patience, energy, meditation and wisdom.

What are the six perfections?

Perfection	Explanation

1. Generosity or giving	• Buddhists should **give without expecting anything in return**.
	• It is therefore important to develop awareness of the reasons for giving, and to gradually purify these in order to give more freely.
	• Tibetan Buddhists talk about three main types of giving:
	  1. Giving **material goods** such as food, clothes and money. These provide immediate relief for people's suffering.
	  2. Giving **protection from fear**. This means helping someone if they are afraid or in trouble.
	  3. Giving **the Dhamma** (the Buddha's teachings). This helps people to help themselves, so has a longer-lasting impact.

2. Morality	• Buddhists try to **follow the five moral precepts** (see page 78). • Mahayana Buddhists aim to follow a **further five precepts**. These include not talking about other people's faults, not being stingy and angry, and not speaking badly of the three refuges. • Meditation and mindfulness help Buddhists to follow the precepts more willingly, without feeling restrained by them.
3. Patience	• A Bodhisattva embodies patience, which is expressed through **tolerance and endurance**. • Buddhists aim to **practise compassion** towards those who show them anger, and **have patience with themselves and others**. • Understanding that suffering is an inevitable part of life (the first noble truth) helps Buddhists to develop the patience needed to endure it.
4. Energy	• Buddhists should put **effort and enthusiasm** into their practice of the Dhamma. • They should develop the **courage and energy** needed to strive for enlightenment. • This may mean looking after their own health, developing their practice, or studying the Buddha's teachings.
5. Meditation	• Meditation helps to **develop the concentration and awareness** needed to achieve wisdom. • It is described further on pages 70–71.
6. Wisdom	• The first five perfections contribute to the development of the sixth one. • By meditating and studying the Buddha's teachings, and by living ethically and morally, Buddhists aim to develop a full understanding of the nature of reality.

A Which **one** of the following is **not** one of the six perfections:

A) Generosity   B) Energy   C) Compassion   D) Wisdom

B Read the following argument in support of the statement, 'The six perfections are more difficult to practise than the five precepts.' Then **write a developed argument** to oppose it.

"The five precepts encourage Buddhists to not do quite specific actions, such as drinking alcohol or telling lies, whereas the six perfections guide Buddhists to develop more general character traits, such as 'generosity' and 'patience'. I think it is easier for a person to give up doing specific bad things than it is to change their character and who they are as a person, so I agree with the statement."

TIP
Remember you don't always have to agree with an argument to write about it. (If this is the case, you could write 'some Buddhists think' or 'some people think' rather than 'I think...')

4 Exam practice

Test the 1 mark question

1 Which **one** of the following is a Buddhist building?

A Church   B Mosque   C Synagogue   D Stupa   **[1 mark]**

2 Which **one** of the following is the best meaning for the term vipassana?

A Calm   B Compassion   C Insight   D Generosity   **[1 mark]**

Test the 2 mark question

3 Give **two** ways in which Buddhists can follow the six perfections.   **[2 marks]**

1) _____

2) _____

4 Give **two** different places of Buddhist worship.   **[2 marks]**

1) _____

2) _____

Test the 4 mark question

5 Explain **two** contrasting Buddhist rituals associated with death and mourning.   **[4 marks]**

● **Explain one ritual.**	*In Pure Land Buddhism, the mourners chant Amitabha's name as they process around the coffin.*
● Develop your explanation with more detail/an example/ reference to a religious teaching or quotation.	*This is because they are hoping the deceased person will be reborn into the pure land where Amitabha lives, from where it is easier to achieve enlightenment.*
● **Explain a second ritual.**	*In Tibet, sky burial is traditional, where the body is left in a high place as a gift to the vultures.*
● Develop your explanation with more detail/an example/ reference to a religious teaching or quotation.	*This tradition started because of a lack of wood for cremation and the ground being too frozen for burial. But now it is more common to cremate the body.*

6 Explain **two** ways in which the five moral precepts influence Buddhists today.   **[4 marks]**

● **Explain one way.**	
● Develop your explanation with more detail/an example/ reference to a religious teaching or quotation.	
● **Explain a second way.**	
● Develop your explanation with more detail/an example/ reference to a religious teaching or quotation.	

7 Explain **two** ways in which Buddhists celebrate Wesak.   **[4 marks]**

4 Exam practice

Test the 5 mark question

8   Explain **two** ways in which Buddhists can perform puja in the home.

Refer to sacred writings or another source of Buddhist belief and teaching in your answer.   **[5 marks]**

● **Explain one way.**	*Buddhists can perform puja in the home by chanting mantras (sequences of sacred syllables).*
● Develop your explanation with more detail/an example.	*Some Buddhists believe mantras call on the spiritual qualities of a Buddha or Bodhisattva, and can help them to develop those qualities.*
● **Explain a second way.**	*Buddhists can also perform puja in the home by making offerings at a shrine to the Buddha.*
● Develop your explanation with more detail/an example.	*These offerings help remind Buddhists of the Buddha's teachings. The act of making offerings also helps to focus the mind.*
● Add a reference to sacred writings or another source of Buddhist belief. If you prefer, you can add this reference to your first way instead.	*Lama Choedak Rinpoche (a Tibetan Buddhist monk) says that, 'The time and effort required to keep the shrine clean and replenished with flowers and other offerings is considered a skilful activity to focus one's mind in the spiritual practices.'*

> **TIP**
> It is acceptable to use a quote from a Buddhist leader or teacher as a 'source of Buddhist belief and teaching'. You do not have to refer to a Buddhist scripture to gain the extra mark.

9   Explain **two** Buddhist beliefs about metta (loving-kindness).

Refer to sacred writings or another source of Buddhist belief and teaching in your answer.   **[5 marks]**

● **Explain one belief.**	
● Develop your explanation with more detail/an example.	
● **Explain a second belief.**	
● Develop your explanation with more detail/an example.	
● Add a reference to sacred writings or another source of Buddhist belief. If you prefer, you can add this reference to your first belief instead.	

10   Explain **two** Buddhist beliefs about kamma.

Refer to sacred writings or another source of Buddhist belief and teaching in your answer.   **[5 marks]**

4 Exam practice

Test the 12 mark question

11   'Meditation is the most important practice for Buddhists.'

Evaluate this statement. In your answer you should:

- refer to Buddhist teaching
- give reasoned arguments to support this statement
- give reasoned arguments to support a different point of view
- reach a justified conclusion.

[12 marks]

REASONED ARGUMENTS IN SUPPORT OF THE STATEMENT ● **Explain why some people would agree with the statement.** ● Develop your explanation with more detail and examples. ● Refer to religious teaching. Use a quote or paraphrase or a religious authority. ● **Evaluate the arguments.** Is this a good argument or not? Explain why you think this.	*For Buddhists the ultimate goal is to achieve enlightenment, and meditation is an important practice that brings Buddhists closer to this. In fact it is so important that there is a whole section of the Eightfold Path dedicated to it. In the Dhammapada the Buddha said that 'even the gods envy those awakened and mindful ones who are intent on meditation', which shows how important the Buddha thought it was.* *Buddhists meditate in order to calm and focus their mind (samatha meditation) so they can then gain insight into the nature of existence (vipassana meditation). This insight is what leads to enlightenment.*
REASONED ARGUMENTS SUPPORTING A DIFFERENT VIEW ● **Explain why some people would support a different view.** ● Develop your explanation with more detail and examples. ● Refer to religious teaching. Use a quote or paraphrase or a religious authority. ● **Evaluate the arguments.** Is this a good argument or not? Explain why you think this.	*Although meditation is very important in Buddhism, some Buddhists might argue that other practices are equally important for achieving enlightenment. For example, ethics is another section of the Eightfold Path. Living ethically and morally (for example by following the five moral precepts) helps to reduce suffering and can lead to a favourable rebirth, which increases progress towards enlightenment.* *Mahayana Buddhists believe that compassion and wisdom are both important for achieving enlightenment. So they may view meditation as important for gaining wisdom, but acting kindly and ethically as important for gaining compassion.*
CONCLUSION ● **Give a justified conclusion.** ● Include your own opinion together with your own reasoning. ● **Include evaluation.** Explain why you think one viewpoint is stronger than the other or why they are equally strong. ● Do not just repeat arguments you have already used without explaining how they apply to your reasoned opinion/conclusion.	*I think that most Buddhists would agree meditation is very important for developing wisdom and achieving enlightenment. But I think that a lot of Buddhists would also say that acting ethically and compassionately is equally important, so for example following the five moral precepts is also an important practice. Mahayana Buddhists would say you cannot have wisdom without compassion, so meditation on its own will not achieve enlightenment.*

TIP

The supporting arguments are good but they need to be fully linked to the statement. An improvement would be to add at the end of the second paragraph, 'So many Buddhists would agree that meditation is the most important practice for Buddhists.'

12 'Vipassana meditation is more important than samatha meditation.'

Evaluate this statement. In your answer you should:

- refer to Buddhist teaching
- give reasoned arguments to support this statement
- give reasoned arguments to support a different point of view
- reach a justified conclusion.

[12 marks]

REASONED ARGUMENTS IN SUPPORT OF THE STATEMENT ● **Explain why some people would agree with the statement.** ● Develop your explanation with more detail and examples. ● Refer to religious teaching. Use a quote or paraphrase or a religious authority. ● **Evaluate the arguments**. Is this a good argument or not? Explain why you think this.	
REASONED ARGUMENTS SUPPORTING A DIFFERENT VIEW ● **Explain why some people would support a different view.** ● Develop your explanation with more detail and examples. ● Refer to religious teaching. Use a quote or paraphrase or a religious authority. ● **Evaluate the arguments**. Is this a good argument or not? Explain why you think this.	
CONCLUSION ● **Give a justified conclusion.** ● Include your own opinion together with your own reasoning. ● **Include evaluation**. Explain why you think one viewpoint is stronger than the other or why they are equally strong. ● Do not just repeat arguments you have already used without explaining how they apply to your reasoned opinion/conclusion.	

13 'Buddhists practise the five moral precepts in order to avoid an unfavourable rebirth.'

Evaluate this statement. In your answer you should:

- refer to Buddhist teaching
- give reasoned arguments to support this statement
- give reasoned arguments to support a different point of view
- reach a justified conclusion.

[12 marks]

TIP

To answer this question, think about <u>why</u> Buddhists might feel that practising the five moral precepts will help to influence their rebirth. How is this related to the idea of kamma?

Check your answers using the mark scheme on pages 163–164. How did you do?
To feel more secure in the content you need to remember, re-read pages 68–79.
To remind yourself of what the examiner is looking for, go to pages 6–11.

5.1 Religious teachings about human sexuality

Essential information:

☐ **Human sexuality** refers to how people express themselves as sexual beings.

☐ **Heterosexual** relationships are between a man and a woman, whereas **homosexual** relationships are between members of the same sex.

☐ The Christian Church teaches that heterosexual relationships within marriage are the ideal, whereas the main concern in Buddhism is for sex to not be harmful to anyone.

> You might be asked to compare beliefs on homosexual relationships between Christianity (the main religious tradition in Great Britain) and another religious tradition.

Attitudes towards sexual relationships

	Christianity	Buddhism and other views
General attitudes towards sexual relationships	• The Christian Church teaches that sex expresses a deep, loving, life-long union that first requires the **commitment of marriage**. • Not all Christians agree with this, but all are against unfaithfulness. • The Bible teaches that heterosexual relationships are part of **God's plan** for humans. • Genesis 1:28 and 2:24 say that a man and woman should be united together and 'increase in number'.	• Buddhism does not favour one form of sexuality over another, or teach that sex before marriage is wrong. • For Buddhists the most important principle is to **not harm others** through sexual activity. ❝There is a middle way wherein sexuality is fully acknowledged and regarded compassionately without the need to indulge in actions which lead to suffering.❞ *Daishin Morgan*
Views on homosexual relationships	• Some Christians oppose homosexual relationships because they believe this goes against God's plan. • The Catholic Church teaches that homosexual sex is a sinful activity. ❝Do not have sexual relations with a man as one does with a woman; that is detestable.❞ *Leviticus 18:22* [NIV] • The Church of England welcomes homosexuals living in committed relationships, but does not allow same-sex marriage in church. Some other Churches do. • Some Christians think loving, faithful homosexual relationships are just as holy as heterosexual ones.	• Buddhist teachings do not oppose homosexual relationships or marriage. • Many Buddhists believe homosexual relationships are not morally different from heterosexual relationships. • It is important there is consent and respect regardless of the gender of the people involved. • Many people in Britain today believe homosexuals should have the same rights as heterosexuals. • This is reflected in the fact that same-sex marriage is now legal in the UK (although same-sex couples are not allowed to get married in many churches).

(A) Write down **two** contrasting religious beliefs about homosexuality. **Develop** both beliefs by explaining in more detail, adding an example, or referring to a relevant religious teaching or quotation.

(B) 'Sex has been devalued in British society.'

Develop the answer below to support this statement. Refer to one religious argument and one non-religious argument.

"Nowadays many people in Britain have lots of different sexual partners."

Essential information:

☐ **Sex before marriage** is sex between two unmarried people. It is common in British society, and accepted by most Buddhists, but goes against the beliefs of many Christians.

☐ **Sex outside marriage** is sex between two people where one or both of them is married to someone else. This is also called **adultery**.

☐ Most religious and non-religious people believe sex outside marriage is wrong.

Sexual relationships before marriage

Sex before marriage is now widely accepted in British society, although it is against the beliefs of many religious people.

Christian views	Buddhist views
• For many Christians, sex expresses a deep, lifelong union that requires the commitment of marriage. It should not be a casual, temporary pleasure. • Anglican and Catholic Churches teach that sex before marriage is wrong. • Some liberal Christians think sex before marriage can be a valid expression of love, particularly if the couple are intending to get married or have a life-long commitment. • Christians believe it is wrong to use people for sex, to spread sexually transmitted infections or to risk pregnancy outside of marriage. ❝Flee from sexual immorality.❞ *1 Corinthians 6:18* [NIV]	• Buddhism teaches that sex before marriage is acceptable, and no less moral than sex after marriage. • What is wrong is to cause harm to others through sex. • Some Buddhists wait until marriage to have sex, but this is likely to be for personal rather than religious reasons, and influenced by local, cultural practices. You might be asked to compare beliefs on sexual relationships before marriage between Christianity (the main religious tradition in Great Britain) and another religious tradition.

Sexual relationships outside marriage

All religions generally teach that adultery is wrong as it involves lies, secrecy and the betrayal of trust. Most non-religious people are against adultery for similar reasons.

Christian views	Buddhist views
• Christians are against adultery as it breaks the marriage vows they make before God, and threatens the stable relationship needed for their children's security. • Jesus once forgave a woman caught committing adultery, but ordered her to leave her life of sin (John 8:1–11). • Adultery is forbidden in one of the Ten Commandments. ❝You shall not commit adultery.❞ *Exodus 20:14* [NIV]	• Most Buddhists would say that adultery is unskilful because it involves deceit and is also likely to cause harm.

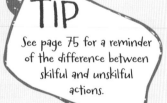

TIP

See page 75 for a reminder of the difference between skilful and unskilful actions.

A Here are two religious beliefs about sexual relationships outside of marriage (adultery). **Develop** one of the points by referring to a relevant religious teaching or quotation.

"Christians think sex outside of marriage (adultery) is wrong because it breaks the vows couples make at their wedding."

"Many Buddhists think sex outside of marriage is wrong because it is likely to cause harm."

B Give **two** points in support and **two** points against the statement, 'It is not always wrong to have sex before marriage.' **Develop** one of them by adding more detail or an example.

RECAP

Essential information:

- [ ] **Contraception** refers to the methods used to prevent a pregnancy taking place. Some prevent conception from taking place (e.g. the pill or condom), while some prevent the fertilised egg from developing (e.g. the 'morning after' pill).

- [ ] **Family planning** is controlling how many children couples have and when they have them.

- [ ] There is widespread acceptance of contraception in Britain among non-religious people. Religious believers are less likely to accept artificial contraception, particularly if it prevents the fertilised egg from developing.

> You might be asked to compare beliefs on contraception between Christianity (the main religious tradition in Great Britain) and another religious tradition.

Religious and non-religious attitudes

Group	Beliefs	Favoured methods
Catholics	• Artificial contraception goes against natural law and the purpose of marriage. • Sex should always be open to creating new life. • Family planning should only involve natural methods of contraception.	The rhythm method (avoiding sex at fertile times of the month).
Anglicans and Non-conformists	• Contraception is allowed for couples to develop their relationship before having children, to space out pregnancies, to avoid harming the mother's health, or to limit the number of children in a family so they can all be cared for. • In 1930 the Church of England approved artificial contraception used 'in the light of Christian principles'. • Christians who believe life begins at the moment of conception are against methods that prevent the fertilised egg from developing, as this is seen as causing an abortion and a form of murder.	A preference among some for contraception that prevents conception from taking place.
Buddhists	• Most Buddhists believe it is acceptable to use contraception that prevents conception. • Some believe contraception that prevents a fertilised egg from developing is a form of killing and breaks the first moral precept, so is not acceptable. • However they might make exceptions, e.g. if the birth threatens the mother's life, or if she would struggle to care for the child. • Having children is not considered an obligation; it may even be considered better not to have children if one wants to lead a spiritual life.	A preference among some for contraception that prevents conception from taking place.
Non-religious people in British society	• There is widespread acceptance of artificial contraception to help family planning. • Many people think it is responsible to use contraception to prevent unwanted pregnancies, control population growth, and prevent the spread of sexually transmitted diseases.	Any type of contraception.

APPLY

(A) Give **two** religious beliefs about the use of contraception.

(B) 'The Christian Church should not take a view on family planning.'
Evaluate this argument against the statement.

"The Christian Church is right to have a view on family planning as it believes marriage is a sacred bond and children are a gift from God to a married couple. If people selfishly prevent having children, they are going against the purpose of marriage."

TIP
The word 'Give' means you can simply write down two different beliefs. There is no need to go into any detail.

5.4 Religious teachings about marriage

Essential information:

☐ **Marriage** is a legal union between a man and a woman (or in some countries, including the UK, two people of the same sex) as partners in a relationship.

☐ Different religious and non-religious groups vary in their views about the purpose and nature of marriage, and whether **same-sex marriage** is acceptable.

☐ **Cohabitation** refers to a couple living together and having a sexual relationship without being married. It is common in Britain today, but not all Christians agree with it.

The purpose and nature of marriage

Non-religious views
- A legal union between two people in a relationship.
- A serious, lifelong commitment made in public to another person.
- Provides legal and financial benefits.

What is marriage?

Buddhist views
- A social contract rather than a religious duty or sacred act.
- A civil ceremony (monks may bless the marriage but can't conduct the ceremony itself).
- Can be between two people of the same sex.
- Helps the wellbeing of a community and society as a whole by cementing strong, trusting relationships that provide support, protection and happiness.

Christian views
- A gift from God and part of the natural law.
- A covenant (agreement) before God in which the couple promises to live faithfully together till death.
- A unique relationship between a man and woman that allows for the possibility of creating new life.

> ❝ God blessed them and said to them, "Be fruitful and increase in number." ❞ *Genesis 1:28* [NIV]

- A spiritual bond of trust that reflects the love of Christ for the Church.
- The proper place to enjoy sex, raise children in a religious faith, and provide a secure, stable environment for family life.

> ❝ The Church sees marriage between a man and woman, as central to the stability and health of human society. ❞ *House of Bishops of the General Synod of the Church of England*

Cohabitation

- In Britain many couples cohabit before they get married, or without ever getting married.
- They may want to see if the relationship will work before getting married, or may not believe it is necessary to get married.
- **Catholic and Orthodox Churches** oppose cohabitation as they believe sex should only take place within marriage.
- Many **Anglican and Protestant Christians** accept that although marriage is best, people may cohabit in a faithful, loving and committed way without being married.
- **Buddhist** teachings do not go against sex before marriage or cohabitation.

> **TIP**
> Cohabitation is one example of people having contrasting beliefs within a religion. Remember that not all people who belong to the same religion have the same beliefs.

A Here are two religious beliefs about the nature of marriage. **Develop** both of these beliefs by referring to a relevant religious belief, teaching or quotation.

"Marriage is God's gift to human beings."

"Marriage is a social contract between two consenting adults."

B 'Marriage gives more stability to society than cohabitation.'

Evaluate this statement by giving arguments for and against it.

5.5 Divorce and remarriage

Essential information:

☐ In the UK, **divorce** (legal ending of a marriage) is allowed after one year if a marriage cannot be saved. **Remarriage** is when someone marries again while their former husband or wife is still alive.

☐ Some religious groups oppose divorce and remarriage, while others may disapprove but accept they are sometimes the best way to reduce people's suffering.

Reasons for divorce

lack of communication

addiction

adultery

people changing and growing apart

Reasons for divorce

illness or disability

inability to have children

immaturity

domestic violence

work and money pressures

Christian and Buddhist views on divorce and remarriage

Christian views	Buddhist views
• Some Christians believe the **sanctity of the marriage vows** means they must be kept no matter what.	• In Buddhism there is no teaching that states divorce or remarriage are wrong.
• The Catholic Church teaches that **marriage is a sacrament** that is permanent, lifelong and cannot be dissolved by civil divorce. Catholics can separate but not remarry while their partner is still alive.	• But societies where Buddhism is prevalent tend to **disapprove of divorce**, which is seen as a last resort. This means couples put more effort into mending their relationship when it goes wrong.
• Other Christians believe that sometimes divorce is the **lesser of two evils** and should be allowed for compassionate reasons.	• However, clinging to an attachment that produces suffering goes against the Buddha's teachings.
• Protestant Churches (e.g. Methodists) accept civil divorce and allow remarriage in church under certain conditions. Divorced Anglicans can remarry in church with the bishop's permission.	• Most Buddhists would therefore consider divorce when it is not possible to reconcile the relationship, and it is the only way to reduce the couple's suffering.
• These Christians think the Church should **reflect God's forgiveness** and allow couples a second chance for happiness.	• Many Buddhists see remarriage as an opportunity to commit to a new, healthy relationship that increases people's happiness.
• Jesus taught that anyone who divorced and remarried was **committing adultery** (Mark 10:11–12).	
• But Matthew 5:32 says, 'If a man divorces his wife for any cause other than unchastity (unfaithfulness) he involves her in adultery'.	

TIP
Note that Mark 10:11–12 suggests divorce is always wrong, but Matthew 5:32 suggests it is acceptable in cases of unfaithfulness.

Christian and Buddhist responses to couples having marriage problems

- Christian churches may offer counselling, prayer and sacraments to support the couple.
- They may refer the couple to outside agencies such as Relate and ACCORD.
- Christians may be encouraged to bring forgiveness and reconciliation into their marriage.
- Buddhists may be encouraged to practise the five moral precepts more fully.

(A) Explain **two** reasons why couples get divorced.

(B) 'Divorce is never right.'

Write a paragraph to explain whether you agree or disagree with this statement. Then write a paragraph from another point of view.

TIP
Even when you favour one side of an argument, it is always good to be able to identify a contrasting view.

RECAP

Essential information:

☐ There are different types of **families** (people related by blood, marriage or adoption) in Britain, including nuclear families, extended families, and families with same-sex parents.

☐ In most families, parents and children are expected to fulfil certain roles and obligations to each other. For example, parents are expected to care for their children, and children are expected to obey their parents.

Types of family

Nuclear family

- A mother, father and children.
- The most common family type in the West.
- For Christians, it fulfils God's plan for a man and woman to be united together and increase in number (Genesis 1:28 and 2:24).

Extended family

- Includes grandparents and other relatives as well.
- In Biblical times, many people lived in extended families for extra support.
- Extended families are still common in Buddhist countries such as Thailand and Sri Lanka.

Families with same-sex parents

- When a homosexual couple raise children together.
- Some Christians disapprove of same-sex parents as they believe children should grow up with a male and female role model as parents.
- Other Christians, and most Buddhists, think it is more important for children to be in a secure and loving family regardless of the gender of their parents.

Polygamous families

- When a man has two wives.
- Illegal in the UK.
- For Christians, it goes against God's plan for marriage to be between one woman and one man, and can lead to sexual immorality (1 Corinthians 7:2).
- Not the favoured family model in Buddhism as it is considered likely to cause suffering to those involved.

Role of parents and children

In Christianity and Buddhism, parents and children are expected to fulfil certain roles or duties.

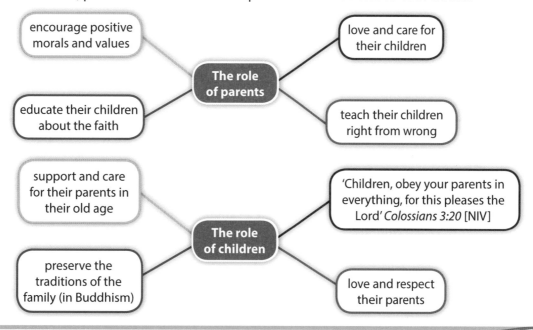

The role of parents
- encourage positive morals and values
- love and care for their children
- educate their children about the faith
- teach their children right from wrong

The role of children
- support and care for their parents in their old age
- 'Children, obey your parents in everything, for this pleases the Lord' *Colossians 3:20* [NIV]
- preserve the traditions of the family (in Buddhism)
- love and respect their parents

APPLY

(A) Give **two** religious beliefs about the nature of the family.

(B) 'Children should grow up in a loving, secure family whatever the gender of their parents.'

List arguments for and against the statement. Include religious views.

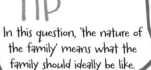

TIP

In this question, 'the nature of the family' means what the family should ideally be like.

RECAP

Essential information:

☐ The family is the main building block of society where **procreation** (bringing babies into the world) takes place.

☐ Happy, healthy families create **stability** for their members and society, helping to **protect children** and keep them safe from harm.

☐ For Christians and Buddhists, another purpose of the family is to **educate children in their faith** (bringing up children according to the religious beliefs of the parents).

The purpose of families

Procreation
- Mainly takes place within the family.
- There is more emphasis in Christianity (and especially Catholicism) on procreation as a purpose of the family.
- In Buddhism there are no religious pressures or expectations to have children.

Stability and the protection of children
- Families provide secure, stable environments for children to grow up in.
- Families offer mutual support and protection for their members.

> 66 Children thrive, grow and develop within the love and safeguarding of a family. Within the family we care for the young, the old and those with caring needs. 99
> *The Church of England website*

The purpose of families

Educating children in a faith
- **Christian** parents are expected to be good role models and teach their children Christian values.
- They should teach children about the faith and nurture their spiritual lives, which they may do through daily prayer.
- Some parents send their children to faith schools or groups run by their church for religious education.
- Most **Buddhist** parents teach their children Buddhist beliefs and practices, and how to show devotion and respect towards the Buddha.
- They will teach their children good morals and values (such as the five moral precepts – see page 78).
- They will usually involve their children in religious ceremonies and gatherings.
- Some may send their children to monasteries to be educated.

APPLY

Ⓐ Here are two religious beliefs about the role of parents in a religious family. **Develop** both points by explaining in more detail, adding an example, and referring to a relevant quotation from scripture or sacred writings.

"Buddhist parents teach their children moral values."

"Christian parents bring their children up in their faith."

Ⓑ **Evaluate** this argument to support the statement, 'Families should do more for their elderly relatives in Britain today.'

"When children leave home and move away from their parents, they may not realise the difficulties this can cause when their parents become old and infirm. If they live far away, they may not be able to do very much for their elderly relatives. Christians, though, believe they must 'Honour their father and mother' so they should still try to support elderly family members financially, take the time to Skype so they still feel part of the family, and keep their parents in their prayers."

TIP

The 'purpose of families' means what families are for, or why families are needed in society.

RECAP

Essential information:

☐ **Gender equality** means that men and women should be given the same rights and opportunities as each other.

☐ Issues standing in the way of gender equality include **gender prejudice** (holding biased opinions about people based on their gender), **sexual stereotyping** (having a fixed idea or image of how men and women will behave), and **gender discrimination** (acting against someone on the basis of their gender).

Gender discrimination and prejudice

The Sex Discrimination Act in 1975 made gender discrimination illegal in the UK. Despite this, it still occurs today.

Views on gender prejudice and discrimination, and the roles of men and women, vary between people based on their religious and personal beliefs.

> in Catholicism, women are not allowed to be ordained as priests

> in Theravada Buddhism, nuns are generally seen as subservient to monks

Examples of gender prejudice and discrimination

> in the UK, some women are paid less than men for doing the same jobs

> in the UK, women make up roughly half the workforce, but men hold a higher proportion of senior positions

In the UK	Christian views	Buddhist views
• In the past, men had more power and rights than women. • Traditional roles involved men working to support the family, and women caring for the home and raising children. • Today, most people in the UK are against gender prejudice and discrimination, but it still occurs. • The roles of men and women have become more flexible, and childcare is often shared more equally between parents. • Who takes on what role in a family may be decided by financial considerations or the different skills of the parents.	• Christians believe all people are created equal in the image of God (Genesis 1:27). ❝There is neither Jew nor Gentile, neither slave nor free, nor is there male and female, for you are all one in Christ Jesus.❞ *Galatians 3:28* [NIV] • The command to love one's neighbour means discrimination is wrong. • Jesus treated women with respect and welcomed them as disciples. • Some traditional Christians think husbands should rule over their wives, based on a literal interpretation of Genesis 3:16. • Most Christians today see marriage as an equal partnership.	• In the Buddha's time women were seen as inferior to men. • The Buddha ordained women as nuns, although was at first reluctant to do so. • The *Aparimitayur Sutra* suggests women must be reborn as men before they can achieve enlightenment. Some Buddhists still believe this today. • In contrast, the *Lotus Sutra* teaches that men and women are equal in their ability to attain enlightenment. • Many Buddhists today believe men and women should have equal status, and that gender discrimination expresses a lack of loving kindness. • E.g. the Triratna Buddhist Order has the same ordination process for men and women.

APPLY

(A) Give **two** religious reasons why gender equality is important.

(B) 'Men and women do not have equal rights.'

Develop this argument in support of the statement by explaining in more detail, adding an example and referring to a religious teaching or quotation.

"Despite the Sex Discrimination Act making gender discrimination illegal, women still get paid less than men for similar jobs. Often women face unfair questions at interviews. Looking at big businesses, there are still many more men than women in top positions. Even some religions expect women to stay home and look after children."

5 Exam practice

Test the 1 mark question

1 Which **one** of the following is **not** a reason why some marriages fail?

   A Domestic violence   B Adultery   C Addiction   D Stability   **[1 mark]**

2 Which **one** of the following describes a nuclear family?

   A A couple, children and grandparents   B A couple and their children

   C A couple, children, aunts and uncles   D A couple without children   **[1 mark]**

Test the 2 mark question

3 Give **two** religious beliefs about gender equality.   **[2 marks]**

   1) _____

   2) _____

4 Give **two** religious beliefs about cohabitation.   **[2 marks]**

   1) _____

   2) _____

> **TIP**
> Remember the main religious tradition of Great Britain is Christianity.

Test the 4 mark question

5 Explain **two** contrasting beliefs in contemporary British society about sex before marriage. In your answer you should refer to the main religious tradition of Great Britain and one or more other religious traditions.   **[4 marks]**

● **Explain one belief.**	Many Christians think that sex before marriage is wrong because this devalues sex.
● Develop your explanation with more detail/an example/ reference to a religious teaching or quotation.	They believe sex expresses a deep, lifelong union that first requires the commitment of marriage. It should not be a casual, temporary pleasure.
● **Explain a second contrasting belief.**	Buddhism teaches that sex before marriage is acceptable, and no less moral than sex after marriage.
● Develop your explanation with more detail/an example/ reference to a religious teaching or quotation.	What is wrong is to cause harm to others through sex, as expressed in the third moral precept.

6 Explain **two** contrasting religious beliefs about divorce. In your answer you must refer to one or more religious traditions.   **[4 marks]**

● **Explain one belief.**	
● Develop your explanation with more detail/an example/ reference to a religious teaching or quotation.	
● **Explain a second contrasting belief.**	
● Develop your explanation with more detail/an example/ reference to a religious teaching or quotation.	

> **TIP**
> You can answer this question from the perspective of two denominations of Christianity or from two religions.

7 Explain **two** contrasting religious beliefs about human sexuality. In your answer you must refer to one or more religious traditions.   **[4 marks]**

5 Exam practice

Test the 5 mark question

8 Explain **two** religious beliefs about the nature of marriage.

Refer to sacred writings or another source of religious belief and teaching in your answer. **[5 marks]**

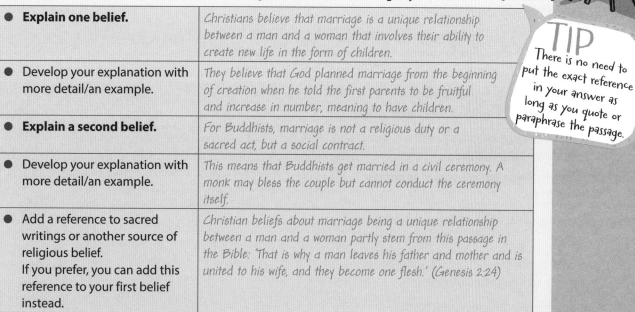

● **Explain one belief.**	*Christians believe that marriage is a unique relationship between a man and a woman that involves their ability to create new life in the form of children.*
● Develop your explanation with more detail/an example.	*They believe that God planned marriage from the beginning of creation when he told the first parents to be fruitful and increase in number, meaning to have children.*
● **Explain a second belief.**	*For Buddhists, marriage is not a religious duty or a sacred act, but a social contract.*
● Develop your explanation with more detail/an example.	*This means that Buddhists get married in a civil ceremony. A monk may bless the couple but cannot conduct the ceremony itself.*
● Add a reference to sacred writings or another source of religious belief. If you prefer, you can add this reference to your first belief instead.	*Christian beliefs about marriage being a unique relationship between a man and a woman partly stem from this passage in the Bible: 'That is why a man leaves his father and mother and is united to his wife, and they become one flesh.' (Genesis 2:24)*

TIP
There is no need to put the exact reference in your answer as long as you quote or paraphrase the passage.

9 Explain **two** religious beliefs about the purpose of families.

Refer to sacred writings or another source of religious belief and teaching in your answer. **[5 marks]**

● **Explain one belief.**	
● Develop your explanation with more detail/an example.	
● **Explain a second belief.**	
● Develop your explanation with more detail/an example.	
● Add a reference to sacred writings or another source of religious belief. If you prefer, you can add this reference to your first belief instead.	

10 Explain **two** religious beliefs about the role of children in a religious family.

Refer to sacred writings or another source of religious belief and teaching in your answer. **[5 marks]**

5 Exam practice

Test the 12 mark question

11 | 'The love and care parents show in bringing up their children is all that matters; the sex of the parents is unimportant.'

Evaluate this statement. In your answer you:

- should give reasoned arguments in support of this statement
- should give reasoned arguments to support a different point of view
- should refer to religious arguments
- may refer to non-religious arguments
- should reach a justified conclusion.

[12 marks]

Plus SPaG 3 mar

REASONED ARGUMENTS SUPPORTING A DIFFERENT POINT OF VIEW ● **Explain why some people would support a different view.** ● Develop your explanation with more detail and examples. ● Refer to religious teaching. Use a quote or paraphrase or a religious authority. ● **Evaluate the arguments.** Is this a good argument or not? Explain why you think this.	*It is true that the love and care parents show in bringing up their children is the most important thing for a good family life. Without love and care, children would grow up deprived of stability and security. But the statement says 'the sex of the parents is unimportant' and that is where people may have different views.* *Some Christians disapprove of same-sex parents because they think God made people male and female so that they would 'be fruitful and increase in number' (Genesis 1:28). Same-sex couples cannot do this naturally. Some think the ideal for children is to grow up with a male and female role model as parents, and that an important role of religious parents is to bring up their children in their faith. If their religion disagrees with homosexual relationships, then it is difficult for same-sex parents to bring their children up within a religion that they might feel disapproves of their behaviour.*
REASONED ARGUMENTS IN SUPPORT OF THE STATEMENT ● **Explain why some people would agree with the statement.** ● Develop your explanation with more detail and examples. ● Refer to religious teaching. Use a quote or paraphrase or a religious authority. ● **Evaluate the arguments.** Is this a good argument or not? Explain why you think this.	*On the other hand, many liberal Christians and Buddhists think that it is more important that children are raised in a secure and loving family regardless of the gender of their parents. There is nothing to say same-sex parents are not religious even if particular faiths disapprove of their relationships. Many can still bring their children up to love God or live spiritual and morally good lives.*
CONCLUSION ● **Give a justified conclusion.** ● Include your own opinion together with your own reasoning. ● **Include evaluation.** Explain why you think one viewpoint is stronger than the other or why they are equally strong. ● Do not just repeat arguments you have already used without explaining how they apply to your reasoned opinion/conclusion.	*In conclusion, I think that whether parents are good at bringing up children depends on the individuals and not on their gender. Some heterosexual couples spoil their children or even abuse them which does not show good parenting. Many children live in single-parent families so do not have the benefit of a male and female role model anyway. The most important thing any family should have is love, and this is at the heart of all religions.*

TIP
In this answer the studen begins by presenting a different point of view, followed by arguments supporting the statemen It doesn't matter which order the arguments appear in, as long as you remember to include bot sides.

TIP
Religious attitudes to some issues vary <u>within</u> religions well as <u>between</u> religions, s helps to say 'some Christia or 'liberal Christians' to sh you understand that not Christians share the same views.

12   'Marriage is the proper place to enjoy a sexual relationship.'

Evaluate this statement. In your answer you:

- should give reasoned arguments in support of this statement
- should give reasoned arguments to support a different point of view
- should refer to religious arguments
- may refer to non-religious arguments
- should reach a justified conclusion.

[12 marks]
Plus SPaG 3 marks

REASONED ARGUMENTS IN SUPPORT OF THE STATEMENT ● **Explain why some people would agree with the statement.** ● Develop your explanation with more detail and examples. ● Refer to religious teaching. Use a quote or paraphrase or a religious authority. ● **Evaluate the arguments.** Is this a good argument or not? Explain why you think this.	**TIP** When evaluating a statement like this one, do not simply list what different people think about the issues, for example 'Christians would agree that the best place to enjoy sex is in marriage. Buddhists think...' Remember to explain the reasons why they hold these opinions and to add an evaluation of how convincing you find these views to be.
REASONED ARGUMENTS SUPPORTING A DIFFERENT VIEW ● **Explain why some people would support a different view.** ● Develop your explanation with more detail and examples. ● Refer to religious teaching. Use a quote or paraphrase or a religious authority. ● **Evaluate the arguments.** Is this a good argument or not? Explain why you think this.	
CONCLUSION ● **Give a justified conclusion.** ● Include your own opinion together with your own reasoning. ● **Include evaluation.** Explain why you think one viewpoint is stronger than the other or why they are equally strong. ● Do not just repeat arguments you have already used without explaining how they apply to your reasoned opinion/conclusion.	

13   'It is wrong for religious couples to use artificial contraception within marriage.'

Evaluate this statement. In your answer you:

- should give reasoned arguments in support of this statement
- should give reasoned arguments to support a different point of view
- should refer to religious arguments
- may refer to non-religious arguments
- should reach a justified conclusion.

[12 marks]
Plus SPaG 3 marks

Check your answers using the mark scheme on pages 164–165. How did you do?
To feel more secure in the content you need to remember, re-read pages 84–91.
To remind yourself of what the examiner is looking for, go to pages 6–11.

6.1 The origins of the universe and the value of the world

RECAP

Essential information:

☐ The **Big Bang theory** suggests there was a massive expansion of space that set the creation of the universe in motion. This theory is accepted by most Christians and Buddhists.

☐ Christians also use the Genesis creation stories to explain the origins of the universe, which they believe was created by God.

☐ Buddhism sees the universe as being cyclical, with no creator.

The Big Bang theory

The Big Bang theory is currently the leading scientific explanation for how the universe began. It suggests the following events happened to form the universe as we know it today:

The universe started with a tiny, dense collection of mass	→	A massive expansion of space took place and the condensed matter was flung in all directions	→	As the universe expanded and cooled, the matter became stars grouped into galaxies	→	The universe has continued to expand over billions of years to form the cosmos as we know it today

Religious views on the origins of the universe

Christian views	Buddhist views
• Christians believe the universe was **designed and made by God** out of nothing.	• Buddhists do not generally believe in a creator of the universe.
• The creation story in Genesis 1 says that God made the universe and all life in it in six days (see page 15).	• Buddhism has a **cyclical vision of the universe** – each universe is followed by another one. There is no beginning or end to the whole process.
• Some **Fundamentalist Christians** believe the creation story describes exactly how the universe was created. Others believe the six days describe six longer periods of time.	• Buddhists can accept the Big Bang theory, as it does not necessarily state there was nothing before the Big Bang happened.
• **Liberal Christians** do not believe the Genesis creation story is a literal account of what actually happened. They believe the creation story is symbolic, with the main message being that God created the universe. They might look to science to understand how God did this.	• Buddhists consider it more important to find a way out of suffering than to understand the origins of the universe.
	• E.g. in the Buddha's parable of the man hit by a poisoned arrow, it is more important the man receives treatment (relief from suffering), not that he finds out where the arrow came from.

The value of the world

Christians view the earth as a priceless gift from God, loaned to humans as a result of his love. The beauty of the world can give a sense of **awe** and **wonder**, and devout respect for God's power of creation.

Buddhists value the world because it provides and sustains life. It also provides the conditions needed to achieve enlightenment. Buddhism teaches that although the world belongs to nobody, it is everyone's responsibility to look after it.

APPLY

(A) Give **two** contrasting beliefs about how the universe was created.

(B) 'The Big Bang theory explains how God created the universe.'

Develop one argument that agrees with this statement and one argument that disagrees with it.

6.2 The use and abuse of the environment

RECAP

Essential information:

☐ Most Christians believe God gave humans the responsibility to care for the world and protect the environment. This idea is known as stewardship.

☐ Buddhist teachings such as dependent arising and the five moral precepts encourage Buddhists to protect the environment.

☐ The overuse of natural resources (particularly those that are non-renewable) is a problem in the world today.

The duty of humans to protect the world

Christian beliefs about how people should interact with the environment stem from the ideas of stewardship and dominion.

Stewardship means Christians have a duty to look after the environment on behalf of God. This is implied in Genesis 2:15, when God puts Adam into the Garden of Eden to 'work it and take care of it'.

- This responsibility has been passed down to the rest of humanity, which means it is the role of all humans to look after the world for God. If they use the world wrongly, they are destroying what belongs to God.
- In return for caring for the world, humans may use it to sustain life.

> ❝Rule over the fish in the sea and the birds in the sky and over every living creature that moves on the ground.❞
> *Genesis 1:28* [NIV]

Genesis 1:28 teaches that God gave humans **dominion** (power and authority) over the world. A minority of Christians interpret this as meaning that humans can do whatever they want with the world. But most Christians want to care for the world as God's stewards.

Most **Buddhists** are aware of the importance of avoiding damage to the environment and of looking after the world for future generations. Reasons for this include the following:

Dependent arising (see page 51) teaches that all life is interconnected. All creatures depend on a healthy planet to survive.	If people misuse the environment, they will cause suffering for themselves and others. This contradicts the Buddhist aspiration to reduce suffering.	The first moral precept encourages Buddhists to avoid causing harm to living beings. This means looking after the world as the home of all living things.

> ❝I believe that not only should we keep our relationship with our other fellow human beings very gentle and non-violent, but it is also very important to **extend that kind of attitude to the natural environment.**❞
> *Tenzin Gyatso (the Dalai Lama)*

The use of natural resources

- **Natural resources** are materials found in nature (such as oil and trees) that can be used by people to make more complex products.
- Some natural resources (such as oil and gas) are non-renewable, which means they will eventually run out. Once they do, the world may have to adapt considerably in order to live without them.
- Reducing the use of natural resources, recycling more, using renewable energy sources (which do not run out), and helping to protect the environment are all ways that people can help to preserve the world for future generations.

APPLY

(A) **Explain** why it is important to develop renewable energy sources.

(B) 'Stewardship is more likely to encourage people to look after the earth than dominion.'

Give **two** arguments that agree with this statement and **develop** each one.

TIP
Remember that 'stewardship' and 'dominion' have specific religious meanings in the context of Christianity.

RECAP

Essential information:

☐ Air, land and water pollution are a major threat to life on earth.

☐ Christians and Buddhists show their concern by taking action to help to protect the earth.

What are the main types of pollution?

Pollution means to contaminate something, especially the environment. As the use of technology increases and the world's population grows, pollution becomes more of a problem, putting human and animal life at risk.

Pollution type	Cause	Possible problems caused
Air	Fumes from factories and transport	Asthma, diseases such as lung cancer, global warming, climate change and acid rain
Land	Poor disposal of waste	Chemicals pollute the earth causing poisoned wildlife, inefficient farming and poisoned food
Water	Dumping waste into rivers and seas	Oil spills and plastic waste kill birds and marine life

Religious views about pollution

Christians want to reduce pollution. They might base their views on the following beliefs and teachings:

- The world is on loan to humans, who have been given the responsibility by God to look after it (Genesis 1:28).
- The parable of the Talents (Matthew 25:14–30) warns that God will be the final judge about how responsible humans have been in looking after the earth.
- Pollution is not loving towards others – Jesus teaches Christians to 'love your neighbour' (Luke 10:27).

> ❝ The earth is the Lord's and everything in it. ❞ *Psalms 24:1* [NIV]

Buddhists are also keen to reduce pollution. One reason for this is that pollution directly or indirectly causes harm to all living creatures. This means it contradicts the first moral precept.

Examples of action that has been taken by Christians or Buddhists to help tackle pollution include the following:

- **Pope Francis has called on everyone to take action** to help protect the environment.
- In his open letter, 'On the Care of Our Common Home', he stressed the need to reduce pollution, use renewable energy and recycle more.

- **Some Christian groups work in their local communities** to clean up the environment, for example by litter-picking.
- Religious believers might also **join secular environmental organisations** such as Greenpeace and Friends of the Earth, which aim to tackle pollution on a wider scale.

- **The Holy Isle Project** is an example of a Buddhist project that aims to protect the local environment and reduce waste.
- Tibetan Buddhists who live on Holy Isle take care of the island's environment.
- E.g. they have planted 35,000 trees, reduced the amount of sewage entering the sea, and created a nature sanctuary for wildlife.

APPLY

Ⓐ Explain **two** religious beliefs about why polluting the earth is wrong.

Ⓑ 'Individual people cannot do anything to solve the global problem of pollution.'

Improve this argument against the statement by **developing** the points made, for example by adding examples and referring to religious teachings.

"Individual people can help to clean up their local environment, and if everyone does this then an impact will be felt worldwide. Also, individual people can donate to charities that have the resources to tackle pollution on a global scale."

6.4 The use and abuse of animals

Essential information:

☐ Many Christians believe animals should be treated kindly, but humans are more important.

☐ Buddhists believe it is important to treat animals with loving-kindness (metta) and compassion (karuna). Many Buddhists are vegetarians or vegans.

Religious attitudes towards animals

Christians believe animals were created by God for humans to use and care for. Many believe humans are more important than animals as they were created in the image of God, but animals should still be treated kindly.

Most **Buddhists** believe animals should be treated with kindness and compassion. The principle of kamma (see page 75) teaches that causing harm to animals is unskilful and will lead to suffering. It also goes against the first moral precept (see page 78). The Eightfold Path teaches that Buddhists should not make a living from activities that cause harm to others, including animals (see page 59).

> You might be asked to compare beliefs on animal experimentation between Christianity (the main religious tradition in Great Britain) and another religious tradition.

Animal experimentation

Scientists use animals to test new products such as cosmetics, medicines and food, to make sure they are safe for human use.

Christian views	Buddhist views
• Most Christians believe that if testing is proved to be necessary, and the welfare of the animals is considered, it is justified to ensure human safety. • Many believe animals can be used to help save human lives.	• Some Buddhists are against animal experimentation because they believe animals should not be harmed (see above). • Others believe it is acceptable if it is the only way to save many human lives.

The use of animals for food

Vegetarians do not eat meat or fish, while **vegans** do not eat animals or food produced by animals (such as eggs). Vegans also try not to use products that have caused harm to animals (such as leather).

Christian views	Buddhist views
• Christianity has no rules about eating meat. • Romans 14:3 says Christians should be sensitive to the beliefs of others about what they wish to eat. • Most Christians eat meat. They believe God gave humans animals to use for food. ❝ Everything that lives and moves about will be food for you. ❞ *Genesis 9:3* [NIV] • Some vegetarians and vegans point out that if crops were grown on land currently used to raise animals for meat, there would be much more food to go round, and this would please God.	• Many Buddhists are vegetarian or vegan because they believe this reduces the harm caused to animals. • Some Mahayana scriptures state the Buddha insisted his followers should not eat meat or fish. • This is because it does not show compassion, and creates an atmosphere of fear among all living beings. ❝ All tremble at violence; all fear death. Comparing [others] with oneself, one should not kill or cause to kill. ❞ *The Buddha in the Dhammapada, verse 129* • Other scriptures include references to the Buddha and his monks eating meat.

(A) Explain **two** religious reasons why some people do not eat meat.

(B) 'Experimenting on animals is wrong because it is cruel.'

Develop this point of view and elaborate it with religious teachings. Make sure to explain how the teachings are relevant to the argument.

RECAP

Essential information:

☐ **The theory of evolution** is the theory that higher forms of life have gradually developed (evolved) from lower ones.

☐ Many Christians think it is possible to believe both the creation stories in Genesis and the theory of evolution.

☐ Buddhism teaches that life began when the conditions were right for it to do so. This view is based on dependent arising.

The theory of evolution

In 1859, in a book called *On the Origin of Species by Means of Natural Selection*, Charles Darwin put forward the theory of evolution. Darwin suggested that as the earth cooled, conditions became right to support life. Simple organisms then evolved over many years into other species:

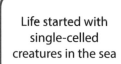

| Life started with single-celled creatures in the sea | → | Over a long period of time they evolved into creatures capable of living on land | → | Humans started evolving around 2.5 million years ago | → | They developed into humans with the same anatomy as us about 200,000 years ago |

Creatures were able to change or **adapt** into their environment and thrived. This is called survival of the fittest.

Christian beliefs about the origins of life

- Genesis 1 says that **God created all life**, with human life being created last.
- Genesis 2 tells how **God created the first man**, Adam, from the soil and breathed life into him.
- Some time later, while Adam was asleep, God took one of his ribs and used it to **create a woman**, Eve. Eve was created to help Adam, and to live in a close relationship with him and with God.

Many Christians do not believe this to be literally true (although some do). Instead they interpret the story as showing that humans are special to God because they were created in his image.

Fundamentalist Christians do not believe in the theory of evolution. They believe God created each species separately. Some believe life was created exactly as described in Genesis 1 and 2.

The majority of Christians accept the theory of evolution but believe that God is the creator: he started the process and evolution explains how life developed afterwards.

Buddhist views on the origins of life

- The Buddha said that anything (including life) can come into existence when the necessary conditions are there. This process does not rely on a creator God – it just happens.
- Buddhism teaches it is not possible to identify a beginning or end to the earth. Instead the earth is in a continuous process of change.
- When the conditions were right on earth, plants and animals came into being. As conditions continued to change, life continued to evolve.
- This means that Buddhist ideas do not conflict with the theory of evolution.

> **TIP**
> Buddhist views about the origins and evolution of life are influenced by the teaching of dependent arising. See page 51 for more on this.

APPLY

A Explain **one** scientific teaching and **one** religious teaching about the origins of life.

B Choose one of the theories about the origin of life and give your opinion on whether you agree with it. Write **two developed reasons** to support your opinion.

RECAP

Essential information:

☐ Abortion is legal in the UK provided doctors agree it meets certain criteria.

☐ Christians and Buddhists generally oppose abortion, although some agree with it in certain situations (such as if the child would have a very poor quality of life).

You might be asked to compare beliefs on abortion between Christianity (the main religious tradition in Great Britain) and another religious tradition.

Abortion in the UK

- **Abortion** is the deliberate removal of a foetus from the womb in order to end a pregnancy.
- In the UK, an abortion can take place in a licensed clinic if two doctors agree there is a risk to the physical or mental health of the mother, the baby, or existing children in the family.
- Abortion can only happen during the first 24 weeks of pregnancy unless the mother's life is in danger or the foetus is severely deformed. In these cases there is no time limit.

Christian and Buddhist attitudes towards abortion

Christian views	Buddhist views
• Christians believe in the **sanctity of life**. This means human life is sacred as it is made in the image of God. All human life should be valued and respected. • Many Christians who believe **life begins at the moment of conception** think abortion is wrong, as it is taking away life that is given by God. • However, some Christians think **abortion is sometimes acceptable**, e.g. if the pregnancy is the result of rape or the child would have a very poor quality of life.	• In general, abortion is seen as a **form of killing** which goes against the first moral precept and so is unskilful. • However, Buddhists **may sometimes favour abortion**, such as when the baby is likely to be born with a serious disability, or have a poor quality of life. • Some Buddhists believe that deciding to have an abortion is a **question of personal choice**. • Buddhist views on abortion **differ from country to country** depending on social norms and traditions.

Further arguments for and against abortion

Religious and non-religious people might also be pro-choice (for abortion) or pro-life (against abortion) for the following reasons:

For	Against
• Pro-choice groups believe the mother's life is more important. • The mother has to carry the baby, give birth to it and bring it up, so she should have the right to choose whether to continue with the pregnancy. • Life doesn't start until birth (or from the point when the foetus can survive outside the womb), so abortion does not involve killing. • It is cruel to allow a severely disabled child to be born.	• Pro-life groups argue that as life begins at conception, abortion is a form of murder. • It is possible for disabled children to enjoy a good quality of life, so they should be allowed to live. • Unwanted children can be adopted into families that will care for them. • Those who choose abortion can suffer from depression and guilt afterwards.

APPLY

(A) Explain **two** religious teachings that may be used to argue against abortion.

(B) 'If the child's quality of life is not going to be good, abortion is the best option.'

Write a developed argument to support this statement, and a developed argument to support a different point of view.

TIP
The commandment 'do not kill' is often used when discussing Christian views on abortion. If you use it as part of an answer, you should explain it is only relevant if someone believes that life begins at conception or some point before an abortion happens.

6.7 Euthanasia

RECAP

Essential information:

☐ **Euthanasia** is the painless killing of a patient who is suffering from an incurable and painful illness, or who is in an irreversible coma.

☐ Christians and Buddhists generally oppose euthanasia, although some may agree with it when it seems to be the most loving and compassionate action to take.

 You might be asked to compare beliefs on euthanasia between Christianity (the main religious tradition in Great Britain) and another religious tradition.

What is euthanasia?

Euthanasia describes a situation in which someone helps another person to die by deliberately giving them life-ending medication. There are three different types of euthanasia:

voluntary: the ill person asks for their life to be ended because they don't want to live any more	**involuntary:** the person is capable of expressing a choice but is not given the opportunity to do so	**non-voluntary:** the person is too ill to ask to die, possibly in a coma, but the doctor ends their life as it is thought to be in their best interests

- Euthanasia is sometimes described as **'active euthanasia'** because it involves active, deliberate steps to end a person's life. It is **illegal in the UK**.
- Doctors may decide to withdraw medical treatment that is keeping someone alive if they believe the person cannot recover or if the person asks then to. This is called a **non-treatment decision** and is **legal in the UK**. It is also sometimes called **passive euthanasia**.

Christian and Buddhist attitudes towards euthanasia

Christian views	Buddhist views
• Many Christians believe euthanasia is a form of murder and **interferes with God's plan** for a person's life.	• Many Buddhists oppose euthanasia because it **goes against the first moral precept**.
• They believe that euthanasia is **against the sanctity of life,** and **only God has the right to take away life**.	• At the same time, many Buddhists would **respect the right of the individual** to do what they wish with their own life.
• They might argue that if euthanasia were legal, the very old **could feel pressure to end their lives** in order not to burden their family.	• Some Buddhists would argue it could be **compassionate to help someone end their life** if they are suffering a lot.
• They might argue that **suffering brings people closer to God** and helps them to understand Jesus' suffering.	• The **state of mind** of the person at death is important, as it influences their rebirth (see page 75). If a person is helped to die quickly and peacefully, this could benefit their future consciousness.
• The Salvation Army has said that euthanasia and assisted suicide 'undermine human dignity and are morally wrong'.	• At other times, a natural death (eased by meditation and painkillers) might be better for a person's kamma.
• Some Christians support euthanasia when it seems the **most loving thing to do**.	• The Dalai Lama has commented that euthanasia **should be avoided except in exceptional circumstances**.
• They may argue that as **God gave people free will** they should be able to choose when to end their lives.	

APPLY

Ⓐ **Explain** one argument in favour of euthanasia. Then explain a Christian or Buddhist teaching that opposes euthanasia.

Ⓑ 'Euthanasia should be allowed in the UK.'

Explain your opinion and include your reasoning. **Refer to religious teachings** as part of your answer.

 TIP
You can use the Christian teaching 'love your neighbour' in a discussion of euthanasia. However, to use it most effectively, consider to whom an action is most loving and to whom it may not be loving.

6.8 Death and the afterlife

RECAP

Essential information:

☐ Christians and Buddhists both believe death is not the end.

☐ Many Christians believe that after death they are judged by God and spend eternity in heaven or hell.

☐ Many Buddhists believe that after death they are reborn. Rebirths then continue until enlightenment.

Christian beliefs about death and the afterlife

Christians believe Jesus' resurrection is evidence for an afterlife. Many Christians believe that after death, they are **judged by God** and will either be **eternally with God** (heaven) or **eternally without God** (hell). The desire to be close to God motivates them to **have faith in Jesus** and **follow his teachings**.

Further beliefs about the afterlife include the following:

- Catholics believe in a middle stage called purgatory, where souls are purified to allow them into heaven.
- Some Christians believe judgement happens as soon as a person dies.
- Others believe Jesus will return on a future Day of Judgement when all souls will be judged.
- Some believe people will be in heaven in their physical bodies, while others believe it is just their souls that enter heaven.
- Some believe that God, who is the source of all good, would not condemn people to hell and that all go to heaven. Others believe that all who go to hell deserve their fate.

> ❝ For God so loved the world that he gave his one and only Son, that **whoever believes in him shall not perish but have eternal life**. ❞
> *John 3:16* [NIV]

TIP

Christian beliefs about the afterlife are discussed in more detail on pages 20–21.

Buddhist teachings about death and the afterlife

- Many Buddhists believe death is a **process** rather than a single moment. The consciousness passes on from the physical body over a period of hours or days.
- Most Buddhist traditions teach that people are **reborn** after they die. This means that at some point after death, the person's consciousness enters another life at the point of its conception.
- The quality of the rebirth is dependent upon the **ethical quality of the person's actions** in their previous life (their kamma). Skilful behaviour builds 'merit', which leads to a favourable rebirth.
- Many Buddhists believe that what happens after death depends on their **state of mind** when they die.
- Someone who becomes **enlightened** is freed of future rebirths.

TIP

For more on how a person's kamma affects their future rebirth, see page 75.

> ❝ **Having reached perfection**, fearless, without craving, without blemish, he has cut off the darts of existence. **This body is his last.** ❞
> *The Buddha in the Dhammapada, verse 351*

APPLY

(A) Explain **two** religious teachings about the afterlife.

(B) 'Beliefs about the afterlife should motivate religious believers to spend their lives helping others.'

By referring to two different religions, **develop** an argument to support this statement. Then develop an argument which supports a different point of view.

Test the 1 mark question

1   Which **one** of the following is the meaning of the term euthanasia?

| A | A type of abortion | B | A method of animal testing |

| C | A painless death | D | A scientific view about the origin of the earth | **[1 mark]**

2   Which **one** of the following is the leading scientific theory for how life on earth developed?

| A | Sustainable development | B | The sanctity of life |

| C | Dependent arising | D | The theory of evolution | **[1 mark]**

Test the 2 mark question

3   Give **two** religious reasons for reducing pollution.   **[2 marks]**

1) _____

2) _____

4   Give **two** religious beliefs about the treatment of animals.   **[2 marks]**

1) _____

2) _____

> **TIP**
> Here the beliefs are 'contrasting' because one is against euthanasia and one is for euthanasia. But you could also give two beliefs that are <u>both</u> for or against euthanasia, but for different reasons. If the reasons are different enough, this would still count as giving 'contrasting' beliefs.

Test the 4 mark question

5   Explain **two** contrasting beliefs in contemporary British society about euthanasia.
In your answer you should refer to the main religious tradition of Great Britain and one or more other religious traditions.   **[4 marks]**

● **Explain one belief.**	Christians believe in the sanctity of life so most think that euthanasia is wrong.
● Develop your explanation with more detail/an example/reference to a religious teaching or quotation.	The sanctity of life means that life is God-given and sacred. This means that life is valuable and should be treated with respect – not ended prematurely.
● **Explain a second contrasting belief.**	Buddhists believe that while euthanasia generally goes against the first moral precept, it may reduce suffering and so may be acceptable in certain circumstances.
● Develop your explanation with more detail/an example/reference to a religious teaching or quotation.	If someone is living with unbearable suffering, it may be more compassionate to help them to die, rather than prolong their suffering until they die of natural causes.

6   Explain **two** similar religious beliefs about animal experimentation. In your answer, you must refer to one or more religious traditions.   **[4 marks]**

● **Explain one belief.**	
● Develop your explanation with more detail/an example/reference to a religious teaching or quotation.	
● **Explain a second similar belief.**	
● Develop your explanation with more detail/an example/reference to a religious teaching or quotation.	

6 Exam practice

7 Explain **two** contrasting religious beliefs about the value of the world.

In your answer, you must refer to one or more religious traditions. **[4 marks]**

Test the 5 mark question

8 Explain **two** religious beliefs about what happens when a person dies.

Refer to sacred writings or another source of religious belief and teaching in your answer. **[5 marks]**

● **Explain one belief.**	*Christians believe in the resurrection of the dead.*
● Develop your explanation with more detail/an example.	*Christians believe Jesus' resurrection proved there is life after death because he came back to life after being crucified, so those who believe in him can also have eternal life in heaven.*
● **Explain a second belief.**	*Buddhists believe that when people die they will be reborn into a new body.*
● Develop your explanation with more detail/an example.	*The kind of rebirth that someone can expect depends upon their kamma, that is if they have lived a skilful or unskilful life.*
● Add a reference to sacred writings or another source of religious belief. If you prefer, you can add this reference to your first belief instead.	*The Christian belief in resurrection is supported by John 11 in the Bible: Jesus said to her, "I am the resurrection and the life. He who believes in me will live, even though he dies; and whoever lives and believes in me will never die"' (John 11:25–26).*

9 Explain **two** religious beliefs about the duty of human beings to protect the earth.

Refer to sacred writings or another source of religious belief and teaching in your answer. **[5 marks]**

TIP
There is no need to include the exact Bible reference and doing so will not earn you any additional marks.

● **Explain one belief.**	
● Develop your explanation with more detail/an example.	
● **Explain a second belief.**	
● Develop your explanation with more detail/an example.	
● Add a reference to sacred writings or another source of religious belief. If you prefer, you can add this reference to your first belief instead.	

10 Explain **two** religious beliefs about the origins of the universe.

Refer to sacred writings or another source of religious belief and teaching in your answer. **[5 marks]**

6 Exam practice

Test the 12 mark question

11 'Religious believers should not eat meat.'

Evaluate this statement. In your answer you:
- should give reasoned arguments in support of this statement
- should give reasoned arguments to support a different point of view
- should refer to religious arguments
- may refer to non-religious arguments
- should reach a justified conclusion.

[12 marks]

Plus SPaG 3 ma

REASONED ARGUMENTS IN SUPPORT OF THE STATEMENT ● **Explain why some people would agree with the statement.** ● Develop your explanation with more detail and examples. ● Refer to religious teaching. Use a quote or paraphrase or a religious authority. ● **Evaluate the arguments.** Is this a good argument or not? Explain why you think this.	*Eating meat involves the killing of animals to provide the meat. This is seen by many religious believers as cruel and unnecessary, and they are quite happy to be vegetarians. For example, Buddhists would agree with this statement as they believe that all life, in whatever form, should be respected. They believe the first moral precept teaches you should not harm other living beings.* *Buddhists also believe there are karmic consequences for unskilful actions (such as harming animals), and killing animals is not showing compassion for life.* *Some people might argue that Christians should not eat meat because it means that overall there is less food to go round (as animals take up more resources and land to farm than crops), which contributes to poverty and suffering that is not pleasing to God.*
REASONED ARGUMENTS SUPPORTING A DIFFERENT VIEW ● **Explain why some people would support a different view.** ● Develop your explanation with more detail and examples. ● Refer to religious teaching. Use a quote or paraphrase or a religious authority. ● **Evaluate the arguments.** Is this a good argument or not? Explain why you think this.	*Most Christians do eat meat because they believe it is a good source of protein or they like the taste of it. Although they believe animals should not be treated cruelly, they believe they were created by God for human use. In Genesis it says that after the flood, God told Noah that animals could be used for food. Also in the New Testament it implies that Jesus ate fish and saw nothing wrong with fishing as an occupation. Although some Christians choose to be vegetarian, the majority believe it is acceptable to eat meat as humans have been given the power to rule over animals (Genesis 1:28).*
CONCLUSION ● **Give a justified conclusion.** ● Include your own opinion together with your own reasoning. ● **Include evaluation.** Explain why you think one viewpoint is stronger than the other or why they are equally strong. ● Do not just repeat arguments you have already used without explaining how they apply to your reasoned opinion/conclusion.	*So there is a difference of opinion concerning whether it is right to eat meat. Although I can see why some people prefer not to kill animals, I believe meat is important for a balanced diet. Also many farmers would lose their livelihoods if people stopped eating meat. In my opinion it would be unfair on religious believers if they were prevented from enjoying meat. I can see that if your religion opposes eating meat then you would need to keep the rules of your faith. However, within Christianity this does not apply as God expressly gave Noah permission to eat meat.*

TIP
The Buddhist content above is an excellent chain of reasoning. It starts with an introductory statement, leading to an opinion, followed by development of the point that refers to religious teachings.

TIP
This is a good conclusion because it includes reference to the arguments already made and supports them with more reasoning, not just the same as before.

12 'In the UK, the law should be changed to make it easier for women to have abortions.'

Evaluate this statement. In your answer you:

- should give reasoned arguments in support of this statement
- should give reasoned arguments to support a different point of view
- should refer to religious arguments
- may refer to non-religious arguments
- should reach a justified conclusion.

TIP
Make sure you focus on whether the law should be changed, not just on whether abortion is right or wrong.

[12 marks]
Plus SPaG 3 marks

REASONED ARGUMENTS IN SUPPORT OF THE STATEMENT ● **Explain why some people would agree with the statement.** ● Develop your explanation with more detail and examples. ● Refer to religious teaching. Use a quote or paraphrase or a religious authority. ● **Evaluate the arguments.** Is this a good argument or not? Explain why you think this.	
REASONED ARGUMENTS SUPPORTING A DIFFERENT VIEW ● **Explain why some people would support a different view.** ● Develop your explanation with more detail and examples. ● Refer to religious teaching. Use a quote or paraphrase or a religious authority. ● **Evaluate the arguments.** Is this a good argument or not? Explain why you think this.	
CONCLUSION ● **Give a justified conclusion.** ● Include your own opinion together with your own reasoning. ● **Include evaluation.** Explain why you think one viewpoint is stronger than the other or why they are equally strong. ● Do not just repeat arguments you have already used without explaining how they apply to your reasoned opinion/conclusion.	

13 'Humans should use the earth's resources however they wish.'

Evaluate this statement. In your answer you:

- should give reasoned arguments in support of this statement
- should give reasoned arguments to support a different point of view
- should refer to religious arguments
- may refer to non-religious arguments
- should reach a justified conclusion.

[12 marks]
Plus SPaG 3 marks

Check your answers using the mark scheme on pages 165–66. How did you do?
To feel more secure in the content you need to remember, re-read pages 96–103.
To remind yourself of what the examiner is looking for, go to pages 6–11.

7.1 The Design argument

RECAP

Essential information:

☐ The **Design argument** says that because everything in the universe is so intricately made, it must have been created by God. Therefore God exists.

☐ Over the centuries, there have been several different ways of illustrating the Design argument in order to explain it.

☐ There are a number of objections to this argument.

Did God create the universe?

- **Christians and other theists** believe in God and that God created the universe.
- Because everything in the universe is so intricate and complex, God must have designed it.
- Genesis 1 supports this view.

Atheists, who don't believe in God, believe the universe was not created but instead evolved naturally.

Agnostics believe there is not enough evidence that God exists or that he created the universe.

- **Buddhism** is usually described as non-theistic (does not involve worship of a creator God), so does not rely on the idea of God to explain the universe.
- Instead Buddhism teaches that all things come into existence when the necessary conditions are present.

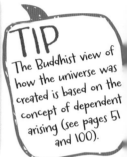
TIP
The Buddhist view of how the universe was created is based on the concept of dependent arising (see pages 51 and 100).

Different versions of the Design argument

William Paley	Isaac Newton	Thomas Aquinas	F. R. Tennant

Paley argued that the workings of a watch are so intricate they must have been designed by a watchmaker. Something so complex cannot be produced by chance. Similarly, the universe is so complex and intricate that it must have been designed by God.	Newton argued that the human thumb, which permits delicate movement such as tying shoelaces, must have been designed, and that such design could only be achieved by God.	Aquinas argued that only an intelligent being could keep everything in the universe in regular order. The fact that the planets rotate in the solar system without colliding is because of God.	Tennant put forward the idea that as everything is just right for humans to develop, it must have been designed. He referred to the strength of gravity being absolutely right, and the force and speed of the explosion caused by the Big Bang being perfect to sustain life.

Objections to the Design argument

- Natural selection happens by chance. Species 'design' themselves through the process of evolution, not through a designer God.
- If God is good, and he designed the universe, why is there so much suffering?
- The order in the universe, which is necessary to support life, makes it look as though it is designed. In reality, the order and structure in nature is imposed by humans to help explain it.

APPLY

(A) Choose **two** arguments in favour of the Design argument and summarise their main points.

(B) 'The Design argument proves that God exists.'

Write **two developed arguments** in response to this statement, one in agreement and one against.

TIP
You should learn the strengths and weaknesses of the Design argument and be prepared to argue the case for each, regardless of what you believe.

7.2 The First Cause argument

Essential information:

☐ The **First Cause argument** states there has to be an uncaused cause that made everything else happen.

☐ Thomas Aquinas put forward an argument which he said proved the existence of God.

☐ There are a number of objections to this argument.

TIP
This five-point chain of reasoning gives a simple overview of the First Cause argument. Try to remember it so you can use it to explain the First Cause argument in your exam.

What is the First Cause argument?

Some Christians argue in favour of the First Cause argument. Their chain of reasoning runs like this:

| Everything that exists or begins to exist must have a cause | → | As the universe exists and had a beginning, it too must have a cause | → | There must be something existing with no cause, which is eternal, to cause everything else to exist | → | The eternal first cause can only be God | → | This means God must exist |

- The key assumption in the First Cause argument is that the **universe had a starting point**.
- Many scientists believe the universe started with the Big Bang.
- Christians and other theists would argue that God caused the Big Bang.
- They would argue that if the universe was eternal, there would be no adequate explanation for its existence, so it must have had a cause.

Thomas Aquinas' First Cause argument

Aquinas argued that everything in the universe is caused to exist. Nothing can become something by itself, and nothing equals nothing and remains nothing unless something is added. As nothing can cause itself to exist, either there is:

- an infinite chain of effects preceded by causes, or
- a first cause that is itself uncaused by anything else (God).

Objections to the First Cause argument

- If everything that exists has a cause, who or what caused God?
- If God is eternal then the universe could be eternal as well.
- The idea that everything has a cause does not necessarily mean the universe has to have a cause as well (or that the cause must be God).
- The Big Bang was a random event and had nothing to do with God.
- Religious creation stories about how God brought the universe into being, such as the ones in Genesis, are myths. The truth they tell is spiritual, not literal.

Buddhism teaches that the universe is cyclical, with no beginning. Consequently, there is no first cause and no need to introduce God as an explanation. There is just a process of endless change without beginning or end.

A Explain **two** reasons why Buddhists do not agree with the First Cause argument.

B 'The First Cause argument proves that God exists.'

"The First Cause argument proves that God exists because it explains how God must be the cause of the universe. The argument shows how the universe (like everything else) must have a cause, and this cause must be eternal. God is the only eternal being, so God must exist."

Write a developed argument in response to this answer, to oppose the statement above.

RECAP

Essential information:

☐ **Miracles** are seemingly impossible events that cannot be explained by natural or scientific laws, and are thought by Christians to be the action of God.

☐ Some Christians think miracles prove God's existence. They show God's love and help to strengthen a believer's faith.

☐ Atheists and agnostics argue that miracles may be lucky coincidences or have scientific explanations that we don't yet know about.

> You might be asked to compare beliefs on miracles between Christianity (the main religious tradition in Great Britain) and another religious tradition.

Different attitudes to miracles

Christians and theists	Atheists and agnostics	Buddhists
• If there is no scientific explanation for an event, it must be caused by something outside nature, i.e. God. • The fact that some people convert to Christianity after experiencing a miracle is proof of God's existence. • 69 healing miracles have officially been recognised by the Catholic Church as taking place at Lourdes (a pilgrimage site in France). • Jesus performed miracles.	• Miracles are no more than lucky coincidences. • They may have scientific explanations we don't yet know about. • Some miracles are deliberately made up for fame or money. • Miracle healings may be the result of mind over matter or misdiagnosis.	• Tradition says that meditators may develop miraculous powers, but that these are not necessarily signs of spirituality. • Nor do they prove the existence of God. • Buddhist scriptures are also full of apparently miraculous events. • These are usually not interpreted literally. Instead they are considered to be symbolic, intended to express spiritual truths.

Examples of miracles

Here are two examples of religious miracles, one from Christianity and one from Buddhism:

- In 1902, the French woman Marie Bailly was diagnosed with tubercular peritonitis, which made her abdomen swell and meant she couldn't eat.
- She asked to visit Lourdes, but on arrival was so ill she had to be taken to hospital, where doctors told her she was dying.
- She returned to Lourdes, where holy water was poured on her abdomen and she prayed to Mary.
- She returned to good health.

- Once when the Buddha was meditating, a heavy rainstorm occurred.
- Mucalinda, the king of the serpents, encircled the Buddha and spread his hood over him to give him protection from the rain.
- After seven days when the Buddha finished meditating, Mucalinda uncoiled himself, took on the appearance of a youth, and bowed before the Buddha.

APPLY

(A) **Explain** how some Christians use miracles to prove their faith in God.

(B) Finish the argument below. Then **write a reasoned argument** to express a different point of view

"When atheists argue against miracles I believe they are right because..."

TIP
Memorise at least one example of a miracle, as you may be required to write about it in your exam.

7.4 Further arguments against the existence of God

Essential information:

☐ Some people use science and the existence of **evil** (the opposite of good) and **suffering** (when people have to live with unpleasant conditions) to question the existence of God.

☐ They argue that God was invented to explain what science couldn't, and a good and all-powerful God would not create a world with evil and suffering in it.

☐ Christians respond by saying there does not have to be a conflict between religion and science, and that evil and suffering exist because of free will.

How science may challenge belief in God

Arguments against the existence of God	Christian and Buddhist responses
• Some atheists think religious beliefs, especially about God, were invented by people to answer questions about the universe that in the past could not be explained. 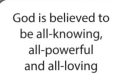 • Similarly, questions about hardship and suffering, such as disease or the failure of crops, could best be explained as punishment by God for wrongdoing. • Science can now answer many questions that in the past couldn't be answered without the idea of God. • In the future, science will be able to answer all questions, so the idea of God is no longer necessary or helpful. • The fact that science is close to creating human life provides further evidence there is no God.	• Many **Christians** see no conflict between science and religion, as they believe the Genesis creation stories should not be interpreted literally. • This means they can accept scientific theories about the origins of the universe. • They believe science reveals the laws by which God created the universe. ❝The big bang […] does not contradict the divine act of creation. Rather, it requires it. ❞ *Pope Francis* • Fundamentalist Christians argue it is wrong to change religious truths to fit scientific laws, which they believe other Christians are doing when they view the creation stories as myths. • In general, **Buddhists** do not regard science as presenting a challenge to Buddhist teachings.

Evil and suffering as an argument against the existence of God

Atheists argue that the existence of evil and suffering proves God does not exist:

God is believed to be all-knowing, all-powerful and all-loving → If this is true, God should be aware of evil → If God is aware of evil, he should want to use his powers to prevent the effects of it → God doesn't do this, so he doesn't exist

Christian responses	Buddhist responses
• Suffering and evil are a result of free will. • They were brought into God's perfect world by Adam and Eve, who used their free will to disobey God. • Giving humans the ability to choose what they do gives them the power to make bad choices. • If there was nothing bad in the world, no one would be able to exercise compassion, learn from their mistakes, or actively choose good over bad.	• Buddhism teaches ethical responsibility: because people can choose their actions, they can choose to act in an evil way. • People act in evil ways because they are in the grip of greed, hatred and ignorance (the three poisons). • Because of kamma, they will suffer as a result of their actions. • Suffering is an inevitable part of life but can be overcome through enlightenment.

(A) Explain **two** reasons why atheists might believe that evil and suffering prove God doesn't exist, and **two** ways that Christians might counter their reasoning.

(B) **Write two logical chains of reasoning**, one to agree that science is correct in challenging the existence of God, and the other to disagree.

TIP
Remember that a logical chain of reasoning can express an opinion, give a reason to support the opinion, and further develop the reason, possibly using religious arguments to elaborate it.

RECAP

Essential information:

☐ For Christians, **special revelation** is when God makes himself known through direct personal experience. For Buddhists, it is when a unique, specific event (such as a vision) gives them greater insight into the nature of reality (or ultimate reality).

☐ In Buddhism, gaining true knowledge of the nature of reality is known as **enlightenment**. It is gained through meditation and other spiritual practices.

You might be asked to compare beliefs on visions between Christianity (the main religious tradition in Great Britain) and another religious tradition.

Special revelation

- **Christians** believe they cannot fully understand God, but they can know something of his nature and purpose through revelations.
- Special revelation is when a person experiences God directly in a particular event.
- Examples from the Bible include Moses receiving the Ten Commandments from God, or Mary finding out from the angel Gabriel that she would give birth to Jesus.
- For **Buddhists**, special revelations can help people to understand the nature of reality.
- For example, a Buddhist may have a vision of a Buddha or Bodhisattva while meditating, who communicates something to them about how to achieve enlightenment.

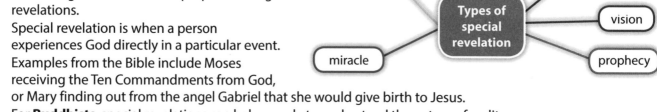

hearing God's call · dream · **Types of special revelation** · vision · miracle · prophecy

Visions

A **vision** is a type of special revelation. It usually involves seeing an image of a person or spiritual being, and receiving messages from them.

Here are two examples of visions, one from Christianity and one from Buddhism:

TIP
Memorise at least one example of a vision, as you may be required to write about it in your exam.

- Acts 9:1–19 describes a vision that persuaded Saul, a Jew, to convert to Christianity.
- Saul was travelling to Damascus when he experienced a blinding light and was spoken to by Jesus.
- Afterwards he committed himself to the Christian faith (whose followers he had previously persecuted).

- Bahiya was a holy man who lived in the western part of India.
- After doubting if he was really enlightened, he had a vision of a deva (a spiritual being) who confirmed he wasn't as wise as he could be.
- The deva advised him to seek out the Buddha.
- Bahiya did so, travelling hundreds of miles on foot to reach him, and became enlightened shortly afterwards.

Buddhism and enlightenment

Buddhists do not believe in God. However, they use meditation and other spiritual practices to discover the meaning of ultimate reality by gaining true knowledge (enlightenment). In striving for enlightenment, they aim to discover how to end suffering and achieve happiness.

APPLY

(A) Using one detailed example, **explain** the meaning of special revelation.

(B) 'Those who see visions are only hallucinating.'

Write a detailed argument that shows what you think about this statement.

RECAP

Essential information:

☐ **General revelation** is coming to understand God or the nature of reality through ordinary, common events that can be experienced by everyone.

☐ Coming to know the divine through observing the natural world or by reading scripture are two examples of general revelation.

Examples of general revelation

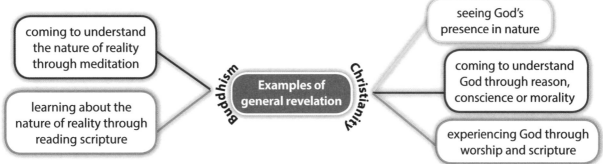

Buddhism:
- coming to understand the nature of reality through meditation
- learning about the nature of reality through reading scripture

Examples of general revelation

Christianity:
- seeing God's presence in nature
- coming to understand God through reason, conscience or morality
- experiencing God through worship and scripture

Nature as a way of understanding the divine

- Many Christians believe they can gain insight into God through the natural world.
- E.g. they believe God is revealed through his creation to be creative, clever and powerful.
- This may lead to awe and wonder at God's power, which may result in stronger faith.
- Atheists and humanists might argue that observing nature can give them a greater understanding of the world but not of God.

 You might be asked to compare beliefs on nature as general revelation between Christianity (the main religious tradition in Great Britain) and another religious tradition.

> " The heavens declare the glory of God; the skies proclaim the work of his hands […] night after night they reveal knowledge. " *Psalms 19:1–2* [NIV]

Scripture as a way of understanding the divine

For Christians, the Bible can help to reveal what God is like and how he wants people to live. For Buddhists, scriptures can help to reveal the nature of reality.

There are different ways to interpret scripture:

Christians	Atheists	Buddhists
• **Fundamentalist Christians** believe the Bible contains God's actual words. These must not be changed or questioned. • **Liberal Christians** believe the Bible was inspired by God but the words must be seen in their original context and understood differently in today's world.	• The Bible consists of the authors' opinions rather than the word of God. • Scripture does not prove God is real or reveal anything about God.	• Scriptures are the 'enlightened word', i.e. they express the enlightened mind (usually the mind of the Buddha). • Some Buddhists believe scriptures contain a sacred power that can positively affect people who hear their words.

APPLY

(A) Explain **two** ways in which Christians believe general revelation helps them to understand God.

(B) 'It is impossible to believe that ancient texts, written such a long time ago, can help people to believe in God today.'

Evaluate this statement.

7.7 Different ideas about the divine

RECAP

Essential information:

☐ Christians view God as being omnipotent, omniscient, personal, impersonal, immanent and transcendent.

☐ Some of these ideas also apply to the Buddha, although the Buddha is usually seen as a person who achieved enlightenment, rather than an all-powerful and all-knowing creator God.

Descriptions of God's nature

The limitations of language make describing an unseen, infinite God very difficult. However, certain terms can be used to help describe God's nature, including the following:

Omnipotent
- Almighty and all-powerful.
- Capable of doing anything (including creating the universe).

Omniscient
- All-knowing.
- Aware of everything that has happened in the past, present or future.

Personal
- Has human characteristics, e.g. being merciful and compassionate.
- People can have a relationship with God through prayer.

Transcendent
- Is beyond and outside life on earth.
- Not limited by the world, time or space.
- Does not act within the world or intervene in people's lives.

Immanent
- Is present in the universe and involved with life on earth.
- Acts in history and influences events.
- People can experience God in their lives.

Impersonal
- Has no human characteristics.
- Is unknowable and mysterious.
- Is more like an idea or a force than a person.

TIP
You could be examined about any of these terms, so make sure you understand all of them.

Can God be immanent and transcendent, personal and impersonal?

Although it may seem contradictory, some Christians believe God is both immanent and transcendent, and personal and impersonal. This is possible because God is a mystery, beyond human understanding.

- God's **immanence** is revealed in Jesus, and in the work of the Holy Spirit on earth.
- But God is also the **transcendent** creator of the universe.
- God is **personal** because he allows followers to join in a relationship with him.
- But he can also be viewed as an **impersonal** force or power.

a **symbol of human potential**

a **supremely compassionate force** that actively reaches out to beings to relieve their suffering

an **immanent, ever-present reality** with which followers can enter into a relationship through meditation and devotion

a **person** – a teacher and example to be followed

a **transcendent figure** to be worshipped

not regarded as a God, or seen as omnipotent or omniscient

The nature of the Buddha

Buddhists may think of the Buddha in different ways, as shown in the diagram to the right.

APPLY

A Give **two** terms to describe God's nature and explain what they mean.

B 'No being can have the qualities and nature that Christians believe God has.'

Write **two developed points of view** about this, one in favour and one that expresses a different opinion.

TIP
In your answer you could compare Christian ideas about the nature of God with how Buddhists see the Buddha.

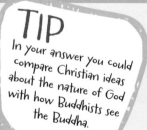

114

Essential information:

☐ Theists believe that revelation and enlightenment are valuable sources of knowledge about the divine.

☐ Revelations are difficult to prove because they are subjective, personal experiences.

☐ What some theists may regard as revelations, non-theists may understand in other ways.

The value of revelation

For some **Christians**, revelation can:

- provide proof of God's existence
- help to start a religion
- enable believers to have a relationship with God
- help believers to understand how God wants them to live.

For some **Buddhists**, revelation can help them to understand the true nature of reality. This in turn helps to reduce their suffering and, through enlightenment, can lead to a state of profound freedom, peace, wisdom and compassion.

TIP

Buddhists themselves do not generally speak in terms of revelation. But insights gained into the nature of reality through practices such as meditation and reading scripture can be thought of as a type of revelation. Just remember that it is the nature of reality, rather than God, that is being revealed.

Revelation: reality or illusion?

Revelation cannot be proved, so how can believers have confidence in a revelation? They may ask themselves:

Question	Explanation and examples
Does their revelation match the real world?	• The more the revelation aligns with what actually happens, the more likely it is to be real. • E.g. a revelation that claims people can fly is unlikely to be believed. A revelation that claims the water in a holy place can cure people, and it then does, is more likely to convince believers.
Does it fit with other revelations accepted by a religion?	• If it contradicts a long-held belief of a religion, it is less likely to be accepted as a true revelation. • However, beliefs may change over time (e.g. about slavery or homosexual relationships), so this is not always the case.
Does it change the faith or the life of a person?	• E.g. Nicky Cruz, a gang leader in New York in the 1950s, was converted to Christianity through the teaching of a Christian street preacher called David Wilkerson, whose words and example came as a revelation to Cruz. For him, this was true.
How can different religions have different revelations? They can't all be correct.	• Atheists might argue that the existence of conflicting revelations prove they cannot all be real. • Different interpretations of revelations can also lead to conflicting ideas about the divine. • Theists might reply by saying that different religions offer different paths to the divine. The meaning a religion places upon a particular revelation depends on the beliefs of that religion.

Alternative explanations for the experiences

Atheists might argue that revelations may be wishful thinking, caused by drugs or alcohol, or the result of a physical or mental illness. A person might have made a genuine error or they might be deliberately lying for fame or money.

(A) Give **three** alternative explanations for revelations and develop each one.

(B) 'Revelation proves that God exists.'

Write a reasoned answer to express a non-theist response to this statement.

Test the 1 mark question

1　Which **one** of the following describes a person who believes in God?

　A　Atheist　　　B　Agnostic　　　C　Theist　　　D　Humanist　　　**[1 mark]**

2　Which **one** of the following is **not** an attribute of God?

　A　Compassionate　　B　Mortal　　　C　Transcendent　　D　Eternal　　**[1 mark]**

Test the 2 mark question

3　Give **two** people who have put forward a Design argument for the existence of God.　　**[2 marks]**

　1) _____

　2) _____

4　Give **two** possible causes of suffering.　　**[2 marks]**

　1) _____

　2) _____

Test the 4 mark question

5　Explain **two** contrasting beliefs in contemporary British society about the Design argument for God's existence.

In your answer you must refer to one or more religious traditions. You may refer to a non-religious belief.　　**[4 marks]**

● **Explain one belief.**	*Christians believe that the beauty and intricacy of nature proves that God created the world.*
● Develop your explanation with more detail/an example/ reference to a religious teaching or quotation.	*William Paley said that just as a watch's intricate workings show evidence of design, so does the universe, which is more complex than a watch.*
● **Explain a second contrasting belief.**	*Atheists disagree with the Design argument because they do not believe there is a God.*
● Develop your explanation with more detail/an example/ reference to a religious teaching or quotation.	*They think that the natural world evolved after the Big Bang, a random event, and through natural selection creatures designed themselves without a need for God.*

> **TIP**
> Remember, 'contrasting' means different. Here the answer refers to Christianity and contrasts it with an atheist view.

6　Explain **two** contrasting beliefs about miracles.　　**[4 marks]**

● **Explain one belief.**	
● Develop your explanation with more detail/an example/ reference to a religious teaching or quotation.	
● **Explain a second contrasting belief.**	
● Develop your explanation with more detail/an example/ reference to a religious teaching or quotation.	

7　Explain **two** similar beliefs about general revelation.　　**[4 marks]**

7 Exam practice

Test the 5 mark question

8 Explain **two** religious beliefs about visions.
   Refer to sacred writings or another source of religious belief and teaching in your answer.   **[5 marks]**

● **Explain one belief.**	*Christians believe that God can be revealed to people in a special, direct way through visions.*
● Develop your explanation with more detail/an example.	*Some people who have had visions may as a result have a dramatic conversion from one way of life or faith to another.*
● **Explain a second belief.**	*Buddhists also believe in the possibility of visions but do not think they reveal the nature of God. Instead, they may reveal some aspect of reality or enlightenment.*
● Develop your explanation with more detail/an example.	*A vision in Buddhism may encourage someone to change their life, such as when Bahiya had a vision of a deva that told him he wasn't really enlightened. He then searched for the Buddha, received his teaching, and became enlightened.*
● Add a reference to sacred writings or another source of religious belief. If you prefer, you can add this reference to your first belief instead.	*An example of a vision in the Bible is in Acts 9:1–19, where it says Saul (who later became Paul) received a vision of Jesus on the Damascus Road. Saul was temporarily blinded and when he regained his sight he changed from persecuting Christians to preaching the gospel of Jesus to everyone.*

TIP
You don't have to quote directly from scripture or sacred writing – it is acceptable to give a summary in your own words instead, as the student has done here.

9 Explain **two** religious beliefs about special revelation.
   Refer to sacred writings or another source of religious belief and teaching in your answer.   **[5 marks]**

● **Explain one belief.**	
● Develop your explanation with more detail/an example.	
● **Explain a second belief.**	
● Develop your explanation with more detail/an example.	
● Add a reference to sacred writings or another source of religious belief. If you prefer, you can add this reference to your first belief instead.	

TIP
This question is not an evaluation question, so do not give your opinion or write arguments against special revelation. Don't forget to include a source of religious teaching in the answer.

10 Explain **two** religious ideas about God.
    Refer to sacred writings or another source of religious belief and teaching in your answer.   **[5 marks]**

Test the 12 mark question

11 'The First Cause argument proves that God exists.'

Evaluate this statement. In your answer you:

- should give reasoned arguments in support of this statement
- should give reasoned arguments to support a different point of view
- should refer to religious arguments
- may refer to non-religious arguments
- should reach a justified conclusion.

[12 marks]

Plus SPaG 3 mar

REASONED ARGUMENTS IN SUPPORT OF THE STATEMENT	The First Cause argument says that everything that exists has a cause. It is obvious to everyone that the universe exists because we live in it! Therefore the universe too must have a cause – something must have started it. But that something had to be eternal and not caused by something else, otherwise that other thing would be the cause, and so on. Christians believe that God is the eternal, almighty cause that began the process of creation of everything we know. The Bible says that God merely said, 'Let there be light' and it was created. So God was the eternal being that set off the Big Bang which led to evolution and the world as we know it today.
● **Explain why some people would agree with the statement.**	
● Develop your explanation with more detail and examples.	
● Refer to religious teaching. Use a quote or paraphrase or a religious authority.	
● **Evaluate the arguments.** Is this a good argument or not? Explain why you think this.	
REASONED ARGUMENTS SUPPORTING A DIFFERENT VIEW	Atheists are people who do not believe there is a God. They would argue that the First Cause argument does not prove there is a God because there are flaws in the logic – the argument contradicts itself. For example, if everything has a cause, what caused God? Buddhists believe in a cyclical universe that has no beginning or end. This way of seeing things takes away the need for a first cause, and so for Buddhists the First Cause argument doesn't apply.
● **Explain why some people would support a different view.**	
● Develop your explanation with more detail and examples.	
● Refer to religious teaching. Use a quote or paraphrase or a religious authority.	
● **Evaluate the arguments.** Is this a good argument or not? Explain why you think this.	
CONCLUSION	In conclusion, I think that although the First Cause argument may seem convincing because it depends on something everyone can observe – that everything that happens has a cause – in the end it fails to convince me that God is the First Cause of the universe. The argument relies on the universe having a beginning and a cause, but just because things in our world have causes does not necessarily mean the universe itself had one. Christians may use the Bible's creation stories to support their arguments in favour of the statement, but as I am an atheist, I am not persuaded by myths.
● **Give a justified conclusion.**	
● Include your own opinion together with your own reasoning.	
● **Include evaluation.** Explain why you think one viewpoint is stronger than the other or why they are equally strong.	
● Do not just repeat arguments you have already used without explaining how they apply to your reasoned opinion/conclusion.	

TIP

This conclusion is good because it doesn't just repeat points already made to justify the opinion. It is also clearly linked to the statement in the question.

12 'The existence of miracles proves that God exists.'

Evaluate this statement. In your answer you:

- should give reasoned arguments in support of this statement
- should give reasoned arguments to support a different point of view
- should refer to religious arguments
- may refer to non-religious arguments
- should reach a justified conclusion.

[12 marks]

Plus SPaG 3 marks

REASONED ARGUMENTS IN SUPPORT OF THE STATEMENT	
● **Explain why some people would agree with the statement.**	
● Develop your explanation with more detail and examples.	
● Refer to religious teaching. Use a quote or paraphrase or a religious authority.	
● **Evaluate the arguments.** Is this a good argument or not? Explain why you think this.	
REASONED ARGUMENTS SUPPORTING A DIFFERENT VIEW	
● **Explain why some people would support a different view.**	
● Develop your explanation with more detail and examples.	
● Refer to religious teaching. Use a quote or paraphrase or a religious authority.	
● **Evaluate the arguments.** Is this a good argument or not? Explain why you think this.	
CONCLUSION	
● **Give a justified conclusion.**	
● Include your own opinion together with your own reasoning.	
● **Include evaluation**. Explain why you think one viewpoint is stronger than the other or why they are equally strong.	
● Do not just repeat arguments you have already used without explaining how they apply to your reasoned opinion/conclusion.	

13 'The existence of evil and suffering proves that God does not exist.'

Evaluate this statement. In your answer you:

- should give reasoned arguments in support of this statement
- should give reasoned arguments to support a different point of view
- should refer to religious arguments
- may refer to non-religious arguments
- should reach a justified conclusion.

[12 marks]

Plus SPaG 3 marks

Check your answers using the mark scheme on page 166. How did you do?

To feel more secure in the content you need to remember, re-read pages 108–115.

To remind yourself of what the examiner is looking for, go to pages 6–11.

8.1 Introduction to religion, peace and conflict

Essential information:

☐ Some Christians (such as Quakers) believe war is always wrong, while others believe war is acceptable under certain conditions.

☐ Buddhism teaches there are no justifiable reasons for war, and people cannot relieve their own suffering by making others suffer.

☐ The concepts of peace, justice, forgiveness and reconciliation are important both in the aftermath of conflict and as tools to prevent war from happening in the first place.

Key concepts of peace, justice, forgiveness and reconciliation

Peace	Justice
• **Peace** is the absence of conflict and war, which leads to happiness and harmony.	• **Justice** is bringing about what is right and fair, according to the law, or making up for a wrong that has been committed.
• The aim of war may be to create peace, but this can be hard to achieve because of the instability and resentment left after a war ends.	• Justice is linked to equality, and the idea that it is just to give everyone the same opportunities.
• Peace is also a feeling of happiness and tranquillity that can come through prayer and meditation, which helps people to avoid conflict.	• If certain governments or parts of the world are seen to be the cause of inequality and injustice, conflict may result.
• **Christians** believe God will bring peace to the world at some time in the future (Isaiah 2:4).	• **Christians** believe that God, as the ultimate judge, will establish justice at some point in the future (Isaiah 2:4).
• **Buddhism** teaches that violence comes from the mind, and so to create peace people must develop it within themselves.	• **Buddhism** teaches that non-violent methods should be used to bring about justice. 

Forgiveness	Reconciliation
• **Forgiveness** is showing compassion and mercy, and pardoning someone for what they have done wrong.	• **Reconciliation** means restoring friendly relationships after conflict.
• Forgiveness does not necessarily mean no action should be taken to right a wrong, but when conflict is over forgiveness should follow.	• It requires a conscious effort (and sometimes much work) to rebuild the relationship.
• **Christians** are taught to forgive others if they wish to be forgiven (the Lord's Prayer). They believe God sets the example by offering forgiveness to all who ask for it in faith.	• Reconciliation doesn't mean ignoring the past but building a constructive relationship for the future.
• For **Buddhists** forgiveness is important because it expresses loving-kindness, and allows them to let go of anger and hatred.	• For **Buddhists**, letting go of blame and resentment is important in reconciliation.

(A) Give **two** religious beliefs about forgiveness. **Develop** each belief by explaining in more detail, adding an example, or referring to a relevant quotation from sacred writings or another source of religious belief and teaching.

(B) Make a list of **three arguments for and three arguments against** the statement, 'Religious believers should not take part in wars.'

RECAP

Essential information:

☐ In the UK the right to **protest** (express disapproval, often in a public group) is a fundamental democratic freedom, but it is illegal to protest violently.

☐ **Terrorism** (the unlawful use of violence, usually against innocent civilians, to achieve a political goal) is a much more serious form of violent protest.

☐ Christianity and Buddhism are against violent protest and terrorism.

Violence and protest

- All religions generally agree that conflict should be avoided if possible, but they have different views about when violence may be justified.
- Protests allow people to express their objection to something in public, but protests can sometimes turn violent.
- Many Christians and Buddhists believe that protesting to achieve what is right is acceptable as long as violence is not used.

 You might be asked to compare beliefs on violence between Christianity (the main religious tradition in Great Britain) and another religious tradition.

Here are two examples of peaceful protests organised by religious leaders:

- In the 1950s and 1960s, the Christian pastor Dr Martin Luther King Jr organised peaceful protests against unjust racist laws in the USA.
- These succeeded in changing US law and bringing civil rights to all its citizens of any race.

- In the 1990s, the Cambodian Buddhist monk Ghosananda led peaceful marches in protest at a repressive Vietnamese government.
- His aim was to encourage reconciliation and peace after decades of civil conflict.

Terrorism

- Some individuals or groups use terrorism to further their cause by killing innocent people.
- Suicide bombers, gunmen shooting into crowds, and using vehicles to injure pedestrians are examples of terrorism.
- Terrorists aim to make society aware of their cause, frighten people and push authorities into giving way to their demands.
- Terrorists may link their cause with a religion but **no religion promotes terrorism.**
- Most **Christians** are against terrorism and prefer more peaceful ways of resolving issues.
- Many **Buddhists** believe it is important to condemn terrorism because it expresses hatred.
- A Buddhist response to terrorism should express love rather than hatred. Revenge and retaliation are not appropriate answers.

TIP
Learning specific examples such as these can help you to develop your answers and gain more marks.

❝ The purpose of terrorism lies not just in the violent act itself. It is in producing terror. It sets out to inflame, to divide, to produce consequences which [terrorists] then use to justify terror. ❞

Former UK Prime Minister Tony Blair

APPLY

Ⓐ Give **two** reasons why religious believers may wish to protest.

Ⓑ 'Terrorism is never justified.'

Develop this argument to support the statement by explaining in more detail, adding an example, or referring to a relevant religious teaching or quotation.

"Terrorism kills innocent people. It uses violence to frighten and intimidate ordinary citizens who are just going about their daily lives. It can never be justified no matter what the cause."

8.3 Reasons for war

RECAP

Essential information:

☐ Some reasons for war include **greed** (selfish desire for something), **self-defence** (acting to prevent harm to yourself or others), and **retaliation** (deliberately harming someone as a response to them harming you).

☐ Christianity and Buddhism teach that war should never be motivated by greed or retaliation.

☐ Many Christians believe fighting in self-defence is morally acceptable, while most Buddhists believe there is no just reason to go to war, even in self-defence.

Greed, self-defence and retaliation as reasons for war

Greed

- Wars may be fought out of greed to gain more land or control of important resources (such as oil).
- **Christianity** teaches that greed is wrong.

> ❝For the love of money is a root of all kinds of evil. ❞ *1 Timothy 6:10* [NIV]

- **Buddhism** teaches that greed is one of the three poisons (see page 57), and one of the main causes of suffering.
- It teaches there are always unhealthy consequences to actions based on greed.

Retaliation

- Wars are sometimes fought in retaliation against a country that has done something very wrong.
- **Christians** try to follow the advice of Jesus, who taught that retaliation is wrong.

> ❝But I tell you, do not resist an evil person. If anyone slaps you on the right cheek, turn to them the other cheek also.❞ *Matthew 5:39* [NIV]

- For **Buddhists,** retaliation is a form of vengeance and expresses hatred (another one of the three poisons).
- It therefore increases suffering and should be avoided.

> ❝For not by hatred are hatreds ever quenched here, but they are quenched by nonhatred. This is the ancient rule.❞ *The Dhammapada*

Reasons for war

Self-defence

- People might fight in self-defence when their country is under attack, or to help defend other nations who are under threat.
- E.g. during the Second World War the UK fought to defend itself against Nazi invasion, and also to defeat what it saw as an evil threat to the whole of Europe.
- Many Christians believe fighting in self-defence is morally acceptable, providing all peaceful ways of solving the conflict have been tried first.
- In Buddhism the most fundamental ethical principle is not to take life, even in self-defence.
- E.g. the Vietnamese monk Thich Nhat Hanh said that killing is never justified, and people should instead develop compassion towards those who wish to harm them.
- Not all Buddhists agree and some are willing to fight in self-defence.

> **TIP**
> Remember that the reasons for a war are complex and usually cannot be simplified to one motive.

APPLY

A Which **one** of the following is **not** a reason for war?

A) Self-defence   B) Greed   C) Retaliation   D) Forgiveness

B Use the table below with arguments for and against the statement, 'Retaliation is a justifiable reason for war.' **Write a paragraph** to explain whether you agree or disagree with the statement, having evaluated both sides of the argument.

For	Against
If a country has attacked you for no reason, you have every right to get back at them by harming them. They started the conflict so should expect a response.	Retaliation is wrong because it simply continues the cycle of violence and is not the way to lasting peace.
The Bible teaches, 'An eye for an eye, a tooth for a tooth', so you should be able to retaliate when an enemy causes you harm. It's a matter of justice which is an important principle.	Retaliation is different from self-defence. It may sometimes be justifiable to defend your country to protect others from harm, but retaliation is a kind of spiteful action, taken to punish the enemy for something they've done.

RECAP

Essential information:

☐ **Nuclear weapons** are weapons that work by a nuclear reaction. They devastate huge areas and kill large numbers of people.

☐ Other types of **weapons of mass destruction** (weapons that kill large numbers of people and/or cause great damage) include chemical weapons and biological weapons.

☐ No religion supports the use of these weapons, although some religious believers do support nuclear deterrence (stockpiling nuclear weapons to deter or prevent an enemy attack).

 You might be asked to compare beliefs on weapons of mass destruction between Christianity (the main religious tradition in Great Britain) and another religious tradition.

The use of nuclear weapons

- US forces used atom (nuclear) bombs on the Japanese cities of Hiroshima and Nagasaki during the Second World War. In response Japan surrendered, ending the war.
- Some people say that as the atom bombs ended the war, their use was justified.
- Since then, many countries have developed powerful nuclear weapons as a deterrent.

Weapons of mass destruction

- In addition to nuclear weapons, other weapons of mass destruction are **biological weapons** (using living organisms to cause disease or death) and **chemical weapons** (using chemicals to harm humans and destroy the natural environment).
- The production, stockpiling and use of these weapons is illegal worldwide.
- Despite this, many countries still possess them.

Religious views

Christian views	Buddhist views
• Only God has the right to end life. • One of the Ten Commandments is, 'You shall not murder' (Exodus 20:13). • Weapons of mass destruction kill huge numbers of innocent civilians, so their use can never be justified. • Their use goes against the teachings of Jesus. ❝any use of nuclear weapons would violate the sanctity of life and the principle of dignity core to our faith traditions❞ *Steve Hucklesby* • Some Christians see the stockpiling of nuclear weapons as a useful deterrent to maintain peace and prevent attack.	• Weapons of mass destruction cause large-scale suffering and their use goes against the first moral precept, which is to abstain from taking life. • Most Buddhists believe nuclear weapons should be abolished, as there is always a risk they will be used as long as they exist. • They also believe the real problem is not the weapons themselves but the attitudes of human beings. • Where there is hatred, it will seek a means to hurt others. ❝For peace, the basic thing to do is not to remove nuclear weapons but to remove the fear, anger and suspicion in us.❞ *Thich Nhat Hanh*

APPLY

(A) Explain **two** contrasting beliefs in contemporary British society about weapons of mass destruction.

(B) 'There are no good reasons for countries to possess nuclear weapons.'

Develop an argument to support this statement. **Refer to a relevant religious teaching or quotation** in your answer.

 TIP
Make sure you choose <u>contrasting</u> viewpoints when answering this question.

8.5 The just war

Essential information:

- A **just war** is a war that meets internationally accepted criteria for fairness.

- The just war theory gives the conditions that must apply to make a war justifiable, and the rules on how the war must be fought to make sure it is ethical.

- The just war theory was developed by Christians and is accepted by many Christians today, although most think it is much better to prevent war from happening at all. Buddhist teachings do not support the idea of a just war.

The just war theory

- The just war theory was developed by Christian thinkers including Augustine (in the fourth century) and Thomas Aquinas (in the thirteenth century).
- Many **Christians** believe that fighting a just war is acceptable, but it is much better to find peaceful ways to resolve conflicts.
- Some Christians disagree with the just war theory because it defends the concept of war.
- **Buddhists** have a commitment to non-violence and most believe war cannot be justified in any circumstance, even in self-defence.

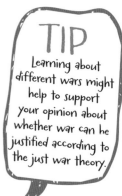

TIP
Learning about different wars might help to support your opinion about whether war can be justified according to the just war theory.

For a war to be 'just' it must meet the following conditions and rules:

	Condition/rule	Explanation
The **six conditions** for a just war	Must be fought for a **just cause**	E.g. fought in self-defence or to defend others, not to gain territory or in retaliation.
	Must be declared by the **correct authority**	E.g. the government or lawful rulers of the country.
	Must have a **just intention**	E.g. fought to promote good or defeat wrongdoing. The good gained by winning should outweigh the evil which led to the war.
	Must be a **last resort**	All other ways of solving the problem (e.g. diplomacy) must have been tried first.
	Must have a reasonable **chance of success**	It is unjust to ask people to fight in a war if it is probable the war will be lost and they will be killed.
	Must be **proportional**	Excessive force should not be used and innocent civilians must not be killed.
The **three rules** for fighting a just war	Must be fought by **just means**	Innocent civilians should not be targeted or harmed.
	Only **appropriate force** should be used	This includes the type of force and how much is used.
	Internationally agreed conventions must be obeyed	The Geneva Convention lays down the rules that must be obeyed in war.

A Give **two** conditions of a just war.

B 'The just war theory is the best religious response to whether it is right to fight.'

Develop each of these arguments for and against the statement by explaining in more detail, adding an example, or referring to a relevant religious teaching or quotation.

For	Against
The just war theory is the best religious response to whether it is right to fight in a war because it is accepted by the United Nations and most religions. It prevents governments from going to war for selfish reasons.	The just war theory is not the best religious response to whether it is right to fight because it accepts that war is sometimes right, when it is not right ever. The best religious response is to say that war is always wrong.

RECAP

Essential information:

- A **holy war** is a war fought for a religious cause or God, controlled by a religious leader.
- Most Christians and Buddhists today believe that violence should not be used to defend the faith.
- Although all religions generally promote peace and harmony, religion is sometimes seen as a cause of violence in the contemporary world.

What is a holy war?

- A holy war is **fought for a religious cause**, such as to defend the faith from attack.
- It must be **authorised by a religious leader**.
- It is believed those who take part **gain spiritual rewards**.
- **The Crusades** are examples of holy war. These were battles between Christians and Muslims in the eleventh to fourteenth centuries. Both believed God was on their side.
- Most **Christians** today believe it is better to defend the faith through words rather than violence.
- **Buddhism** teaches that no war can be justified, even in self-defence, so does not support the concept of holy war.

Religion as a cause of violence

Christian views	Buddhist views
• Most Christians today do not respond violently to an attack on their faith.	• There is a basic commitment to non-violence in Buddhism.
• Most Christians accept Jesus' teaching that not only violence, but the anger that leads to violence, is wrong (Matthew 5:21–22).	• Buddhism teaches that instead of responding to violence with violence, people should conquer the violent tendencies within themselves, and have confidence this will have a positive impact on the world.
• Jesus said, 'Put your sword back in its place, for all who draw the sword die by the sword' (Matthew 26:52).	

Although all religions generally promote peace and harmony, there are examples of recent conflicts that have had a religious aspect to them, or examples of violence that have been justified as helping to defend the faith. For example:

During 'the Troubles' in Northern Ireland (1968–1998), conflict between Catholics and Protestants led to acts of discrimination and violence. However, many consider this to have been a political conflict rather than a religious one.

In the twentieth century, some Japanese Buddhist monks supported war against China and Korea. They believed the war was helping to ensure the survival and spread of the Buddha's teachings.

In recent years in Myanmar, some Buddhists have felt threatened by the minority presence of Muslims in the country and used violence against them. Many other Buddhists around the world have condemned this action.

APPLY

(A) Give **two** features of holy wars.

(B) **Evaluate** this argument to support the statement, 'There is no place for a holy war in contemporary Britain.'

"There is no place for a holy war in Britain today. People have religious freedom. No one has to fight for the right to worship God in the way they wish. Jesus taught people to 'turn the other cheek' and not retaliate against someone who is being nasty to you. So even though the Christian religion seems under attack at times, it is not right to use violence against those who insult Christian beliefs."

TIP
Do **not** use the conflict in Northern Ireland as an example of a holy war.

RECAP

Essential information:

☐ **Pacifism** is the belief of people who refuse to take part in war and any other form of violence.

☐ Many Christians are not pacifists because they believe war is sometimes necessary in self-defence, while many Buddhists are pacifists and believe war is never justified.

☐ **Peacemaking** is the action of trying to establish peace, and a **peacemaker** is someone who works to establish peace in the world or in a certain part of it.

What is pacifism?

Pacifists believe that:

* war and violence can rarely or never be justified
* it is best to prevent war from becoming a possibility by promoting justice and peace
* prayer and meditation can help people to be at peace with themselves and others.

 You might be asked to compare beliefs on pacifism between Christianity (the main religious tradition in Great Britain) and another religious tradition.

Christian views	Buddhist views
• The Religious Society of Friends (Quakers) is a Christian denomination that strongly supports pacifism. • Christian pacifists follow Jesus' example and teaching: ❝ Blessed are the peacemakers, for they shall be called children of God. ❞ *Matthew 5:9* [NIV] • Many Christians are not pacifists because they believe war can be justified under certain criteria (see page 124).	• Buddhist teachings strongly promote pacifism. • The first moral precept teaches that Buddhists should not harm or kill any living being. • The Buddha taught that Buddhists should try instead to develop compassion for all beings and that violence should be avoided. • Buddhism teaches that to live in peace, Buddhists must try to create a world that favours peaceful states of mind.

Modern-day peacemakers

Many pacifists and peacemakers believe it is important to resist oppression and injustice in non-violent ways, to help create a just and equal world where conflict is not necessary. For example, Buddhism teaches that peace comes from within each person, but people also need to work to improve society so it is easier to develop this sense of peace.

Three examples of modern-day peacemakers are Mairead Corrigan, Betty Williams and Thich Nhat Hanh.

TIP
You need to be able to talk about individuals involved in peacemaking and the work they have done.

Mairead Corrigan and Betty Williams

* A Catholic and Protestant from Northern Ireland who formed the 'Peace People' organisation in 1976.
* Organised peace marches and other events throughout the UK to bring Catholics and Protestants together, and to call for peace between the two sides in Northern Ireland.
* Awarded the 1976 Nobel Peace Prize.

Thich Nhat Hanh

* A Vietnamese Buddhist monk who supports non-violent protest.
* Combines meditative practices with non-violent protest.
* A pioneer of engaged Buddhism, which aims to use the Buddha's teachings to improve social justice.
* Believes that to create peace, Buddhists must work to change the structures of society that influence people's mental states and behaviour.

APPLY

(A) Explain **two** contrasting beliefs in contemporary British society about pacifism.

(B) **Write down two arguments** in support of the statement, 'Promoting justice and human rights is the best way of preventing conflict'. Now **develop** each argument by explaining in more detail or by giving examples.

8.8 Religious responses to victims of war

Essential information:

☐ Victims of war may include those directly involved in the fighting, their families and dependents, and refugees whose homes and societies have been destroyed.

☐ There are many organisations that offer help and care for victims of war (such as Caritas and the Tzu Chi Foundation). Christians and Buddhists support organisations such as these.

Providing help to victims of war

There are many organisations that help the victims of war, from those providing shelter and supplies for refugees to those providing medical and psychological care for members of the military.

Christian views	Buddhist views
• Christians support such organisations because Jesus taught people to 'love your neighbour as yourself' (Mark 12:31). • In the parable of the Good Samaritan (Luke 10:25–37), Jesus taught that everyone is everybody else's neighbour, regardless of race, age, gender, religion or political beliefs. 	• Buddhists support such organisations because they believe all suffering should be stopped. • Many Buddhists believe victims of war need psychological and spiritual help in addition to the basic necessities required for survival. • Victims should be encouraged to develop compassion towards the aggressors, as this not only helps the victims but also enables the aggressors to change. > "When another person makes you suffer, it is because he suffers deeply within himself […] He does not need punishment; he needs help." *Thich Nhat Hanh*

Organisations that help victims of war

Two examples of religious organisations that help victims of war are Caritas and the Tzu Chi Foundation.

Caritas
- A Catholic organisation that helps the poor and promotes justice worldwide.
- Inspired by the teachings of Jesus and the Catholic Church.
- Aims to provide practical help to those suffering through conflict.
- In 2015, provided food and shelter to refugees fleeing the civil war in Syria.
- Also provided translators and legal services so the refugees could make informed decisions about their futures.

Tzu Chi foundation
- A Buddhist organisation founded in Taiwan.
- Inspired by the Bodhisattva goal to help all beings become free from suffering.
- Runs educational, welfare, health and cultural projects.
- Opened a clinic in Istanbul to help with the medical needs of Syrian refugees.
- All treatment in this clinic is free. Refugee Syrian doctors work in the clinic to help reduce language barriers and make meaningful use of their skills.

A Give **two** ways in which religious believers help victims of war.

B 'The point of war is to kill the enemy, not help them to survive.'

Write one paragraph to support this view and another paragraph which gives a different point of view.

Test the 1 mark question

1 Which **one** of the following best expresses the religious ideal of bringing about what is right and fair?

A Peace   B Forgiveness   C Justice   D Defence   **[1 mark]**

2 Which **one** of the following are **not** weapons of mass destruction?

A Chemical weapons   B Nuclear weapons

C Biological weapons   D Conventional weapons   **[1 mark]**

Test the 2 mark question

3 Give **two** conditions of a just war.   **[2 marks]**

1) _____

2) _____

4 Give **two** reasons why many religious people do **not** support violent protest.   **[2 marks]**

1) _____

2) _____

Test the 4 mark question

5 Explain **two** contrasting beliefs in contemporary British society about whether countries should possess weapons of mass destruction. In your answer you should refer to the main religious tradition of Great Britain and one or more other religious traditions.   **[4 marks]**

● **Explain one belief.**	*Many Christians might approve of countries possessing some weapons of mass destruction as a deterrent.*
● Develop your explanation with more detail/an example/ reference to a religious teaching or quotation.	*They would believe that possessing them is necessary in order to prevent war and help to keep the peace.*
● **Explain a second contrasting belief.**	*No religion agrees with the use of weapons of mass destruction, but some Buddhists would also disagree with countries possessing them.*
● Develop your explanation with more detail/an example/ reference to a religious teaching or quotation.	*The first moral precept is to cause no harm to others and the possession of weapons of mass destruction would provide temptation to use them.*

TIP

Read the question carefully. It asks for beliefs about whether countries should 'possess' weapons of mass destruction, not whether they should 'use' them.

6 Explain **two** contrasting beliefs in contemporary British society about pacifism. In your answer you should refer to the main religious tradition of Great Britain and one or more other religious traditions.   **[4 marks]**

● **Explain one belief.**	
● Develop your explanation with more detail/an example/ reference to a religious teaching or quotation.	
● **Explain a second contrasting belief.**	
● Develop your explanation with more detail/an example/ reference to a religious teaching or quotation.	

8 Exam practice

7 Explain **two** similar religious beliefs about forgiveness. In your answer you must refer to one or more religious traditions. **[4 marks]**

Test the 5 mark question

8 Explain **two** religious beliefs about helping victims of war.

Refer to sacred writings or another source of religious belief and teaching in your answer. **[5 marks]**

● **Explain one belief.**	*One Christian belief about helping victims of war is that Christians should treat everyone as if they were a neighbour to them.*
● Develop your explanation with more detail/an example.	*Victims of war may be suffering because they have lost everything including people they love, so even if Christians do not know them, they should not ignore their suffering but offer to help them in whatever way they can.*
● **Explain a second belief.**	*Buddhists believe that all suffering should be relieved, whatever its cause, so it is important to relieve the suffering of war victims.*
● Develop your explanation with more detail/an example.	*Buddhists might say that even the aggressors in a war need compassion as well, because they too will suffer as a consequence of their unskilful actions.*
● Add a reference to sacred writings or another source of religious belief. If you prefer, you can add this reference to your first belief instead.	*The Buddhist monk Thich Nhat Hanh says, 'When another person makes you suffer, it is because he suffers deeply within himself [...] He does not need punishment; he needs help.'*

9 Explain **two** reasons why some religious people believe it is right to fight in a war.

Refer to sacred writings or another source of religious belief and teaching in your answer. **[5 marks]**

● **Explain one reason.**	
● Develop your explanation with more detail/an example.	
● **Explain a second reason.**	
● Develop your explanation with more detail/an example.	
● Add a reference to sacred writings or another source of religious belief. If you prefer, you can add this reference to your first reason instead.	

10 Explain **two** religious beliefs about reconciliation.

Refer to sacred writings or another source of religious belief and teaching in your answer. **[5 marks]**

8 Exam practice

Test the 12 mark question

11 'The just war theory is the best religious response to whether it is right to fight.'

Evaluate this statement. In your answer you:

- should give reasoned arguments in support of this statement
- should give reasoned arguments to support a different point of view
- should refer to religious arguments
- may refer to non-religious arguments
- should reach a justified conclusion.

[12 marks]
Plus SPaG 3 ma

REASONED ARGUMENTS IN SUPPORT OF THE STATEMENT ● **Explain why some people would agree with the statement.** ● Develop your explanation with more detail and examples. ● Refer to religious teaching. Use a quote or paraphrase or a religious authority. ● **Evaluate the arguments.** Is this a good argument or not? Explain why you think this.	*Although religious people think it is better to avoid war and violence, if faced with a decision about whether or not it is right to fight, the just war theory can give them some guidance. The theory has several criteria including that the war must be declared by a leader of a state, it should be proportional in the amount of force that is used and civilians should be protected.* *The theory is a good response because it makes sure wars are not fought about something unimportant or in a way which breaks internationally agreed rules. This is important because God wants people to protect innocent people rather than killing them. The just war theory was invented by Thomas Aquinas so that is why Christians follow it. Also the Bible teaches 'You shall not murder'. If wars are not just wars, more people will die, and they may be fighting for a wrong reason.*
REASONED ARGUMENTS SUPPORTING A DIFFERENT VIEW ● **Explain why some people would support a different view.** ● Develop your explanation with more detail and examples. ● Refer to religious teaching. Use a quote or paraphrase or a religious authority. ● **Evaluate the arguments.** Is this a good argument or not? Explain why you think this.	*Buddhism generally opposes all arguments in favour of war, including the idea of a just war. According to Buddhism, violence is not the way to promote peace because it usually just provokes more violence. The Dalai Lama says, 'We can never obtain peace in the outer world until we make peace with ourselves.' This suggests that improving the world is not just about changing governments but also about changing the attitudes of people, which are what lead to aggression.*
CONCLUSION ● **Give a justified conclusion.** ● Include your own opinion together with your own reasoning. ● **Include evaluation.** Explain why you think one viewpoint is stronger than the other or why they are equally strong. ● Do not just repeat arguments you have already used without explaining how they apply to your reasoned opinion/conclusion.	*In conclusion, I would agree with the statement that the just war theory is the right religious response. I have sympathy with the views of pacifists, and ideally war should be avoided, but in the real world there are always countries that will bully other countries or try to take their land or resources, so war is sometimes necessary. It is better to have rules that limit the damage war can do, and the just war theory helps in that way.*

TIP
This opening shows an excellent chain of reasoning. It starts by giving strong support to the statement and then demonstrates detailed knowledge of what the just war theory says. In the second paragraph it goes back to the issue of whether it is a good religious response and includes Christian teaching

TIP
This is a good example of a justified conclusion as the student gives reasons for their opinion.

12 'Religion is the main cause of wars.'

Evaluate this statement. In your answer you:

- should give reasoned arguments in support of this statement
- should give reasoned arguments to support a different point of view
- should refer to religious arguments
- may refer to non-religious arguments
- should reach a justified conclusion.

[12 marks]
Plus SPaG 3 marks

TIP

When evaluation questions ask whether something is the 'main' cause or 'best' response, or whether a religious belief is the 'most important' belief, they are asking you to think about whether other causes/responses/beliefs are more significant or whether there can be many of equal merit.

REASONED ARGUMENTS IN SUPPORT OF THE STATEMENT

- **Explain why some people would agree with the statement.**

- Develop your explanation with more detail and examples.

- Refer to religious teaching. Use a quote or paraphrase or a religious authority.

- **Evaluate the arguments.** Is this a good argument or not? Explain why you think this.

REASONED ARGUMENTS SUPPORTING A DIFFERENT VIEW

- **Explain why some people would support a different view.**

- Develop your explanation with more detail and examples.

- Refer to religious teaching. Use a quote or paraphrase or a religious authority.

- **Evaluate the arguments.** Is this a good argument or not? Explain why you think this.

CONCLUSION

- **Give a justified conclusion.**

- Include your own opinion together with your own reasoning.

- **Include evaluation.** Explain why you think one viewpoint is stronger than the other or why they are equally strong.

- Do not just repeat arguments you have already used without explaining how they apply to your reasoned opinion/ conclusion.

13 'Religious people should be the main peacemakers in the world today.'

Evaluate this statement. In your answer you:

- should give reasoned arguments in support of this statement
- should give reasoned arguments to support a different point of view
- should refer to religious arguments
- may refer to non-religious arguments
- should reach a justified conclusion.

[12 marks]
Plus SPaG 3 marks

Check your answers using the mark scheme on pages 166–167. How did you do?
To feel more secure in the content you need to remember, re-read pages 120–127.
To remind yourself of what the examiner is looking for, go to pages 6–11.

9.1 Crime and punishment

RECAP

Essential information:

☐ Crime and punishment are both governed by the law.

☐ Not all good actions are required by law and not all evil actions break the law.

What are crime and punishment?

- A **crime** is an offence that breaks the law set by the government. People who commit crimes face legal consequences.
- In the UK, people who commit crimes are arrested and questioned by police.
- They then appear before a court where a judge or jury determines their **punishment** (something done legally to somebody as a result of being found guilty of breaking the law).
- In the UK, the most serious crimes are punished with a life sentence in prison, while less serious ones might result in a shorter time in prison, community service or a fine. No legal punishment is allowed to deliberately cause harm to the offender.

Good and evil intentions and actions

- Some people assume a **good action** is an action that does not break a law. However, there are also many good actions which exist outside the law (such as giving to charity or helping people in need).
- Likewise, there are some actions that are not against the law but might be considered evil by some people (such as adultery or abortion). Generally, **evil actions** are considered to cause suffering and harm to others.

Christian views	Buddhist views
• Teachings in the Bible warn against having any evil or wrong thoughts and intentions. ❝You have heard that it was said, 'You shall not commit adultery.' But I tell you that anyone who looks at a woman lustfully has already committed adultery with her in his heart. ❞ *Matthew 5:27–28* [NIV] • Evil actions such as using violence are considered to be sinful and against God. • Many Christians would claim there is no such thing as an evil person, because God created people to be good. • However, because of original sin (see page 22), all humans have a tendency to do evil things even though they are not evil in themselves.	• Buddhism doesn't generally speak of 'good' and 'evil' but rather of skilful and unskilful actions and intentions (see page 75). • Not all unskilful actions are illegal (for instance, it is not illegal to be unkind to someone). • Equally, not all skilful actions are legal (there are countries where it is illegal to practise Buddhism, for instance). • The principle of kamma teaches that the intention behind an action is very important. • Whether an action causes harm to someone, or agrees with the five moral precepts, can help to determine if it is skilful or not. • Buddhists believe it is correct to follow the law unless this seriously restricts their capacity to act in a skilful way.

APPLY

(A) Give **two** ways in which a crime might be punished in the UK.

(B) 'Intentions are more important than actions.'

Write a developed argument for this statement and another developed argument against it. Elaborate your arguments with religious teaching.

TIP

When faced with a statement that you have a strong opinion on, you must also focus on an alternative opinion, even if you strongly disagree with it.

RECAP

Essential information:

☐ There are many different reasons why people commit crimes, from poverty and addiction to greed and hatred.

☐ Christians and Buddhists believe crime is very rarely justified.

Reasons why some people commit crime

Reason	Explanation	Christian views	Buddhist views
Poverty	There are millions of people in the UK who live in **poverty**, who cannot always afford to buy food. Some believe the only way out of this is to steal. However, stealing for any reason is against the law, and those who steal food or other essentials can be arrested and punished.	Stealing is wrong, but people should do what they can to help make sure nobody finds themselves in the position of having to steal because of poverty.	Stealing contradicts the second moral precept (to abstain from taking what is not freely given) and causes harm to others.
Upbringing	Some young people grow up in a household where crime is a part of life. A troubled upbringing (for example because of neglect or abuse) might also lead a person to turn to crime.	Parents should teach their children the right way to behave through their own words and actions.	People need supportive conditions growing up in order to develop sensitivity to others and to learn how to behave ethically.
Mental illness	Some forms of **mental illness** (a medical condition that affects a person's emotions or moods) may lead to crime. E.g. anger management problems may lead to violence.	Treating the causes of the illness is the most loving and compassionate way of dealing with people with mental illness.	Everyone sees reality in a distorted way, which leads people to inflict suffering on themselves and others.
Addiction	Taking illegal drugs is in itself a criminal act. A person's **addiction** (physical or mental dependency) may make them commit further crimes to be able to buy drugs. Legal drugs such as alcohol can also cause crime such as violence, rape and drunk driving if taken to excess.	Christians are against taking illegal drugs and support rehabilitation as a way of defeating an addiction. Most Christians believe alcohol is acceptable in moderation.	People under the influence of drugs lose awareness and so are less sensitive to others. The fifth moral precept encourages Buddhists not to take drugs (including alcohol).
Greed	Some people want personal possessions they do not need and cannot afford. Their **greed** may lead them to steal them.	The Ten Commandments forbid envy, and it is envy that often causes greed.	Acting out of greed is unskilful and leads to suffering.
Hate	Hate, the opposite of love, can lead to violence or aggression.	Jesus taught Christians to love everybody, including their enemies.	Hatred is one of the three poisons and one of the main causes of suffering.
Opposition to an unjust law	Sometimes people break a law they believe to be unjust in order to protest against it. These could be laws based on inequality or that deny basic human rights.	Some Christians may agree with this but only if no violence is involved and nobody gets harmed.	Buddhists might disobey a law that expresses prejudice and hatred.

APPLY

Ⓐ Give **two** religious responses to the reasons why people commit crimes.

Ⓑ 'Addiction is the only good excuse for committing crimes.'

Write down your own thoughts about this and **develop them by adding religious views**.

> **TIP**
> Remember that while Christianity and Buddhism condemn crime, they do not condemn criminals. Most Christians and Buddhists believe criminals should be treated with compassion and forgiveness, even though the crimes they committed were wrong.

9.3 Religious attitudes to lawbreakers and different types of crime

Essential information:

☐ Christians believe criminals should be punished according to the law but also treated compassionately.

☐ Buddhism does not agree with the idea of punishment, although accepts the need to protect society from offenders. Most Buddhists prefer to focus on the rehabilitation and reformation of offenders.

Religious attitudes to lawbreakers

Many **Christians** may disapprove of the crime but don't hate the criminal who committed it. They believe that:

- Offenders **must be punished by the law** according to how serious their crime was.
- Offenders **have basic rights** so should not be given a punishment that is inhumane or harmful.
- Through their punishment offenders should be **helped to become responsible members of society** so they do not reoffend.
- The parable of the Sheep and the Goats teaches that helping prisoners is good.

Buddhism does not favour the idea of punishment as it is rooted in the idea of vengeance and causes suffering to the offender. However, Buddhists do believe there will be consequences for people who act unskilfully, either because of the law or because of the principle of kamma.

Buddhism also teaches that everyone can change, so the **rehabilitation and reformation** of the offender is important. For example, Buddhist scriptures describe how the murderer Angulimala had killed many people, but when he met the Buddha, the Buddha did not try to punish him for his crimes. Instead he encouraged Angulimala to live a better life. Angulimala gave up crime and became a follower of the Buddha.

> **TIP**
> You could use the story of Angulimala in your exam to show how Buddhists believe reformation is more important than punishment.

Religious attitudes towards three different types of crime

Type of crime	Christian views	Buddhist views
Hate crime (usually targeted at a person because of their race, religion, sexuality, disability or gender)	• Christians condemn hate crimes because they believe God created all humans equal and no one should be singled out for inferior treatment. • When Jesus taught his followers to 'love your neighbour' (Mark 12:31), he meant showing compassion, care and respect to everybody.	• Hatred is one of the three poisons and the direct opposite of the emotions that Buddhists aim to develop: loving-kindness and compassion. • This means there is no justification for hatred or intolerance. • A person who acts from hatred causes harm to themselves and others.
Theft (less serious than some crimes but still results in the victim suffering a loss)	• Theft goes against the Ten Commandments (Exodus 20:15). • Christians do not agree with any theft, including theft caused by need rather than greed.	• Theft breaks the second moral precept. • It also strengthens the habit of greed (one of the three poisons). • It expresses a lack of respect and empathy for others.
Murder (viewed by many as the most serious crime)	• Murder is wrong because only God has the right to take life. • It goes against the Ten Commandments (Exodus 20:13).	• Murder breaks the first moral precept. • It inflicts suffering not only on the victim but also on their family and friends.

APPLY

(A) **Explain** the similarities and differences between a hate crime and murder.

(B) 'Religious believers should hate the crime but not the criminal who committed it.'

Explain your opinion and develop it with religious teachings.

RECAP

Essential information:

☐ Three aims of punishment are **retribution** (to get your own back), **deterrence** (to put people off committing crimes) and **reformation** (to change someone's behaviour for the better).

☐ Christians and Buddhists generally support reformation as the best aim of punishment.

Retribution, deterrence and reformation

	Explanation	Christian views	Buddhist views
Retribution – to get your own back	• Society, on behalf of the victim, is getting its own back on the offender. • Criminals should be made to suffer in proportion to how serious their crimes are. • E.g. in the case of murder, the murderer should be killed as a punishment.	• Paul teaches, 'Do not be overcome by evil, but overcome evil with good' (Romans 21:21). • Many Christians focus on other aims of punishment, which they believe are less harmful and more positive. • Some Christians support the death penalty by quoting, 'life for life, eye for eye, tooth for tooth' (Exodus 21:23–24). But most think this means, for example, that murderers should be punished severely but not killed.	• Retribution is a form of violence and therefore wrong. • A person will suffer anyway, because of the principle of kamma (see page 75). ❝We should not seek revenge on those who have committed crimes against us, or reply to their crimes with other crimes.❞ *Tenzin Gyatso (the Dalai Lama)*
Deterrence – to put people off committing crimes	• The idea of deterrence is to use punishment as an example and warning to others. • If the punishment is harsh, it may deter the offender from repeating the crime and others from copying it. • In some countries, punishments are carried out in public as a form of deterrence.	• Although most Christians have no real problem with the idea of deterrence, they do not support punishments that are excessively harsh. • They oppose carrying out punishments in public because these could humiliate offenders rather than treating them with respect.	• Deterrence may not work if people are in grip of the three poisons. • Buddhists might agree it is important to protect society from certain criminals by imprisoning them, but the motive here is the protection of society – not punishment or deterrence.
Reformation – to change someone's behaviour for the better	• Reformation aims to use punishment that helps offenders to give up crime and realise their behaviour is harmful. • This may involve therapy and counselling, community service, and meeting the victims. • It is hoped offenders will change their attitude and become law-abiding members of society.	• Most Christians favour reformation over other aims of punishment. • This is because it is positive rather than negative, and works with individuals to improve their life chances. • It should not be a replacement for punishment but should happen alongside punishment.	• A criminal should be encouraged to recognise the suffering they have caused, apologise to their victims, and even undertake corrective action. • Buddhism favours a justice system where criminals are encouraged to change and become more responsible and sensitive to others.

APPLY

(A) **Explain** what each of the three aims of punishment are.

(B) **Write a developed argument** to support your own opinion about whether offenders should be punished severely. Include some religious teachings in your answer.

> **TIP**
> Protection is another aim of punishment (where criminals are imprisoned to protect the rest of society).

9.5 Religious attitudes to suffering and causing suffering to others

Essential information:

Christians and Buddhists believe in not causing suffering to others.

They also believe it is important to help those who are suffering.

For Christians, suffering is not caused by God but is a result of human free will. For Buddhists, suffering is simply an inevitable part of life.

Christian attitudes towards suffering

- Whatever the cause, Christians believe they **have a duty to help those who are suffering**.
- Christians try to **follow the example of Jesus**. He helped many whom he saw were suffering and told his followers to do the same.
- Christians should also **try not to cause others to suffer**.
- When they do cause others to suffer, they should **apologise and to try to repair the damage they have caused** in order to restore relationships.
- Where it is unavoidable, suffering may **strengthen a person's character and faith**.

> **❝** We also glory in our sufferings, because we know that suffering produces perseverance; perseverance, character; and character, hope. **❞**
> *Romans 5:3–4 [NIV]*

TIP
The use of free will is discussed in more detail on page 22.

How can a loving God allow people to suffer?

- Christians believe it is wrong to blame God for the suffering that results from human actions.
- This is because God gave humans **free will**: the ability to make decisions for themselves.
- God has also given plenty of guidance on how to use free will responsibly.
- The teachings and example of Jesus will reduce suffering if followed.
- The role of the law is to give more 'compulsory' guidance about the best way to use free will, together with punishments for those who cause suffering by committing crimes.

Buddhist attitudes towards suffering

The main goal of Buddhism is to **overcome suffering and achieve enlightenment**. Chapters 3 and 4 discuss this in much more detail, but the main points to remember are repeated here:

- Buddhism teaches that suffering is an **inevitable part of life**.
- Buddhists aim to overcome suffering by first **accepting it is a fact of existence** (see page 56), and then **following the Eightfold Path** or other Buddhist teachings (see page 59).
- Buddhists try to **avoid causing others to suffer**. In fact most Buddhist teachings or viewpoints revolve around the need to reduce suffering for oneself and others. A few examples include the following:

The basic moral precept in Buddhism is to not harm others (see page 78).	Bodhisattvas choose to remain in the cycle of samsara out of compassion for the suffering of others (see page 62).	The Eightfold Path encourages right livelihood, which means earning a living that does not cause suffering to oneself or others (see page 59).

A Explain **two** contrasting religious beliefs about suffering.

B 'Using violence in self-defence only causes more suffering.'

Think carefully about this statement and **write a developed argument** to support your opinion on it.

RECAP

Essential information:

☐ A **prison** is a secure building where offenders are kept for a period of time set by a judge. In the UK, people who commit more serious crimes are sent to prison.

☐ **Corporal punishment** is punishment that causes physical pain. It is illegal in the UK and not supported by Christianity or Buddhism.

☐ **Community service** is a way of punishing offenders by making them do unpaid work in the community. It is approved of by most Christians and Buddhists.

 You might be asked to compare beliefs on corporal punishment between Christianity (the main religious tradition in Great Britain) and another religious tradition.

Prison

Features	Christian views	Buddhist views
• The main punishment is a loss of liberty. • Prisoners are locked in cells for some of the day, and have to do manual work for little money. • Reserved for more serious crimes.	Many Christians support the use of prisons for more serious crimes. They also believe prisoners should be treated well, and involved in positive activities and education that help them to reform.	The primary aim of prison should be to protect society from dangerous criminals. Prison may also provide time and space for rehabilitation.

Corporal punishment

Features	Christian views	Buddhist views
• Punishes offenders by inflicting physical pain. • Considered to be a breach of human rights laws. • Illegal in the UK and many other countries. • Muslim countries such as Iran and Saudi Arabia use corporal punishment (e.g. caning) for offences such as gambling and sexual promiscuity.	Christians do not support corporal punishment. It does not seek to reform an offender, so can be seen as a negative and harmful punishment. It does not show respect for the individual.	Corporal punishment expresses violence and encourages resentment rather than reformation. It does not solve the underlying cause of crime.

Community service

Features	Christian views	Buddhist views
• Includes work in the community, such as cleaning graffiti, decorating or clearing wasteland. • Used for more minor offences, such as vandalism or benefit fraud. • May include treatment for addiction or medical conditions, counselling and education. • In some cases, a meeting may be set up so the victim can tell the offender the impact their crime had and the offender can apologise. 	Most Christians approve of community service as it allows offenders to make up for what they have done wrong, deters them from committing future offences, and reforms them by making them realise the consequences of their actions. Another positive is that no harm is done to the offender.	Most Buddhists approve of community service that helps to rehabilitate the criminal. It needs to directly address the crime and help the criminal see the impact of their actions. To be most effective, it should also address the needs of the victims.

APPLY

(A) Explain **two** similar religious beliefs about corporal punishment.

(B) 'Criminals should not be treated well.'

Make a list of the religious arguments you would use when evaluating this statement. Sort them into arguments in support of the statement and arguments against the statement.

TIP
Here you could explain one Christian belief against corporal punishment, and a similar Buddhist belief against corporal punishment.

RECAP

Essential information:

☐ Christians and Buddhists emphasise the importance of **forgiveness** (showing mercy and pardoning someone for what they have done wrong).

☐ Many Christians believe forgiveness is not a replacement for punishment.

 You might be asked to compare beliefs on forgiveness between Christianity (the main religious tradition in Great Britain) and another religious tradition.

Christian attitudes towards forgiveness

Forgiveness is a **key belief in Christianity**. Jesus taught forgiveness and showed it in his actions:

*   When he was dying on the cross, **Jesus forgave those who crucified him**: 'Father forgive them, for they do not know what they are doing' (Luke 23:24).
*   When asked how many times a person should be forgiven, Jesus said 'not seven times, but seventy-seven times' (Matthew 18:21–22). Christians interpret this to mean there should be **no limit to the amount of forgiveness they show to someone**.

The Lord's Prayer shows that Christians believe **God expects them to show forgiveness** to others. In turn, **God will forgive them** for the sins they commit ('Forgive us our sins as we forgive those who sin against us').

Many Christians argue that **forgiveness should not be a replacement for punishment**. They believe the offender should be forgiven as far as possible, but should also be punished to ensure justice is done (and to help the offender reform themselves).

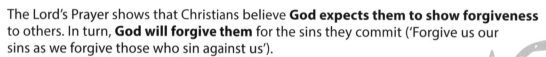

TIP
Remember that forgiving a crime is not the same as forgetting a crime. It means acknowledging the crime happened while letting go of any anger or resentment towards the criminal.

Buddhist attitudes towards forgiveness

*   For Buddhists, forgiveness involves **letting go of anger and resentment**, as well as the desire for the offender to suffer through punishment.
*   Buddhism teaches that **if people do not forgive they will suffer**, because they will continue to be angry and resentful. This means people should also forgive others for the sake of their own health and welfare.
*   Forgiving a criminal does not mean their actions will not have consequences. They will still be punished by the law or because of the **principle of kamma** (which says that unskilful actions lead to suffering).

> ❝ 'He abused me, he struck me, he overcame me, he robbed me.' Of those who wrap themselves up in it hatred is not quenched. ❞
> *The Buddha in the Dhammapada, verse 3*

*   Someone who has acted unskilfully should **confess and apologise before hoping for forgiveness**.
*   Once someone has confessed, it is considered to be unskilful not to accept their apology.
*   Apology and forgiveness can sometimes **bring about reconciliation**.

The example of Anh-Huong Nguyen

Ann-Huong Nguyen is a Vietnamese Buddhist who believed she should forgive pirates for committing evil acts including rape. In order to do this, she developed understanding of the conditions in which the pirates lived. For her, understanding and compassion led to forgiveness.

APPLY

(A) Give **two** ways in which Christian beliefs about forgiveness are different from Buddhist beliefs.

(B) 'Nobody should expect to be forgiven more than once.'

Write a **logical chain of reasoning** that agrees with this statement, and another one that gives a different point of view.

TIP
A logical chain of reasoning could include four things:
· an opinion
· a reason for the opinion
· development of the reason
· the addition of religious teaching and examples.

RECAP

Essential information:

☐ The **death penalty** (when a criminal is put to death for their crime) is illegal in the UK but still exists in some other countries.

☐ Many Christians and Buddhists oppose the death penalty.

> You might be asked to compare beliefs on the death penalty between Christianity (the main religious tradition in Great Britain) and another religious tradition.

Arguments for and against the death penalty

The death penalty was abolished in the UK in 1969. It is also illegal in most of Europe, but still exists in some states in the USA, China and in many Muslim countries, such as Saudi Arabia.

Arguments for and against the death penalty include the following:

For or against	Explanation
Against 	• There is a chance of **killing an innocent person**. • E.g. three people executed in the UK in the 1950s have since been pardoned, because new evidence has cast serious doubt over their guilt.
	• There is **little evidence the death penalty is an effective deterrent**. • E.g. the UK murder rate is no higher than in countries that have the death penalty. • Often the threat of punishment does not enter into the murderer's thinking.
	• It is **not right to take another person's life**. This does not show forgiveness or compassion.
	• Society can still be protected by **imprisoning criminals** instead of executing them.
For	• The **principle of utility** states an action is right if it produces the maximum happiness for the greatest number of people affected by it. • If the use of the death penalty is proven to protect society – therefore creating happiness for a greater number of people – it can be justified.
	• It is **justified retribution** for people who commit the worst possible crimes.
	• It **protects society** by removing the worst criminals so they cannot cause harm again.

Religious attitudes to the death penalty

Most Christians and Buddhists do not support the death penalty, although some do. Their views may be based partly on the arguments given above, and partly on the religious teachings given below.

Christian views	Buddhist views
• The **sanctity of life** is the idea that all life is holy as it is created by God, and only God can take it away. This teaching is used to oppose the death penalty. • Ezekiel 33:11 teaches that wrongdoers should be reformed (not executed). • Some Christians agree with the death penalty and use teachings from the Old Testament to support their views. " Whoever sheds human blood, by humans shall their blood be shed. " *Genesis 9:6* [NIV]	• Most Buddhists oppose the death penalty because it breaks the first moral precept and does not allow the possibility of rehabilitation. • It also makes revenge part of the criminal justice system. • It is not possible to relieve the suffering of the victim by making the offender suffer. • Thailand, a largely Buddhist country, has capital punishment for more than 30 crimes. This shows that Buddhist principles don't always impact on government policy.

APPLY

(A) Give **two** religious teachings about the death penalty.

(B) **Write a paragraph** to support the statement, 'Religious believers should not support the death penalty.'

9 Exam practice

Test the 1 mark question

1 Which **one** of the following punishments is illegal in the UK?

  A Corporal punishment B Prison   C Paying a fine   D Community service   **[1 mark]**

2 Which **one** of the following suggests an action is right if it follows the principle of utility and promotes the maximum…?

  A Pain   B Sadness   C Happiness   D Profit   **[1 mark]**

Test the 2 mark question

3 Give **two** aims of punishment.   **[2 marks]**

1) _____

2) _____

4 Give **two** reasons why some people commit crimes.   **[2 marks]**

1) _____

2) _____

Test the 4 mark question

5 Explain **two** contrasting beliefs in contemporary British society about whether the death penalty should exist in the UK. In your answer you should refer to the main religious tradition of Great Britain and one or more other religious traditions.   **[4 marks]**

● **Explain one belief.**	*Some Christians believe the death penalty is correct because it follows the Old Testament teaching of an 'eye for an eye and a tooth for a tooth'.*
● Develop your explanation with more detail/an example/ reference to a religious teaching or quotation.	*An eye for an eye and a tooth for a tooth means that an offender should receive back the same as he has done, so if he has murdered someone, he should be killed.*
● **Explain a second contrasting belief.**	*Buddhists disagree with the death penalty because it goes against the first moral precept and the Eightfold Path.*
● Develop your explanation with more detail/an example/ reference to a religious teaching or quotation.	*The first moral precept forbids Buddhists from harming or killing any living being. The 'right action' practice in the Eightfold Path also means Buddhists shouldn't harm others.*

> **TIP**
> Both of the explanations of beliefs in this answer have been clearly developed with religious teaching.

6 Explain **two** contrasting beliefs about community service. In your answer you should refer to the main religious tradition of Great Britain and one or more other religious traditions.   **[4 marks]**

● **Explain one belief.**	
● Develop your explanation with more detail/an example/ reference to a religious teaching or quotation.	
● **Explain a second contrasting belief.**	
● Develop your explanation with more detail/an example/ reference to a religious teaching or quotation.	

> **TIP**
> The 'contrasting' beliefs here could be about the value of community service and whether it is the best method of punishment.

7 Explain **two** similar beliefs that oppose retribution as an aim of punishment.

In your answer you should refer to the main religious tradition of Great Britain and one or more other religious traditions. **[4 marks]**

Test the 5 mark question

8 Explain **two** religious beliefs about reformation as an aim of punishment.
Refer to sacred writings or another source of religious belief and teaching in your answer. **[5 marks]**

● **Explain one belief.**	*A Christian belief is that reformation is a preferable aim of punishment because it seeks to help offenders change their behaviour.*
● Develop your explanation with more detail/an example.	*This means they are less likely to commit any further offences, so they won't hurt anybody else or need to be punished again.*
● **Explain a second belief.**	*A Buddhist belief is that the desire for revenge expresses hatred and leads to suffering, so should be abandoned in favour of reformation.*
● Develop your explanation with more detail/an example.	*Buddhists aim to reduce suffering by showing compassion and loving-kindness towards others. Helping criminals to reform their ways is part of this.*
● Add a reference to sacred writings or another source of religious belief. If you prefer, you can add this reference to your first belief instead.	*Buddhist scriptures tell how the Buddha didn't want to punish the murderer Angulimala. Instead he helped Angulimala to reform his life. This shows how important reformation is to Buddhists.*

9 Explain **two** religious beliefs about forgiveness.
Refer to sacred writings or another source of religious belief and teaching in your answer. **[5 marks]**

● **Explain one belief.**	
● Develop your explanation with more detail/an example.	
● **Explain a second belief.**	
● Develop your explanation with more detail/an example.	
● Add a reference to sacred writings or another source of religious belief. If you prefer, you can add this reference to your first belief instead.	

10 Explain **two** religious beliefs about hate crimes.
Refer to sacred writings or another source of religious belief and teaching in your answer. **[5 marks]**

9 Exam practice

Test the 12 mark question

11   'It is right to forgive all offenders whoever they are and whatever they have done.'
   Evaluate this statement. In your answer you:
   - should give reasoned arguments in support of this statement
   - should give reasoned arguments to support a different point of view
   - should refer to religious arguments
   - may refer to non-religious arguments
   - should reach a justified conclusion.

[12 marks]
Plus SPaG 3 mar

REASONED ARGUMENTS IN SUPPORT OF THE STATEMENT ● **Explain why some people would agree with the statement.** ● Develop your explanation with more detail and examples. ● Refer to religious teaching. Use a quote or paraphrase or a religious authority. ● **Evaluate the arguments.** Is this a good argument or not? Explain why you think this.	*Christians should always forgive anybody who wants to be forgiven. When the disciples asked Jesus how many times they should forgive, suggesting that seven was a fair number, Jesus told them it should be seventy-seven times. In other words, there should be no maximum. Jesus even asked God to forgive the people who crucified him because they didn't know what they were doing. So it should not matter how many times, who is asking to be forgiven or what they have done to be forgiven for.* *According to Buddhism, if people don't forgive, and hang on to resentment and hurt, they will continue to suffer. So forgiveness benefits the victim as well as the criminal. It makes no sense to continue inflicting suffering on oneself through hatred or anger. If someone is forgiven, there is a better chance they will be reformed and try hard to make sure that whatever they have done is never repeated. No sin is unforgiveable and so people, especially religious people, should always forgive.*
REASONED ARGUMENTS SUPPORTING A DIFFERENT VIEW ● **Explain why some people would support a different view.** ● Develop your explanation with more detail and examples. ● Refer to religious teaching. Use a quote or paraphrase or a religious authority. ● **Evaluate the arguments.** Is this a good argument or not? Explain why you think this.	*Some people who are victims of serious crimes find it very difficult to forgive. They cannot imagine how they can ever feel anything but hatred for someone who has wronged them so horribly. A victim of rape may find it hard to forgive their attacker and they are highly unlikely to ever forget it. But time is a great healer and maybe forgiveness is more easily given some years later.* *The line in the Lord's Prayer that says: 'Forgive us our sins, as we forgive those who sin against us' is unrealistic because there are some awful things that should never be forgiven unless the offender shows they are truly sorry and remorseful, and even then, it is almost impossible. Many Jews find it impossible to forgive the Nazis for the Holocaust and why should they be expected to?*
CONCLUSION ● **Give a justified conclusion.** ● Include your own opinion together with your own reasoning. ● **Include evaluation.** Explain why you think one viewpoint is stronger than the other or why they are equally strong. ● Do not just repeat arguments you have already used without explaining how they apply to your reasoned opinion/conclusion.	*In my opinion, forgiveness is an ideal that religions want people to work towards. I think if they become the victims themselves, they may change their mind. We are only human.*

TIP
The first paragraph not only shows good knowledge of the Bible's teaching on forgiveness but also makes its meaning clear.

TIP
This student could improve their conclusion by going into more detail about their views on the statement. For example, they could explain why they think one viewpoint is stronger than the other, or express an opinion about the strength of the religious arguments given in the answer.

9 Exam practice

12 'The use of the death penalty is always wrong.'

Evaluate this statement. In your answer you:

- should give reasoned arguments in support of this statement
- should give reasoned arguments to support a different point of view
- should refer to religious arguments
- may refer to non-religious arguments
- should reach a justified conclusion.

[12 marks]
Plus SPaG 3 marks

REASONED ARGUMENTS IN SUPPORT OF THE STATEMENT ● **Explain why some people would agree with the statement.** ● Develop your explanation with more detail and examples. ● Refer to religious teaching. Use a quote or paraphrase or a religious authority. ● **Evaluate the arguments.** Is this a good argument or not? Explain why you think this.	
REASONED ARGUMENTS SUPPORTING A DIFFERENT VIEW ● **Explain why some people would support a different view.** ● Develop your explanation with more detail and examples. ● Refer to religious teaching. Use a quote or paraphrase or a religious authority. ● **Evaluate the arguments.** Is this a good argument or not? Explain why you think this.	
CONCLUSION ● **Give a justified conclusion.** ● Include your own opinion together with your own reasoning. ● **Include evaluation.** Explain why you think one viewpoint is stronger than the other or why they are equally strong. ● Do not just repeat arguments you have already used without explaining how they apply to your reasoned opinion/conclusion.	

13 'There is no good reason why anyone should commit a crime.'

Evaluate this statement. In your answer you:

- should give reasoned arguments in support of this statement
- should give reasoned arguments to support a different point of view
- should refer to religious arguments
- may refer to non-religious arguments
- should reach a justified conclusion.

[12 marks]
Plus SPaG 3 marks

Check your answers using the mark scheme on pages 167–168. How did you do?
To feel more secure in the content you need to remember, re-read pages 132–139.
To remind yourself of what the examiner is looking for, go to pages 6–11.

10 Religion, human rights and social justice

10.1 Social justice and human rights

Essential information:

☐ **Human rights** are the basic rights and freedoms to which all human beings should be entitled. It is only possible for all people to have these rights if they acknowledge the responsibility to respect and help provide for the rights of others.

☐ **Social justice** means ensuring society treats people fairly whether they are poor or wealthy. It involves protecting everyone's human rights.

Human rights and responsibilities

- In 1948, the United Nations adopted the **Universal Declaration of Human Rights** (UDHR).
- This sets out the rights to which every person should be entitled.
- The UK government is obliged to provide these rights to people living in the UK.

a fair trial — education — marriage — **Examples of human rights** — life — liberty — security — privacy

People can only have human rights if they acknowledge the responsibility to make sure these rights are available. This includes the responsibility to **respect other people's rights**, and the responsibility to **help create access to those rights**. For example:

- Humans have the right to freedom of speech, but the responsibility not to say something that causes offence.
- Children have the right to protection from cruelty, but the responsibility not to bully or harm each other.

Social justice

Social justice is about trying to protect people's rights and opportunities so the least advantaged members of society are treated with the same justice and compassion as more advantaged people.

Christian views	Buddhist views
• There are many teachings in the Bible about the importance of social justice and caring for others. • Some of the Old Testament prophets were quick to condemn injustice and looked forward to a fairer society. For example, the prophet Amos said, 'Let justice roll on like a river and righteousness like a never-failing stream' (Amos 5:24). • Jesus stressed the need to help others, for example in his teaching 'love your neighbour as yourself' (Mark 12:31).	• The Buddha taught that while suffering is inevitable, at the same time people should try to relieve the suffering of others. • Buddhists can do this through social justice projects. Such work expresses compassion and brings communities together. • Engaged Buddhism is a movement in Buddhism that uses the Buddha's teachings to tackle social issues, including injustice.

(A) Give **two** examples of human rights.

(B) 'Everybody's human rights should be protected.'

Write a **detailed argument** agreeing with this statement and a contrasting argument to support a different opinion.

10.2 Prejudice and discrimination

Essential information:

☐ **Equality** means having equal rights, status and opportunities.

☐ Christianity teaches that all people are equal because they have all been made in God's image, while for Buddhists, treating people equally expresses loving-kindness.

☐ Despite this, there are examples of prejudice and discrimination against women and homosexuals in religion today.

In 2014, Libby Lane became the first female bishop in the Church of England.

Gender prejudice and discrimination

- **Prejudice** means holding biased (usually negative) opinions about an individual or a group of people. These opinions are usually based on ignorance and stereotypical ideas about race, religion, gender, sexuality, disability, etc.
- Actions or behaviour arising from holding prejudiced views are called **discrimination**.

> **TIP**
> Christian and Buddhist views on homosexuality and gender equality are also discussed on pages 84 and 91.

Christian views	Buddhist views
• In early Christianity, women were not allowed to be leaders of the Church. **❝**Women should remain silent in the churches […] for it is disgraceful for a woman to speak in the church.**❞** *1 Corinthians 14:34–35* [NIV] • The Catholic and Orthodox Churches still do not allow women to be priests. They argue that men and women are equal but have different roles. • Other Christian denominations are happy to ordain women. They argue the Church should adapt to reflect the importance of equality in today's society.	• The Buddha ordained nuns, although at first was reluctant to do so. • Today, some Buddhist traditions ordain men and women equally (e.g. the Triratna Buddhist Order). • In 2015, the Dalai Lama (the most senior Tibetan Buddhist leader) said he thought there was no reason why a future Dalai Lama could not be a woman. • Some traditional Buddhist schools do not allow women to be fully ordained. • In Theravada Buddhism, nuns are not given the same respect and recognition as monks.

Sexuality

Christian views	Buddhist views
• Some Christians think heterosexual relationships that lead to procreation are what God intended (see Genesis 1:28 and 2:24). • They believe homosexual relationships are sinful. • Others think homosexual relationships are morally acceptable, and it is not loving to condemn people for their sexual orientation.	• Buddhist scriptures say very little about homosexuality, and no Buddhist teaching says homosexual relationships are wrong. • Many Buddhists think the moral precepts apply to any couple, regardless of their sexual orientation.

(A) Explain **one** similarity and **one** difference between Buddhism and Christianity in relation to views on homosexuality.

(B) 'Women should not be allowed to take on leadership positions in a religion.'

Write a **developed argument** to agree with this statement, and another argument to support a different opinion.

You might be asked to compare beliefs on the status of women in religion between Christianity (the main religious tradition in Great Britain) and another religious tradition.

RECAP

Essential information:

☐ Christians and Buddhists generally believe people should have **freedom of religion** (the right to practise whatever religion one chooses), including **freedom of religious expression** (the right to worship, preach and practise one's faith in whatever way one chooses).

☐ These rights are protected by the UK government, and included in the Universal Declaration of Human Rights.

Freedom of religion

In Britain today:

- Christianity is the main religious tradition.
- But nobody is forced to be a Christian because the government protects the freedom of religious expression.
- This gives all individuals the right to follow whichever faith they choose or none.
- Laws forbid the persecution of members of any faith.
- Any person can encourage anybody else to follow their faith, provided they do not preach hatred and intolerance.

> ❝ Everyone has the right to freedom of thought, conscience and religion; this right includes freedom to [...] manifest his religion or belief in teaching, practice, worship and observance. ❞
> *Universal Declaration of Human Rights*

Religious teachings on freedom of religion

Christian views	Buddhist views
• Christian teaching encourages tolerance and harmony. • Different Christian denominations fighting each other or other religions are not following teachings in the Bible. ❝ If it is possible [...] live at peace with everyone. ❞ *Romans 12:18* [NIV] ❝ Be completely humble and gentle; be patient, bearing with one another in love. ❞ *Ephesians 4:2* [NIV]	• The Buddha encouraged people to listen to the teachers of other religions with respect. • Very few Buddhist traditions try to persuade others to become Buddhists. • In Buddhist countries, people are usually free to practise Buddhism as little or as much as they wish. ❝ I always say that every person on this earth has the freedom to practise or not practise religion. It is all right to do either. ❞ *Tenzin Gyatso (the Dalai Lama)*

Despite the fact that Christianity and Buddhism both encourage religious tolerance, there have been examples in recent years where Christians and Buddhists have not been able to live in harmony with people from other denominations or religions. For example:

> In Northern Ireland, different religious and political views have caused conflict for many years between Protestants and Catholics.

> In Myanmar, some Buddhists have shown intolerance and encouraged violence towards Muslims, who are a religious minority.

APPLY

Ⓐ **Explain** the attitudes to freedom of religion from the main religious tradition of Great Britain and one or more other religious traditions.

Ⓑ **Explain** whether you think people should be free to follow any religion they choose without any interference from anyone else. **Refer to religious teachings** in your argument.

 You might be asked to compare beliefs on freedom of religious expression between Christianity (the main religious tradition in Great Britain) and another religious tradition.

RECAP

Essential information:

☐ Prejudice and discrimination based on disability or race is illegal in the UK, but still occurs regularly.

☐ Most Christians and Buddhists oppose any form of prejudice and discrimination.

☐ **Positive discrimination** means treating people more favourably because they have been discriminated against in the past or have disabilities.

Disability

- There are over 500 million people with **disabilities** in the world today (people with physical or mental impairments that affect day-to-day activities).
- Some people show prejudice or discrimination towards those with disabilities.
- Sometimes positive discrimination is used to give disabled people opportunities they would not otherwise have, such as giving wheelchair users front-row positions at a football ground so they can see the match.

Christian views	Buddhist views
• Christians oppose discrimination against disabled people because it does not demonstrate equality or love. • In the Bible, Jesus helped the disabled by healing them, and he taught his followers to 'love your neighbour as yourself' (Mark 12:31).	• There are no explicit Buddhist teachings on disability, but the general Buddhist attitude of karuna (compassion) applies to all those who are suffering in any way, including disabled people (see page 76).

Racism

- Racism means to consider people of different races as inferior and to treat these people badly as a result. Racism is often triggered by skin colour.
- Since 1976, various Acts have been passed that make racism illegal in the UK. Despite this, it still occurs regularly.
- 'Show Racism the Red Card' is one example of a campaign against racism. It is designed to educate football fans and remove racist abuse from football.

Christian views	Buddhist views
• Most Christians oppose racism as they believe all people are equal: 'There is neither Jew nor Gentile, neither slave nor free, nor is there male and female, for you are one in Christ Jesus' (Galatians 3:28). • In the twentieth century, races were kept apart with black people being discriminated against in countries such as South Africa and the USA. • The actions of Christians such as Archbishop Desmond Tutu (South Africa) and Dr Martin Luther King Junior (USA), with the help of others, persuaded their respective governments that racist policies were unfair and needed to be changed.	• The principle of loving-kindness means racism is not acceptable to most Buddhists. • Loving-kindness should be developed towards all people without discrimination. **TIP** Positive discrimination can also be applied to race, e.g. a business might employ someone from an ethnic minority partly to help make the workplace more ethnically diverse.

APPLY

(A) **Explain** why Christians and Buddhists oppose discrimination based on race.

(B) 'All discrimination is wrong.'

Write a developed argument in support of this statement and a developed argument to support a different point of view. You can include your own opinion, but make sure you also **refer to religious teaching**.

TIP
You might find a statement such as this difficult to argue against. But remember there are two forms of discrimination: negative and positive. Could you write an argument in favour of positive discrimination?

Essential information:

☐ Christianity and Buddhism do not teach it is wrong to be wealthy. But they do teach that focusing on wealth can lead to greed and selfishness, and the neglect of spiritual practice.

☐ Both religions also teach it is important to use wealth to help others in need.

Religious attitudes towards wealth

Christian views	Buddhist views
• The Bible teaches that wealth is a blessing from God (1 Chronicles 29:12). • The Bible also teaches that wealth is associated with dangers like greed and selfishness. **"For the love of money is a root of all sorts of evil."** *1 Timothy 6:10 [NIV]* • Jesus did not teach it is wrong to be wealthy, but said that focusing on wealth brings the danger of ignoring God and neglecting the spiritual life. **"You cannot serve both God and money."** *Matthew 6:24 [NIV]*	• For Buddhists, what matters is not how wealthy someone is but how they got their money, their attitude towards it, and what they do with it. • The Buddha grew up in a privileged environment but later renounced this luxury in order to live a simple life (see pages 46–49). • Traditionally, monks and nuns live a simple life with little or no money. • Letting go of wealth is a way of overcoming attachment, which is a spiritual obstacle. • Ordinary Buddhists need to earn their livelihood but at the same time follow the ethical precepts. • The Buddha taught that happiness is not achieved through craving and accumulating wealth but through enlightenment. **"By action, knowledge and Dhamma, by virtue and noble way of life – By these are mortals purified, not by lineage or wealth."** *The Buddha in the Majjhima Nikaya, vol. 3, p. 262*

TIP
If you use this quote in your exam, you must include the words 'For the love of' at the beginning, otherwise you change its meaning.

Religious attitudes towards using wealth

Christian views	Buddhist views

• While everyone needs money to live, Christians believe those with excess money should give it to the Church for its upkeep and mission, including providing for the poor.
• Wealth should be used to help people in need.
• In the Bible, the parable of the Rich Man and Lazarus ends with the rich man in hell for not sharing his wealth with the poor beggar (Luke 16:19–31).
• The parable of the Sheep and the Goats states that those who help the poor are rewarded with a place in heaven (Matthew 25:31–46).
	• The *Adiya Sutta* says a person can use their wealth for three purposes:
	  1. to provide pleasure and satisfaction for themselves, their family and their friends
	  2. to keep themselves safe
	  3. to give offerings to monks, nuns, or the poor.
	• Buddhism places a lot of emphasis on using one's wealth to benefit others.
	• It is also important to give freely without expecting anything in return.

A Explain **two** religious teachings about wealth.

B **Write a developed argument** to support the idea that giving to charity should be compulsory.

 You might be asked to compare beliefs on the uses of wealth between Christianity (the main religious tradition in Great Britain) and another religious tradition.

10.6 Poverty and its causes

Essential information:

☐ Many people throughout the world live in **poverty**, without money, food or basic necessities.

☐ Some of the causes of poverty include debt, unemployment, exploitation and natural disasters.

☐ While many Christians and Buddhists believe it is important to help those living in poverty, they also think the poor have a responsibility to help themselves out of poverty if they are able to do so.

The causes of poverty

- Every person has basic needs in order to live (such as food, shelter and health care), but those living in poverty are not able to meet these needs.
- Poverty is a complex global problem that has many causes. A few of these include the following:

Debt	• Many of the poorest countries owe money to wealthier countries, which they have borrowed for such things as health care and education.
	• Debt is also a reason why individual people go into poverty in the UK, e.g. if they can't pay back money they owe to a bank.
Unemployment	• Unemployment is one of the main causes of poverty in the UK, as not everyone is able to find work or is fit to work.
Natural disasters	• Flooding, drought and other natural disasters are common throughout the world. They can destroy crops and properties, leaving people with no food or shelter.

Responsibilities of those living in poverty

- Even though the Bible says 'the one who is unwilling to work shall not eat' (2 Thessalonians 3:10), **Christians** believe it is important to help those who need assistance.
- Christians also encourage the poor to help themselves by finding work, but realise some are unable to do so.
- **Buddhism** teaches that all poverty deserves compassion, but that people also have a responsibility to themselves to create the conditions needed for a healthy life.

> **TIP**
>
> People have different views on who is responsible for helping those in poverty. Some think it is society's responsibility, especially if people are in poverty through bad luck as a result of how society works. Others think more responsibility should be placed on people to make an effort to get out of poverty or to not get into poverty in the first place.

> **An example of the poor freeing themselves from poverty**
>
> The Dalit people in India are at the bottom of the Hindu caste system. In the 1950s, their leader Dr Ambekar inspired many of them to convert to Buddhism. He taught them to 'educate, agitate and organise' to resist the people and laws keeping them in poverty. He also taught them to develop more self-respect for themselves and each other. Since the 1950s, millions of them have freed themselves from extreme poverty.

(A) Give **two** causes of poverty in Britain.

(B) 'Those living in poverty should help themselves to get out of it rather than relying on the help of others.'

Write a paragraph that gives your opinion on this statement and explains your reasoning. **Refer to religious teachings** as part of your answer.

> **TIP**
>
> Don't forget, you are assessed on your reasoning, not your opinion. This means it doesn't matter what your opinion is as long as you have explained it well.

RECAP

Essential information:

☐ **Exploitation** is the misuse of power or money to get other people to do things for little or unfair reward.

☐ The poor are exploited worldwide in various ways, including by being paid unfairly, being charged excessive interest on loans, and being involved in people-trafficking.

☐ All of these practices go against the teachings of Christianity and Buddhism.

Fair pay

- An important way to stop exploitation of the poor is to make sure they receive **fair pay** for the work they do.
- In the UK, the National Minimum Wage sets the lowest amount an employer can pay a worker per hour.
- In many developing countries, large companies pay their workers very low wages in order to increase their profits.
- For example, in West Bengal in India, hundreds of thousands of people work on tea plantations for around £1 per day, which is about half of what they are legally entitled to.

> **Religious responses**
>
> - Most Christians support fair pay for everyone as this contributes to an equal and just society.
>
> > "Do not exploit the poor because they are poor."
> > *Proverbs 22:22* [NIV]
>
> - Many Buddhists consider it very important to balance profit with ethics.
> - Taking workers' time and energy without paying them a fair wage goes against the second moral precept (to avoid taking what has not been freely given).

Excessive interest on loans

- Poor people sometimes have little choice but to borrow money from loan companies that charge very high rates of interest (**excessive interest on loans**).
- If they cannot repay the loans fast enough, the huge interest rates mean they can quickly end up in debt, as they end up owing much more than the amount they borrowed.

> **Religious responses**
>
> - Buddhism teaches that making money by exploiting the poor is an example of greed (one of the three poisons), and against the second moral precept.
> - Buddhism also teaches that each person has a responsibility to create the conditions for a healthy life, and this includes not getting into debt if they can help it.

People-trafficking

- **People-trafficking** is the illegal movement of people, typically for the purposes of forced labour or commercial sexual exploitation.
- People who are desperate for a better way of life may pay smugglers to get them into a more prosperous country.
- Once in the new country, they have few rights and may be forced by the smugglers to work in poor conditions for little pay.
- Some are kidnapped and forced to work against their will.

> **Religious responses**
>
> - People-trafficking goes against Jesus' teaching to 'love your neighbour as yourself', and it is against the Buddhist moral precepts.
> - Although people-trafficking may not have been a recognised problem when the Buddha was alive, he criticised the caste system in India, which exploited the poor and forced them to work in bad conditions for little money.

APPLY

(A) Explain **two** ways in which poor people might be exploited.

(B) 'Developed countries requiring cheap goods are to blame for exploitation.'

Write two developed arguments, one supporting the statement and one supporting a different opinion. **Refer to religious teaching** in your writings.

TIP
Remember that if you refer to religious teachings in your answer, they need to be relevant to the point you are making.

10.8 Giving money to the poor

Essential information:

☐ There are two main ways to help the poor – by giving **short-term aid** (immediate help that focuses on short-term survival) or **long-term aid** (help over a longer period of time that has a more lasting effect).

☐ Many Christians and Buddhists try to help provide both types of aid, by supporting charities and campaigns that help those living in poverty.

Giving aid

There are two main types of help that can be given to the poor – short-term aid and long-term aid.

	Short-term aid	Long-term aid
Definition	• Help given to communities in a time of disaster or crisis. • Help given directly to the poor to relieve their immediate needs. • Also called emergency aid.	• Help given to communities over a longer period of time, which has a more lasting effect.
Examples	• Providing supplies of food and water after an earthquake. • Giving money directly to homeless people on the streets.	• Providing education to help people find better-paid work. • Providing farmers with tools to improve their efficiency.
Pros	• Important for survival in the short term. • Displays compassion and kindness.	• Helps people to become more self-reliant. • Helps to solve the root causes of poverty.
Cons	• Does not tackle the underlying causes of poverty. • Can make people reliant on whoever is giving out the aid.	• May take time to have an effect. • Does not help with short-term survival.

Christian and Buddhist responses

- **Christians** believe they have been given a responsibility by God to look after the world and the poor.
- Jesus' teachings mean they have a duty to show compassion and to 'love your neighbour as yourself'.
- Many Christians try to balance providing immediate help to those in poverty (short-term aid) with helping people to use their own gifts and talents to get themselves out of poverty (long-term aid).
- Generosity and compassion are important values for **Buddhists**.
- The Buddha taught that Buddhists should give freely, without expecting anything in return.
- For many Buddhists it is also important to give what will be of genuine help. This means some Buddhists might prefer not to give money directly to homeless people, as they cannot be sure how the money will be spent. They may prefer to give to a homeless charity instead.

Christians and Buddhists might donate to charities such as CAFOD or the Karuna Trust to help those living in poverty. Other ways they might help include:

Buying Fairtrade products. These have been made by workers who are paid fairly and work in good conditions.	Supporting soup kitchens, food banks, and charities that provide help for those in poverty or assist them in finding work.	Supporting campaigns that promote greater equality and a just society, such as the Living Wage campaign.

 A Explain **two** ways in which long-term aid helps people to provide for themselves.

B 'Aid simply perpetuates poverty and dependence.'

Prepare one developed argument in favour and one developed argument against this statement.

Test the 1 mark question

1 Which **one** of the following best describes prejudice?

  A Doing something to someone which is unfair   B Misusing power to get people to do things

  C Unfairly judging someone before the facts are known

  D Using violent action to threaten or harm someone   **[1 mark]**

2 Which **one** of the following is **not** an action which goes against human rights?

  A Promoting tolerance   B People-trafficking   C Racial prejudice   D Exploiting the poor   **[1 mark]**

Test the 2 mark question

3 Give **two** ways in which the poor are exploited.   **[2 marks]**

  1) _____

  2) _____

4 Give **two** ways in which a religious person should use their wealth.   **[2 marks]**

  1) _____

  2) _____

Test the 4 mark question

5 Explain **two** contrasting beliefs in contemporary British society about what role women should be allowed in worship. In your answer you should refer to the main religious tradition of Great Britain and one or more other religious traditions.   **[4 marks]**

● **Explain one belief.**	The main religious tradition of Great Britain is Christianity and in many denominations women are allowed to take a full and active role in leading worship.
● Develop your explanation with more detail/an example/ reference to a religious teaching or quotation.	For example, Libby Lane became an Anglican bishop and in the United Reformed and Methodist denominations, women are also allowed to be preachers and ministers.
● **Explain a second contrasting belief.**	In contrast, in Theravada Buddhism nuns are often not given the same respect and recognition as monks.
● Develop your explanation with more detail/an example/ reference to a religious teaching or quotation.	For example, they do not allow women to be fully ordained.

> **TIP**
> This is a good start to the answer. It immediately identifies Christianity as the main religious tradition of Great Britain.

6 Explain **two** contrasting religious beliefs about prejudice based on sexuality.   **[4 marks]**

● **Explain one belief.**	
● Develop your explanation with more detail/an example/ reference to a religious teaching or quotation.	
● **Explain a second contrasting belief.**	
● Develop your explanation with more detail/an example/ reference to a religious teaching or quotation.	

> **TIP**
> 'Prejudice based on sexuality' usually means holding negative opinions about people who are not heterosexual. To answer this question, you could explain different Christian and Buddhist beliefs about homosexuality.

7   Explain two similar religious beliefs about human rights.   **[4 marks]**

Test the 5 mark question

8   Explain **two** religious beliefs about social justice.

      Refer to sacred writings or another source of religious belief and teaching in your answer   **[5 marks]**

● **Explain one belief.**	Buddhists believe social justice is important because it helps to relieve people's suffering.
● Develop your explanation with more detail/an example.	This is shown in the movement of Engaged Buddhism, which uses the Buddha's teachings to tackle social issues.
● **Explain a second belief.**	Christians believe that working to promote social justice brings them closer to God.
● Develop your explanation with more detail/an example.	Many Christians have campaigned to improve human rights, for example Martin Luther King Jr, who led a peaceful movement to achieve social justice for black people who were discriminated against in America.
● Add a reference to sacred writings or another source of religious belief. If you prefer, you can add this reference to your first belief instead.	The parable of the Sheep and the Goats supports this Christian belief: 'Take your inheritance, the kingdom prepared for you since the salvation of the world. For I was hungry and you gave me something to drink, I was a stranger and you invited me in...' (Matthew 25:34–36)

TIP
The parable of the Sheep and the Goats is a useful story to quote when dealing with issues of justice, poverty or helping those in need.

9   Explain **two** religious beliefs about the duty to tackle poverty.

      Refer to sacred writings or another source of religious belief and teaching in your answer.   **[5 marks]**

● **Explain one belief.**	
● Develop your explanation with more detail/an example.	
● **Explain a second belief.**	
● Develop your explanation with more detail/an example.	
● Add a reference to sacred writings or another source of religious belief. If you prefer, you can add this reference to your first belief instead.	

10   Explain **two** religious beliefs about the dangers of wealth.

      Refer to sacred writings or another source of religious belief and teaching in your answer.   **[5 marks]**

Test the 12 mark question

11 'All religious believers must give to charities that help the poor.'

Evaluate this statement. In your answer you:

- should give reasoned arguments in support of this statement
- should give reasoned arguments to support a different point of view
- should refer to religious arguments
- may refer to non-religious arguments
- should reach a justified conclusion.

[12 marks]
Plus SPaG 3 mar▸

REASONED ARGUMENTS IN SUPPORT OF THE STATEMENT ● **Explain why some people would agree with the statement.** ● Develop your explanation with more detail and examples. ● Refer to religious teaching. Use a quote or paraphrase or a religious authority. ● **Evaluate the arguments.** Is this a good argument or not? Explain why you think this.	*If all religious believers gave to charities it would go a long way to ending a lot of poverty in the world. So many people are suffering because they do not have enough money to buy food, clothes and provide a home for themselves. While a lot of food is thrown away in rich countries other people struggle to have one meal a day. So if all religious believers were generous in their giving it would make life a lot more bearable for the poor. Some people are poor because of natural disasters or are refugees from war. They need emergency aid and religious believers should respond and it should be their duty to give to charities that are helping.*
REASONED ARGUMENTS SUPPORTING A DIFFERENT VIEW ● **Explain why some people would support a different view.** ● Develop your explanation with more detail and examples. ● Refer to religious teaching. Use a quote or paraphrase or a religious authority. ● **Evaluate the arguments.** Is this a good argument or not? Explain why you think this.	*However, some religious believers are poor themselves, so will not be able to afford to help others. They are struggling to survive and have no extra money to give to charity. So you can't expect those religious believers to starve in order to give to the poor. Some may prefer to do work to help the charities like distributing and collecting envelopes for Christian Aid. Not all religious believers have to give money; they can help in other ways.*
CONCLUSION ● **Give a justified conclusion.** ● Include your own opinion together with your own reasoning. ● **Include evaluation.** Explain why you think one viewpoint is stronger than the other or why they are equally strong. ● Do not just repeat arguments you have already used without explaining how they apply to your reasoned opinion/conclusion.	*It is true that charities do a lot of good in helping those who are poor. However, it is unfair just to expect religious believers to donate money to the charities. Everyone should try and help if they can whether they are religious or not. Not all religious believers are able to donate money but they can pray or give their time to help charities.*

TIP
This answer could be improved by referring to specific religious teachings. For example, in this section the student could refer to the Christian teaching to 'love your neighbour' and the parable of the Sheep and the Goats, or the instruction in the Buddhist Adiya Sutta to give to the poor and the importance of generosity as one of the six perfections.

TIP
A key word in the statement is 'all'. It hints that some religious believers might not have a duty to give to charities, for example if they are very poor themselves. The student has rightly explained other ways people could help, for example volunteering their time.

12 'Discrimination is always wrong.'

Evaluate this statement. In your answer you:

- should give reasoned arguments in support of this statement
- should give reasoned arguments to support a different point of view
- should refer to religious arguments
- may refer to non-religious arguments
- should reach a justified conclusion.

[12 marks]
Plus SPaG 3 marks

REASONED ARGUMENTS IN SUPPORT OF THE STATEMENT ● **Explain why some people would agree with the statement.** ● Develop your explanation with more detail and examples. ● Refer to religious teaching. Use a quote or paraphrase or a religious authority. ● **Evaluate the arguments.** Is this a good argument or not? Explain why you think this.	
REASONED ARGUMENTS SUPPORTING A DIFFERENT VIEW ● **Explain why some people would support a different view.** ● Develop your explanation with more detail and examples. ● Refer to religious teaching. Use a quote or paraphrase or a religious authority. ● **Evaluate the arguments.** Is this a good argument or not? Explain why you think this.	
CONCLUSION ● **Give a justified conclusion.'** ● Include your own opinion together with your own reasoning. ● **Include evaluation.** Explain why you think one viewpoint is stronger than the other or why they are equally strong. ● Do not just repeat arguments you have already used without explaining how they apply to your reasoned opinion/conclusion.	

> **TIP**
> Don't forget that your spelling, punctuation and grammar are assessed in the 12 mark questions.

13 'Everybody should have the freedom to follow whichever religion they wish to.'

Evaluate this statement. In your answer you:

- should give reasoned arguments in support of this statement
- should give reasoned arguments to support a different point of view
- should refer to religious arguments
- may refer to non-religious arguments
- should reach a justified conclusion.

[12 marks]
Plus SPaG 3 marks

Check your answers using the mark scheme on page 168. How did you do?
To feel more secure in the content you need to remember, re-read pages 144–151.
To remind yourself of what the examiner is looking for, go to pages 6–11.

Apply answers

1 Christianity: beliefs and teachings

Please note that these are suggested answers to the Apply questions, designed to give you guidance, rather than being definitive answers.

1.1 **A** 'We believe in one God' (the Nicene Creed)/ the first of the Ten Commandments. **B** *You might include*: Christians are inspired to follow the teaching of the Bible/ believe they have a relationship with God/ communicate with God through prayer/ find comfort in God in challenging times/ pray and worship/ try to follow Jesus' example.

1.2 **A** Creating humans/ caring for humans/ sending his son, Jesus, to live among humans/ requiring justice. **B** Suffering was brought into God's perfect world by Adam and Eve's disobedience/ the result of human free will/ a test of faith/ without suffering people can't show positive human qualities such as compassion/ by overcoming suffering humans learn to be strong and appreciative of good in the world. *Remember to develop each point with more detail.*

1.3 **A** 1: These persons are God the Father, the Son (Jesus) and the Holy Spirit/ these three persons are named in the Apostles Creed and the Nicene Creed. 2: God the Father is the creator of all life/ acts as a good father towards humankind, who are his children/ is omnipotent, omnibenevolent, omniscient and omnipresent. **B** *Arguments for*: 1, 2, 4, 6, 7. *Arguments against*: 3, 5, 8. *In your justified conclusion you should weigh up both sides of the argument and then say which side you personally find more convincing and why.*

1.4 **A** They value every human being as created by God/ they believe people should look after the natural world. **B** *You might conclude that this is a strong argument because it is true that Christians believe in God's omnipotence and the truth of the Bible. But you might think it is a weak argument because theories of evolution and the Big Bang are widely accepted by many Christians despite not being 'proved'. It doesn't matter whether you think the argument is weak or strong, the important thing is to carefully explain why you think it is weak or strong.*

1.5 **A** Jesus was God in human form/ 'The Word became flesh and made his dwelling among us' (John 1:14 [NIV])/ Jesus was born of a virgin, Mary. **B** *E.g. 'The belief that Jesus was conceived by the Holy Spirit is given in Matthew 1:18, which says, 'His mother Mary was pledged to be married to Joseph, but before they came together, she was found to be pregnant by the Holy Spirit."*

1.6 **A** 1: Jesus' death restored the relationship between people and God. 2: God understands human suffering because Jesus, who is God, experienced it. **B** When Jesus died he took the sins of everyone on himself (the atonement)/ if Jesus had not died he would not have risen from the dead. *The answer could be improved by developing reasons why the crucifixion is an important belief rather than merely describing what took place.*

1.7 **A** The women were told by angels that Jesus had risen/ Jesus appeared to the disciples. **B** Paul wrote, 'And if Christ has not been raised, our preaching is useless and so is your faith' (1 Corinthians 15:14 [NIV])/ 'He rose again according to the scriptures' (the Nicene Creed)/ the resurrection shows the power of good over evil and life over death/ Christians will be resurrected if they accept Jesus/ 'I look for the resurrection of the dead and the life of the world to come' (the Nicene Creed).

1.8 **A** Gives hope of life after death with Jesus/ inspires Christians to live in the way God wants. **B** *In your paragraph you should weigh up both sides of the argument and then say which side you personally find more convincing and why.*

1.9 **A** Christians believe that when they die God will judge them on their behaviour and actions during their lifetime/ as well as their faith in Jesus/ God will judge people based on how they serve others unselfishly. *Refer to the Parable of the Sheep and the Goats to support your points.* **B** *You might include*: the promise of heaven inspires people to be kind to others/ people want to be with Jesus when they die so they follow his teachings/ on the other hand, no one can be sure there is an afterlife, so it is not a good way to get people to behave/ an atheist would question how a loving God could punish people forever in hell. *In your justified conclusion you should weigh up both sides of the argument and then say which side you personally find more convincing.*

1.10 **A** A loving God would not condemn people to hell/ God is forgiving so would offer everyone a second chance to repent. **B** *Arguments in support might include*: the promise of heaven would encourage good behaviour/ the threat of hell would prevent bad behaviour/ belief in heaven takes away the fear of death/ gives hope that people will experience eternal happiness even if their life on earth has been hard. *Other views might include*: atheists don't believe in heaven or hell but still have moral principles/ most people do not consider belief in the afterlife when deciding how to behave/ morality is formed in childhood by parental teaching/ if heaven and hell were made up to encourage good behaviour, it hasn't worked.

1.11 **A** Salvation by grace of God freely given through faith in Jesus/ 'For it is by grace you have been saved' (Ephesians 2:8 [NIV])/ salvation by doing good works/ 'In the same way, faith by itself, if it is not accompanied by action, is dead' (James 2:17 [NIV]). **B** *In deciding whether you find this argument convincing, try to think of what others might say against it.*

1.12 **A** Jesus' death made up for the original sin of Adam and Eve/ Jesus' resurrection was proof that his sacrifice was accepted by God. **B** *There is no 'right' order, but suggested arguments in support*: 4, 5, 2, 8. *Arguments against*: 1, 6, 7, 3. *Missing from this evaluation is any reference to specific Christian teaching, for example a reference to sacred writing. A justified conclusion is also needed.*

2 Christianity: practices

Please note that these are suggested answers to the Apply questions, designed to give you guidance, rather than being definitive answers.

2.1 **A** Private prayer/ singing hymns of praise in church. **B** *Arguments in support might include:* a set ritual is familiar to people/ provides a powerful emotional bond/ liturgical worship may be more formal, so more dramatic/ gives a powerful sense of tradition. *Arguments in support of other views might include:* spontaneous worship is more powerful as it comes from the heart/ charismatic worship involves speaking in tongues so is a powerful emotional experience/ the silence of a Quaker service may be more powerful than one that uses words and hymns/ it depends on an individual Christian's point of view whether one type of service is more powerful than another.

2.2 **A** It is the prayer Jesus taught his disciples/ it is a model of good prayer as it combines praise to God with asking for one's needs. **B** *You might include an example*: a Christian may wish to pray for something personal using their own words, such as the strength to overcome an illness. *Or add a religious teaching*: Jesus said to pray in your room with the door closed so that God who sees in secret will reward you (Matthew 6:6).

2.3 **A** 1: Believers' baptism: full immersion in a pool/ person is old enough to make a mature decision about their faith. 2: Infant baptism: blessed water is poured over the baby's head/ parents and godparents make promises of faith on behalf of the child. **B** *Arguments in support might include*: at baptism the parents promise to bring up the child as a Christian so they would be lying/ it is hypocritical/ the symbolic actions have no meaning for them. *Arguments against might include*: they may not be religious themselves but that doesn't mean they should not give their child a chance to be a member of the Church/ the child receives grace at baptism regardless of their parents' future actions/ the child is cleansed from sin.

2.4 **A** 1: Christians receive God's grace/ by joining in the sacrifice of Jesus/ their faith is strengthened/ they become closer to God. 2: Communion brings the community of believers together in unity by sharing the bread and wine/ this provides support and encouragement for those going through a difficult time/ encourages church members to love others in practical ways. **B** *In your paragraph you should weigh up both sides of the argument and then say which side you personally find more convincing and why.*

2.5 **A** 1: An Orthodox Holy Communion is mainly held behind the iconostasis/ the priest distributes the consecrated bread and wine on a spoon. 2: Holy Communion in the United Reformed Church has an 'open table' so anyone can receive communion/ bread is broken and passed around the congregation/ wine is distributed in small cups. **B** *Arguments for the statement might include:* the ministry of the Word is very important because it focuses on the life and teaching of Jesus/ reminds people of sacred writing in the Old Testament/ provides spiritual education for the congregation through the sermon given by the priest/ allows the community to pray for themselves and others. *Arguments against might include*: Holy Communion services should focus on the consecration and sharing of bread and wine because that is the most important part of the service/ people receive the body and blood of Jesus/ recall Jesus' death and resurrection which saved them from sin.

2.6 1: Lourdes: pilgrims go there to seek healing, both spiritual and physical/ to help the sick bathe in the waters/ to strengthen their faith/ to take part in services with people speaking many different languages from many countries/ it is a busy place with crowds of people, unlike Iona which is quieter and more remote. 2: Iona: pilgrims wish to spend time in quiet prayer, reading the Bible or meditating/ to enjoy the natural beauty of the place so they feel closer to God who created nature/ to worship with others who are like-minded/ some prefer to feel God's presence in silence and solitude rather than in a busy place like Lourdes. **B** On a pilgrimage there are many opportunities for prayer and meditation/ for reading the scriptures/ for reflecting on one's life/ whereas on a holiday people usually spend time enjoying themselves and reading novels rather than scriptures, etc. *A Christian teaching that supports pilgrimage might include*: Jesus withdrew to a lonely place when he wanted to pray/ Bernadette was told by Mary in a vision to build a church in Lourdes and pray for sinners, so Christians are following their traditional teaching by going there.

2.7 **A** By attending services which emphasise Jesus is risen/ by celebrating with family and friends/ giving Easter eggs to children to symbolise new life. **B** *Arguments for might include*: Christmas is very commercialised/ many people think about food, presents and seeing their relatives, not about Jesus/ not many people go to church on Christmas/ some think that in multicultural Britain, celebrating Christmas as a religious festival might offend others. *Arguments against might include*: Christmas is still a religious holiday in Britain/ the royal family go to church on Christmas Day and many Christians attend Midnight Mass/ carol services are held to prepare for the coming of Jesus into the world/ schools have nativity plays about Jesus' birth and often collect presents to give to children who are less fortunate.

2.8 **A** 1: The community of Christians/ holy people of God/ Body of Christ. 2: A building in which Christians worship. **B** The Church is the Body of Christ and as such has a duty to help the needy/ Christians are taught to love their neighbour/ the Parable of the Sheep and the Goats/ the parable of the Good Samaritan.

2.9 **A** Patrol streets in urban areas to support vulnerable people/ challenge gang and knife crime/ listen to people's problems/ help young people who have had too much to drink and may end up in trouble/ try to stop anti-social behaviour/ in this way they show love of neighbour/ 'Faith by itself, if it is not accompanied by action, is dead' (James 2:17 [NIV]). **B** *Two religious arguments might include*: Jesus taught that Christians should help others by showing agape love towards them/ this means being unselfish, caring and putting others' needs before your own, including praying for your neighbours' needs/ Jesus taught Christians should give practical help to others in the parable of the Sheep and the Goats/ he said to feed the hungry, clothe the naked, etc. *Two non-religious arguments against the statement might include*: praying is pointless/ not a practical action/ no one will know if prayer works to help them/ Christians should not have to be street pastors or social workers/ it is the police and social services' responsibility, not the Church's responsibility.

2.10 A By telling non-believers that Jesus Christ, the Son of God, came into the world as its saviour/ by spreading the Christian faith through evangelism. **B** *Arguments for*: 1, 3, 5. *Arguments against*: 2, 4, 6. *You should weigh up both sides of the argument and then say which side you personally find more convincing.*

2.11 A Through organisations that promote evangelism, such as Christ for all Nations/ through personal witness and example. **B** *You should weigh up the argument and suggest how it could be improved – e.g. by referring to the Great Commission (which suggests all Christians have a duty to spread the gospel), or by considering arguments for the statement.*

2.12 A 1: The Church works on a personal level to try to restore relationships between individuals/ between conflicting groups in the community. 2: The Church has sponsored different organisations that work for reconciliation/ e.g. the Irish Churches Peace Project. **B** Jesus taught, 'Love the Lord your God with all your heart and with all your soul and with all your mind. This is the great and first commandment.' (Matthew 22: 37–38 [NIV])/ therefore reconciliation to God is most important/ reconciliation to one's neighbour is second: 'Love your neighbour as yourself' (Matthew 22:39 [NIV]).

2.13 A Smuggling Bibles into the USSR to give comfort to persecuted Christians/ sending money to projects that support persecuted Christians. **B** *A religious argument might include*: it is possible for a Christian to be happy even in times of persecution because they believe they are sharing in the sufferings of Jesus/ their courage can inspire others to become Christians/ persecution strengthens their faith. *A non-religious argument might include*: no one can be happy while being persecuted/ they may be angry at the injustice of their treatment and turn to violence or stop believing in God.

2.14 A 1: Emergency relief includes food, shelter and water to people suffering from a natural disaster or sudden war/ parables such as the Rich Man and Lazarus and the Good Samaritan encourage Christians to help the needy. 2: Long-term aid may include education or new farming equipment that helps to make people independent of aid/ 'If anyone has material possessions and sees a brother or sister in need but has no pity on them, how can the love of God be in that person?' (1 John 3:17 [NIV]). **B** *Arguments for the statement might include*: religious charities can respond quickly to emergencies but it is not their role to provide long-term aid/ the countries themselves should be helping their own people/ long-term aid might make people dependent on religious charities. *Arguments against might include*: religious charities should provide long-term aid because people are still in need/ it will give independence eventually/ it is better to teach people how to make a living for themselves than merely to feed them for a short period of time/ the parable of the Sheep and the Goats teaches that God will judge people on whether they have helped their fellow humans because helping them is helping Jesus Christ.

3 Buddhism: beliefs and teachings

Please note that these are suggested answers to the Apply questions, designed to give you guidance, rather than being definitive answers.

3.1 A He was entertained by female dancers/ lived in a palace/ where there were lotus ponds of many colours/ was always protected by a sunshade/ had three mansions (*as described in the Anguttara Nikaya*). **B** *The answer is rather one-sided. It is good that it includes examples of legendary events in Siddhartha's life, but does not acknowledge there are also many details that are believable. Some of these details could have been included to create a counter-argument. A better answer could have tried to explain the spiritual meaning of the miraculous events. For instance, the supposed miraculous birth of Siddhartha shows he was a special person. Remember: a good answer is likely to include arguments for and against the statement.*

3.2 A The first sight helped Siddhartha realise that everyone will age/ the second sight helped Siddhartha realise that illness is a reality of life/ the third sight helped Siddhartha realise that everyone will die/ these three sights helped Siddhartha to understand the nature of suffering/ realise that suffering is an inevitable part of life/ the fourth sight inspired Siddhartha to find a spiritual answer to the problem of suffering/ inspired him to leave the palace and his life of luxury. **B** *For*: if he hadn't seen the four sights, Siddhartha might never have left the palace and achieved enlightenment/ the four sights made Siddhartha realise that suffering is a problem, which inspired him to search for an answer/ the fourth sight inspired Siddhartha to follow a spiritual life, so this could be seen as the start of Buddhism. *Against*: Siddhartha's enlightenment was more important as this is when he understood how to overcome suffering/ gained enough knowledge about the nature of reality to share it with his followers, so this could be seen as the start of Buddhism.

3.3 A By living in dangerous and hostile forests/ sleeping on a bed of thorns/ eating very little/ studying and practising meditation. **B** *Arguments in support*: 1, 3, 5, 6. *Arguments against*: 2, 4. *E.g. of a justified conclusion*: 'I agree with the statement because Siddhartha's practice of asceticism helped him to develop certain qualities necessary to achieve enlightenment, such as self-disciple and how to meditate. It was also an important part of his development of a middle way, as it helped him to realise that living a life of extremes (either asceticism or luxury) does not help to overcome the problem of suffering.'

3.4 A Mara sent his daughters to tempt Siddhartha/ sent his armies to attack Siddhartha/ offered Siddhartha control of his kingdom/ personally attacked Siddhartha/ questioned Siddhartha's right to sit at the seat of enlightenment. **B** *For*: the Buddha had a series of three insights on the night of his enlightenment/ which gave him the knowledge of why people suffer and how to overcome suffering/ therefore enlightenment is best thought of as having a deep understanding about suffering. *Against*: enlightenment also requires the development of other qualities, not just knowledge/ e.g. compassion is important for Mahayana Buddhists/ other qualities such as peace, tranquillity, freedom are part of enlightenment/ enlightenment also involves living and acting ethically.

3.5 A The truth about the nature of existence/ the teachings of Buddhism/ the Buddhist scriptures/ the path of training the Buddha recommended/ a universal 'law' governing how reality works. **B** *The answer makes a strong argument for why*

the Dhamma is the most important of the three refuges, but it is very one-sided. A better response would explain why the Buddha and Sangha are also important. For example, it might explain that if the Buddha had not discovered the Dhamma, Buddhists might never have been able to understand the way out of suffering. The Sangha is also important for providing support, guidance and friendship for Buddhists. This means all three refuges are important and interlinked.

3.6 A A tree depends on changing conditions to survive (e.g. rain and sunshine)/ a wave depends on changing conditions to form (e.g. wind speed and direction)/ each wave is linked to every other wave/ kamma shows how a person's happiness depends on changing conditions (their actions). **B** *E.g.* 'For instance, the Four Noble Truths apply the principle of dependent arising to the reality of human suffering. The Tibetan Wheel of Life applies it to the process of birth, death and rebirth. It shows that a person's happiness or suffering depends on their actions.'

3.7 A *Ordinary suffering*: sickness/ injury/ missing someone/ being upset at failing an exam, etc. *Suffering because of change*: getting older/ moving to a new city/ losing a friend/ the weather turning bad, etc. **B** *E.g.* 'Through drawing attention to suffering, Buddhism aims to help people understand why they suffer. If they can understand this, then they can overcome suffering by achieving enlightenment. So Buddhism is actually optimistic in saying that everyone can overcome suffering if they are committed enough.'

3.8 A Everything is impermanent/ impermanence affects the world in three different ways/ impermanence leads to suffering because of attachment/ an awareness of impermanence helps to reduce suffering/ as illustrated in the story of Kisa Gotami in the *Therigatha*. **B** *E.g.* 'On the other hand, it is clear that it is not impermanence in itself that causes suffering but our attachment to things. Buddhism teaches that if we can reduce our attachment then we will suffer less. If I recognise that my mobile phone, like all things, will age and eventually break, I will be less upset when this actually happens. So the real problem is not impermanence but wanting things to be permanent.'

3.9 A *Form*: a person's body or objects in the world/ *sensation*: a person's feelings/ *perception*: how someone interprets and understands things/ *mental formations*: a person's thoughts and opinions/ *consciousness*: a general awareness. **B** *E.g.* 'This argument is weak because, first of all, it claims that 'nothing really exists', which is not what anatta teaches. Second, it says that everything is 'just in our mind and not really there'; this would mean that other people are just in our imagination, which is not true. Third, while the argument mentions 'five things', it does not develop this point well. Finally, while there is a brief reference to a sacred source (the Questions of King Milinda), the answer doesn't include the title of the source or give the example of the chariot. Overall, the argument is unconvincing and has limited, relevant information.'

3.10 A The first noble truth is that suffering exists (like a doctor establishing you have an illness)/ the second noble truth is that suffering has a cause (like a doctor finding the cause of the illness)/ the third noble truth is that suffering can end (like a doctor saying there is a cure)/ the fourth noble truth is the means to end suffering (like the treatment a doctor gives you for the illness). **B** *Arguments in support*: 1, 3, 7, 8. *Arguments against*: 2, 4, 5, 6. *E.g. of a justified conclusion*: 'the Four Noble Truths are a very important Buddhist teaching because they teach Buddhists why suffering exists and how to overcome it, which is the main point of Buddhism. For example, the fourth noble truth (the Eightfold Path) shows Buddhists what they need to do to become enlightened. The Four Noble Truths also encompass or link to other important teachings such as the three poisons and the five moral precepts.'

3.11 A Beliefs about dukkha help Buddhists to empathise with and respond to the suffering of others/ help Buddhists not to take refuge in temporary pleasures/ inspire Buddhists to follow the Eightfold Path. **B** *Arguments in favour*: Buddhism teaches that pleasure can only provide temporary happiness/ because all things are impermanent/ overcoming suffering means accepting it exists, rather than trying to distract oneself with temporary pleasures/ if people focus on their own happiness this does not help other people who are suffering. *Arguments in support of different views*: pleasures can remove or distract from suffering/ make a person happy/ there is nothing wrong with seeking pleasure. *E.g. of a justified conclusion*: pleasure can be a good thing/ but it is not the solution to suffering because it is impermanent/ Buddhism teaches that the solution is through understanding what causes suffering (the second noble truth) and overcoming this by following the Eightfold Path (the fourth noble truth).

3.12 A Beliefs about craving motivate Buddhists to practise non-attachment/ e.g. monks and nuns live a very simple lifestyle with few possessions/ encourage Buddhists to understand the Buddha's teachings more fully in order to overcome craving/ e.g. by studying and meditating. **B** Some desires are good/ e.g. a desire to help others or a desire to become enlightened/ the problem is not desire in itself but becoming attached to the desire/ as it is craving which leads to suffering.

3.13 A Nibbana. **B** *E.g.* 'The argument could be better developed. For example, it gives an example of eating ice-cream but doesn't explain how this leads to suffering. It also doesn't consider the difference between non-attachment and not caring. It suggests that to reach nibbana you have to 'stop liking things', which is not what the third noble truth teaches.' *Opposing arguments could include*: non-attachment means recognising that all things are impermanent/ this does not mean people shouldn't care or enjoy things/ but that they should be ready to let go of them when they end.

3.14 A There are three aspects of the Eightfold Path linked to meditation: right speech, right action and right livelihood/ these help Buddhists to become better at meditating/ two aspects of the Eightfold Path are linked to wisdom: right understanding and right intention/ these help Buddhists to develop an understanding of the Buddha's teachings. **B** *E.g. for the statement*: 'the Eightfold Path means the actual practice of Buddhism, which allows Buddhists to make spiritual progress towards enlightenment. Without the Path, Buddhism would be just theoretical and not make a real difference to people's lives. The Path is how Buddhists apply the Buddha's teachings to their lives.' *E.g. against the statement*: 'While the Path is very important, it cannot be fully understood or practised without an understanding of the other three noble truths. For example, the Four Noble Truths can be likened to treating an illness: there is the diagnosis, the cause, the cure and the treatment. Each element is important if the illness is to be cured.'

3.15 **A** Sensation: the feelings that occur when people come into contact with things/ e.g. feeling happy when meeting a friend. Mental formations: a person's thoughts and opinions/ e.g. forming an opinion about a person someone has just met. **B** *For*: the five aggregates help to show that a person has no fixed, independent essence by explaining what people are made up of instead/ the aggregates show how people consist of things that are constantly changing (e.g. a person's feelings or thoughts are always changing). *Against*: the story of Nagasena and King Milinda is more useful because it uses a simple image (a chariot) to show how a person only exists because of the parts they are made up from.

3.16 **A** Buddha-nature. **B** *E.g. 'While Mahayana Buddhists use the term sunyata and Theravada Buddhists use the term anatta, both are talking about the same thing, which is that nothing has a fixed, unchanging nature. Both concepts teach that nothing has an independent self or 'soul', and everything depends on the parts it is made up from. While anatta applies this idea to human beings and sunyata applies it to all things, it is essentially the same idea.'*

3.17 **A** Theravada Buddhists aims to become Arhats, Mahayana Buddhists aim to become Bodhisattvas/ an Arhat is no longer reborn when they die, a Bodhisattva chooses to remain in the cycle of samsara/ the Arhat refers to a human being, whereas Bodhisattvas are sometimes transcendent figures/ Arhats follow the Eightfold Path, Bodhisattvas practise the six perfections. **B** *Arguments for*: an Arhat only needs to develop wisdom whereas a Bodhisattva must develop compassion as well/ as well as living ethically, meditating and developing wisdom, a Bodhisattva must also develop the traits of generosity and patience. *Arguments against*: it is not possible to have wisdom without compassion, so Arhats must also develop both/ there are many similarities between the Eightfold Path and the six perfections.

3.18 **A** Has many flowers and fruits/ has jewel trees/ all the birds have sweet voices/ contains no suffering/ a perfect paradise/ *Larger Sukhavativyuha Sutra*. **B** *E.g. 'Pure Land Buddhism offers an easier way to gain enlightenment because all you have to do is call on Amitabha and you can be reborn in his Pure Land. The Pure Land offers the perfect conditions to reach enlightenment and here Buddhists are taught by Amitabha himself, whereas the Eightfold Path requires much more of Buddhists such as following the five moral precepts and meditating.'*

4 Buddhism: practices

Please note that these are suggested answers to the Apply questions, designed to give you guidance, rather than being definitive answers.

4.1 **A** Main hall: where Buddhists worship and practise together/ meditation hall: where Buddhists meditate/ study hall: for meetings and lectures/ shrine: provides a focal point for worship/ stupa: contains the remains or relics of an important Buddhist. **B** *For*: a monastery is designed for the purpose of worship/ monks and nuns live simple lives which makes it easier to focus on worship/ it is easier to worship with others in a monastery than it is at home. *Against*: Buddhists can worship just as well in a temple or in their homes/ e.g. many Buddhist homes have shrines where Buddhists can express devotion.

4.2 **A** Making offerings at a shrine/ e.g. light, flowers, incense/ taking part in rituals and ceremonies carried out in groups/ meditation/ reciting mantras/ using malas/ chanting sacred texts. **B** *E.g. 'This argument assumes that worship may only be directed towards God, which is not true for Buddhism, where devotion is directed towards the Buddha and other enlightened beings. There is also no evidence to support the claim that Buddhists treat the Buddha like God. For these reasons the argument is unconvincing.'*

4.3 **A** Mindfulness of breathing uses the breath to develop calm/ kasina meditation uses objects as a focus to develop concentration. **B** *E.g. for the statement: 'Meditation is the most important Buddhist practice because it is how Buddhists gain insight into the true nature of reality and this leads to enlightenment. Through contemplating how everything is characterised by the three marks of existence, Buddhists can let of attachment and reach nibbana.' E.g. against the statement: 'The practice of ethics is also very important for reaching enlightenment, as it is also part of the Eightfold Path and six perfections. Through practising ethics, Buddhists transform their minds and learn to become kinder and more compassionate people. This is particularly important for Mahayana Buddhists who want to become enlightened.'*

4.4 **A** During mindfulness of breathing the meditator could focus on the impermanence of their breath, as impermanence is one of the three marks of existence/ walking meditation could be used to focus on the ever-changing sensations and movements that come from walking, in order to see that nothing has a fixed, unchanging nature (anatta). **B** *Arguments for*: vipassana meditation helps Buddhists to develop insight into the nature of reality in order to achieve enlightenment/ samatha meditation is merely a preparation for vipassana meditation/ deity visualisation also has the aim of reaching enlightenment by absorbing the qualities of a Buddha or Bodhisattva. *Arguments against*: the aim of samatha meditation is to develop calm and concentration/ loving-kindness meditation is concerned with developing the quality of metta/ meditation may also have a devotional purpose.

4.5 **A** By visualising a deity and focusing on its spiritual qualities/ imagining themselves as a deity/ by using a thangka or mandala as inspiration/ and trying to visualise it in as much detail as possible. **B** *E.g. 'For example, Buddhists might visualise the Bodhisattva Avalokiteshvara and through doing this call to mind the qualities of compassion that they wish to embody in their own lives. Pure Land Buddhists might visualise Buddha Amitabha in the hope he will help them to be reborn in the pure land.'*

4.6 **A** Belief in the transference of merit might prompt mourners to donate to a worthy cause/ offer cloth to make new robes to a monastery/ belief in impermanence encourages Buddhists to reflect on this idea/ belief in the Buddha means there will be a shrine and offerings to the Buddha/ belief in Amitabha will prompt Pure Land Buddhists to chant Amitabha's name as they process around the coffin. **B** *E.g. 'Buddhists believe that after death they will be reborn. They also believe that funerals may contribute to the rebirth process. For example, Theravada Buddhists believe it is important to transfer merit to the deceased at the funeral to help the deceased achieve a favourable rebirth.'*

4.7 **A** Light up their homes for Wesak to symbolise hope and enlightenment/ make offerings to the Buddha for festivals which commemorate events in his life/ meditate and worship with others in a temple or monastery/ read and study Buddhist scriptures/ go on pilgrimage. **B** *E.g. 'Wesak is a Buddhist festival that celebrates the Buddha's birth, enlightenment and death. It commemorates these three key events in the life of the Buddha. So it does not celebrate the Buddhist belief in enlightenment in general; it celebrates the Buddha's enlightenment in particular, as well as other events in his life.'*

4.8 **A** Generosity/ compassion/ understanding. **B** *E.g. 'The principle of kamma says that a person's happiness or suffering is determined by their actions. It also says that good, ethical actions, such as those motivated by generosity or understanding, will lead to happiness. This encourages ethical behaviour because it leads to happiness both in this life and in future lives.'*

4.9 **A** Beliefs about karuna encourage Buddhists to help relieve the suffering of others/ e.g. by donating to charities such as ROKPA/ encourage Buddhists to be kind towards themselves/ encourage Mahayana Buddhists to stay in the cycle of samsara to help others. **B** *Arguments in support*: 1, 4, 6. *Arguments against*: 2, 3, 5, 7, 8. *E.g. of a conclusion*: *'While it is clear that wisdom is very important, it is equally clear that compassion has a central place in Buddhism. Mahayana Buddhists would say that both are necessary for enlightenment, and even Theravada Buddhists would say it is not possible to have one without the other. So it is difficult to agree that one is more important than the other.'*

4.10 **A** Metta is a general attitude of friendliness and kindness, whereas karuna is a specific response to suffering/ kaurna only arises in relation to people who are suffering, whereas metta applies to all people. **B** *E.g. 'Buddhists believe metta should be developed towards all people, including people they don't like. For example, in loving-kindness meditation, Buddhists aim to develop metta towards 'difficult' people. The Sutta Nipata says that metta should be cultivated 'towards all the word', which naturally includes people you don't like.'*

4.11 **A** To abstain from taking life/ this means not killing or harming any living being/ to abstain from taking what is not freely given/ this means not stealing or manipulating and exploiting others/ to abstain from misuse of the senses or sexual misconduct/ this means not abusing or overindulging in sensual pleasures, or using sex harmfully/ to abstain from wrong speech/ this means not lying or gossiping about others/ to abstain from intoxicants that cloud the mind/ this means not taking drugs or alcohol/ *reference to the Dhammapada (verses 246–247)*. **B** *Arguments for*: truthful speech is one of the five moral precepts/ lying is not honest/ a person may lie to cover up something they have done wrong, but they should accept the consequences of their actions/ a person will suffer after they lie because of kamma. *Arguments against*: the five moral precepts are principles that are followed voluntarily rather than rules that must not be broken/ the most important percept is not to cause harm, so if lying prevents harm then it may be justifiable/ Buddhists believe intentions are important, so if a lie is motivated by genuine kindness then it may be justifiable.

4.12 **A** C) Compassion. **B** *E.g. 'In their general aim, there is a great deal of overlap between the five precepts and the six perfections. All of the perfections relate to the development of spiritual and ethical qualities. The five precepts have the same intention, although they are expressed negatively instead of positively. For example, the most important precept is not to cause harm – this suggests treating others with generosity and patience. It is difficult to conclude that one is more difficult to practise than the other when both overlap so much, and both can practised at deeper and more subtle levels.'*

5 Relationships and families

Please note that these are suggested answers to the Apply questions, designed to give you guidance, rather than being definitive answers.

5.1 **A** *Beliefs must be contrasting*. 1: Some Christians believe homosexual relationships are against God's will/ God's plan for humans was heterosexual relationships/ 'Be fruitful and increase in number…' (Genesis 1:28 [NIV]). 2: Buddhism does not favour one type of sexual relationship over any other/ what matters most is not to cause harm. **B** *An example of a religious argument*: Christians believe sex expresses a deep, lifelong union and casual sex does not represent this. *An example of a non-religious argument*: the acceptance of contraception and legal abortion has made casual sex more common.

5.2 **A** 1: 'You shall not commit adultery' (Exodus 20:14 [NIV]). 2: The third moral precept in Buddhism teaches that people should not cause harm to others through sexual activity/ adultery causes harm and so breaks this precept. **B** *In support*: it can be a valid expression of love for each other/ Buddhism teaches that sex before marriage is no less moral than sex after marriage. *Against*: 'your bodies are temples of the Holy Spirit' (1 Corinthians 6:19 [NIV])/ Anglican and Catholic Churches teach that sex requires the commitment of marriage. *A development may be*: the Catholic Church teaches that sex should be open to the possibility of creating new life/ having sex before marriage risks pregnancy.

5.3 **A** Catholic and Orthodox Churches believe the use of contraception within marriage goes against the natural law/ other Christian churches accept its use e.g. to avoid harming the mother's health/ most Buddhists believe it is acceptable to use contraception that prevents conception. **B** *The argument is strong as it explains why the Church is right to have a view on family planning by referring to specific Christian teachings. It could perhaps be expanded by mentioning relevant passages in the Bible, such as Genesis 1:28 and 2:24.*

5.4 **A** 1: Christians believe marriage should be between a man and a woman/ 'That is why a man leaves his father or mother and is united to his wife, and they become one flesh' (Genesis 2:24 [NIV]). 2: For Buddhists and many non-religious people, marriage is not a sacred duty and may be between people of the same sex. **B** *Arguments for*: marriage is a legal contract/ society is more stable if the rights of all people are protected/ 'The Church sees marriage between a man and a woman, as central to the stability and health of human society' (House of Bishops of the General Synod of the Church of England). *Arguments against*: many marriages end in divorce/ relationships between cohabiting couples can be just as stable and loving.

5.5 **A** Adultery/ addiction/ people changing and growing apart, etc. **B** *For*: children are badly affected by divorce/ for Christians, marriage is a sacrament and reflects the love Christ has for his Church/ Jesus taught that anyone who divorced and remarried was committing adultery (Mark 10:11–12). *Against*: continual arguments or abuse can damage children more than divorce/ some Christians think the Church should reflect God's forgiveness and allow couples a second chance for happiness/ Buddhists might agree with divorce if the marriage is causing a lot of suffering.

5.6 **A** *For*: many non-religious people, Buddhists and some Christians agree the gender of the parents makes no difference to a child's upbringing/ a same-sex couple that gives love and security to their children will make just as good parents as heterosexual ones/ it is the quality of their parenting that matters. *Against*: all religions agree children should grow up in a loving, secure family, but not all would agree the gender of the parents makes no difference/ some people think children should have male and female role models as they grow up/ Christians who oppose homosexual relationships would disagree with same-sex parents because of their homosexuality/ they might argue that homosexual parents cannot provide the moral upbringing a child needs. **B** *Arguments for the statement*: same-sex parents can be just as loving as other parents/ same-sex parents who adopt children are probably more committed to being good parents than other people/ same-sex parents can pass on religious beliefs and moral values to their children. *Arguments against the statement*: children of same-sex parents will not grow up with a male and female role model/ same-sex parents cannot pass on religious faith if their religion disapproves of their relationship/ children of same-sex parents may be teased at school.

5.7 **A** 1: For example, how to show compassion or follow the five moral precepts/ Buddhist parents also teach their children how to show devotion and respect towards the Buddha. 2: Many Christian parents present their babies for baptism/ teach them to pray/ some send them to faith schools. **B** *E.g. 'This argument is good because it suggests why it is important for families to help their elderly relatives, gives specific examples of how families can do this, and includes religious teachings. It could be developed further by giving more reasons for why families should help their elderly relatives, for example because it shows love and compassion (important values in both Christianity and Buddhism).'*

5.8 **A** All people are created equal in the image of God/ the command to love one's neighbour as oneself shows that discrimination is wrong/ gender discrimination expresses a lack of loving-kindness. **B** *E.g. 'For example, some traditional Christians think husbands should rule over their wives. Paul taught that this was wrong when he said, 'There is neither… male nor female, for you are all one in Christ Jesus' (Galatians 3:28 [NIV]).'*

6 Religion and life

Please note that these are suggested answers to the Apply questions, designed to give you guidance, rather than being definitive answers.

6.1 **A** 1: Some Fundamentalist Christians believe God made the universe and all life in it in six days/ Buddhists believe the universe is cyclical in nature, so there is no point when the universe suddenly came into being from nothing. **B** *For*: liberal Christians believe the Genesis creation stories are symbolic, with the main message being that God created the universe/ the Big Bang theory explains how God did this. *Against*: atheists might say that God is not responsible for the Big Bang, this is just something that happened by chance.

6.2 **A** Oil and other non-renewable resources are important sources of energy and will eventually run out/ without renewable energy sources to replace them, people will suffer. **B** For Christians, stewardship means looking after the environment for God/ not being stewards is letting God down/ stewardship means taking care of the planet rather than simply exploiting it/ dominion suggests ruling over the world with power and authority, whereas stewardship emphasises care and love.

6.3 **A** Pollution causes harm to living things including humans/ not good stewardship and therefore against God's wishes (Genesis 1:28)/ may lead to God's fair judgement being harsh (the parable of the Talents)/ pollution causes suffering to the planet and to life, which contradicts the first Buddhist moral precept. **B** *E.g. 'While the impact of just one person seems small, the Buddhist teaching of dependent arising shows that it still has an effect. For example, one person's actions may inspire others to take action to tackle pollution as well.'*

6.4 **A** Many Buddhists do not eat meat because the first moral precept says they should not cause harm to any living beings/ according to kamma, harming living beings will result in suffering/ some Christians argue that if more people were vegetarian there would be more food to go round, which would please God. **B** Animals bred for experimentation have no freedom in their lives and will probably suffer before they die/ most Buddhists believe animals should be treated with kindness and compassion/ harming animals goes against the first moral precept/ the Bible says humans should care for animals (e.g. Proverbs 12:10)/ Christians believe experimenting on animals is not good stewardship.

6.5 **A** 1: The theory of evolution says that life started with single-celled creatures in the sea/ evolved into creatures living on land/ creatures resembling humans evolved around 2.5 million years ago/ this happened because of the survival of the fittest. 2: The Bible teaches that human life was created last/ life was breathed into Adam by God/ Eve was created by God from Adam/ humans were created in God's image. **B** *One opinion is given, i.e. agreement with Genesis, science or a combination of both, and two reasons to support it which may be based on the answers for 6.5 A, perhaps with further content on the existence and/or role of God.*

6.6 **A** Christians believe life is a gift from God and abortion is taking life/ the sanctity of life means life should be valued and respected/ Buddhists believe abortion is taking life and this is unskilful/ goes against the first moral precept. **B** *For*: being brought up with a poor quality of life is not loving/ possibly not the child's preferred option had they been able to choose. *Against*: preventing life is never the best option/ the sanctity of life/ the family should be supported to improve the child's quality of life/ better a poor quality of life than no life.

6.7 **A** *For*: if someone is suffering unbearably and going to die anyway, it may be kinder to help them to die than to keep them alive to suffer more. *Against*: Christians believe euthanasia interferes with God's plan for a person's life/ only God has the

right to take away life/ Buddhists may oppose euthanasia because it goes against the first moral precept. **B** *Your opinion should be supported by arguments for or against the statement, with reference to religious teachings. Arguments for might include*: it is every person's right to decide what to do with their life/ if someone is suffering unbearably they should be able to end their life with dignity/ Buddhism suggests it may be the most compassionate thing to do in some situations. *Arguments against might include*: it is murder ('do not kill')/ interferes with God's plan/ open to abuse/ disrespects the sanctity of life/ only God should take life/ goes against the first moral precept.

6.8 **A** Buddhists believe that when people die they will be reborn according to their kamma/ this process will continue until they become enlightened/ many Christians believe that after death they are judged by God/ they will either be eternally with God (heaven) or eternally without God (hell). **B** *For*: Buddhism teaches that if people live selfish lives, they are likely to be reborn in an unfavourable realm and so suffer/ this motivates them to act ethically/ some Christians believe if they follow Jesus' teachings to help others they are more likely to be judged favourably by God and spend the afterlife in heaven. *Against*: helping others brings its own rewards without needing to think about the afterlife/ religious believers should help others simply because it is a good thing to do.

7 The existence of God and revelation

Please note that these are suggested answers to the Apply questions, designed to give you guidance, rather than being definitive answers.

7.1 **A** The earth and humans were created for a purpose/ the intricacy and complexity of earth shows it cannot have appeared by chance/ the designer can only have been God/ the thumb is evidence of design because it allows precise delicate movement/ everything in the universe is in a regular order so must have been designed/ everything in the universe is perfect to sustain life. **B** *See the answers to 7.1 A for arguments to agree with the statement. Arguments against could include*: natural selection happens by chance/ species are developed by evolution, not a designer/ suffering proves there is no designer God/ order and structure in nature is imposed by humans, not God.

7.2 **A** Buddhists do not believe in God/ do not believe the universe has a beginning/ believe the universe is cyclical. **B** *Points could include*: what caused God?/ the universe may be eternal, not God/ the universe may not need a cause/ the Big Bang was random chance.

7.3 **A** As science cannot explain miracles, they must be caused by something outside nature/ the only thing that exists outside nature is God/ therefore miracles must be the work of God. **B** *E.g. 'There is never enough evidence to prove that miracles are the work of God, instead of having a (perhaps unknown) scientific explanation. People who claim to have witnessed miracles are making them up or mistaken about what they have experienced. On the other hand, anyone who has witnessed a miracle is unlikely to remember it wrongly and there are 69 recorded miracles at Lourdes alone. They cannot all have been remembered wrongly. If Jesus had not performed miracles, they wouldn't have been written down in the Bible, and people who were there at the time would have spoken out if they thought the miracles were made up.'*

7.4 **A** *Reasons might include*: if God was loving, he would not allow suffering/ evil exists because God does not/ an all-knowing and all-powerful God would know about suffering and do something to prevent it. *Counter-arguments might include*: suffering is caused by wrong use of free will which God gifted to humans/ without evil, there would be no good/ suffering allows others to show love and compassion. **B** *E.g. 'Science challenges the existence of God because it gives explanations for things that used to be explained with God, which means God is no longer needed as the answer to these things. For example, some people would say the Big Bang theory removes the need to believe that God created the universe. However, others believe science can help to explain God's creation. For example, the Big Bang theory explains how God created the universe, and the theory of evolution explains how God brought life to earth and developed it to what it is like now.'*

7.5 **A** A specific experience of God such as a dream, vision, prophecy or miracle. *Any example from scripture, tradition, history or the present day can be given, e.g. Bahiya's vision of a deva.* **B** *E.g. 'I don't think the statement can be true because visions can have a profound effect on people's lives, which would be unlikely to happen if they were not real. For example, Saul converted to Christianity after he saw a blinding light and heard Jesus' voice. The way he changed his life as a result of this vision means it probably did happen. Also, he certainly didn't expect to experience God in this way because he was very opposed to Christianity. However, at the same time we don't really know what Saul experienced. It is possible that the writers of the Bible dramatised a process of conversion and there was no vision.'*

7.6 **A** By gaining greater insight about God from events in nature/ e.g. the natural world reveals God to be creative, clever and powerful/ by learning about God's past actions through reading scripture/ by learning about God's relationship with people through reading scripture. **B** *Arguments for might include*: as the texts were written so long ago it is difficult to verify their accuracy/ ancient texts are not relevant to the modern world. *Arguments against might include*: ancient texts contain eternal truths/ can still help people today to learn about God/ can still inspire those in the modern world.

7.7 **A** Omniscient: all-knowing, aware of everything that has happened/ omnipotent: all-powerful, capable of doing anything/ transcendent: beyond and outside life on earth, etc. **B** *E.g. 'Christians would agree with this statement because nobody but God is all-powerful, all-knowing or eternal. Humans and other beings are subject to limits that God is not, so they cannot possibly be like him. On the other hand, it is possible for people to display some of the same qualities that God has, although not so perfectly. For example, God is benevolent, and people can also show love and kindness towards others. Some Buddhists might also say that the Buddha shares qualities with God. For example, some see him as a transcendent figure.'*

7.8 **A** Drugs or alcohol can make a person lose touch with reality/ wishful thinking means people can persuade themselves that something has happened purely because they want it to/ hallucinations can be symptoms of some illnesses/ some people might lie to become famous or rich, as it is hard to disprove their lies/ some may genuinely believe they have had a revelation but there may be a perfectly normal explanation that they do not know about. **B** *E.g. 'There is no way to prove that a revelation means God does exist. There are perfectly normal explanations for what people say are revelations, so they cannot be considered as evidence for God. For example, they might just be hallucinations caused by illness, or made up by someone to get attention. There is no way to know if a person's 'revelation' is genuine or not, so it cannot act as proof that God exists.'*

8 Religion, peace and conflict

Please note that these are suggested answers to the Apply questions, designed to give you guidance, rather than being definitive answers.

8.1 **A** Christians have a duty to forgive others if they wish to be forgiven/ the Lord's Prayer says, 'Forgive us our sins as we forgive those who sin against us'/ Buddhists practise forgiveness because it allows them to let go of hatred and resentment/ it also expresses loving-kindness. **B** *Arguments for*: Christianity teaches that killing is wrong/ Jesus' teaching does not support war/ Jesus told people to love their enemies/ wars express violence and hatred, rather than compassion (the basic Buddhist principle). *Arguments against*: some Christians believe in the just war theory/ it is sometimes necessary to take part in war for self-defence/ war can help create a more just and fair society (e.g. if it is being used to end an oppressive dictatorship).

8.2 **A** There is an injustice/ they believe in loving their neighbours. **B** 'You shall not murder' (Exodus 20:13 [NIV])/ Buddhists believe it is important to condemn terrorism because it expresses hatred/ there are peaceful and democratic ways to express protest and draw attention to important issues.

8.3 **A** D) Forgiveness. **B** *Read the statements carefully. You should weigh up both sides of the argument and then say which side you personally find more convincing.*

8.4 **A** *Beliefs must be contrasting.* All religions are against the use of weapons of mass destruction/ Christians believe life is sacred (sanctity of life)/ only God has the right to end life/ nothing can justify the use of WMDs which target innocent people/ some people think all nuclear weapons should be abolished as there is always a risk they will be used/ some people agree with the possession of nuclear weapons as a deterrent/ to maintain peace and prevent attack/ some people think the use of nuclear weapons in war can be justified/ e.g. they ended the Second World War. **B** If nuclear weapons were used, they could kill huge numbers of people and destroy much of the earth/ 'You shall not murder' (Exodus 20:13 [NIV])/ many Buddhists believe that as long as nuclear weapons exist, there is a risk they could be used/ there are less threatening ways to maintain peace.

8.5 **A** Just cause/ proper legal authority/ just intention/ last resort/ chance of success/ proportional. **B** *For*: the just war theory says war should be a last resort/ all other means of settling disputes should be tried first/ limited retaliation is accepted by some Christians based on the teaching 'eye for eye, tooth for tooth' (Exodus 21:24 [NIV]). *Against*: Quakers believe war is never justified/ most Buddhists believe war cannot be justified in any circumstance, even self-defence/ responding to violence with more violence solves nothing.

8.6 **A** Fighting for God or a religious cause/ authorised by a high religious authority. **B** *E.g. 'This is a good argument because it gives reasons why there is no place for a holy war today (e.g. 'no one has to fight for the right to worship God'), and includes reference to religious teachings (e.g. 'turn the other cheek'). It finishes with a sentence that sums up why holy war is not the right response to an attack on the Christian faith in Britain today. It could perhaps be developed further by including reference to other religions in contemporary Britain.'*

8.7 **A** *Beliefs must be contrasting.* Many Christians are not pacifists because they believe war can be justified under certain circumstances/ as explained by the just war theory/ many Buddhists are pacifists who refuse to take part in war or violence of any kind/ the Buddha taught that violence should be avoided and Buddhists should try instead to develop compassion for all beings. **B** One of the causes for war is when people feel an injustice has been done/ e.g. if a group of people in a country feel they are being treated unfairly by the government they could retaliate, leading to a civil war/ if everyone has access to basic human rights, this might prevent conflict that tries to gain these rights by force/ e.g. if everyone had access to food this might prevent conflict in regions where food is very scarce.

8.8 **A** By raising money to help refugees through organisations such as Caritas and the Tzu Chi **Foundation/ by going to war-torn areas to deliver emergency supplies to victims. B *E.g. for the statement: 'To win a war there should be a strong, decisive victory against the enemy. Killing the enemy demonstrates strength and resolve. War should also be ended as quickly as possible, and this means casualties are sometimes unavoidable. For example, many Japanese died as a result of the atom bombs being dropped in the Second World War, but these won the war.' E.g. against the statement: 'The point of war is to win and create peace, not to kill the enemy. Showing compassion towards the enemy means there will hopefully be less tension when the war ends, making reconciliation easier. Helping the enemy to survive also demonstrates Christian teachings such as Jesus' teaching to love your neighbour and Paul's teaching to live at peace with everyone.'***

9 Religion, crime and punishment

Please note that these are suggested answers to the Apply questions, designed to give you guidance, rather than being definitive answers.

9.1 **A Prison/ community service/ fine. B** ***For the statement***: intentions are the reasons for actions/ loving and compassionate intentions usually bring about good actions/ **'But I tell you that anyone who looks at a woman lustfully has already committed adultery with her in his heart' (Matthew 5:28 [NIV])/ Buddhist ethics suggest the intention behind an action is very important and determines its moral quality. *Against the statement*:** nobody is helped or harmed by intentions but they may be by actions/ 'faith by itself, if it is not accompanied by action, is dead' (James 2:17 [NIV])/ Buddhism teaches that skilful actions lead to happiness, unskilful actions lead to suffering.

9.2 **A *E.g. in response to the reason of poverty*: Christians believe stealing is wrong, and they should help to create a society where it is not necessary to steal because of poverty/ Buddhists believe stealing is wrong because it contradicts the second moral precept and causes harm to others. B *Arguments for the statement might include*:** addiction takes away choice/ a person may need to commit crimes to fund their addiction. *Arguments against might include*: some other reasons (e.g. poverty and mental illness) are also good reasons for committing crimes/ addicts should be helped to defeat their addiction so they do not commit crimes/ Christians and Buddhists believe crime is very rarely justified/ taking drugs goes against the fifth moral precept in Buddhism.

9.3 **A** Hate crimes usually involve violence and possibly killing/ murder is unlawful killing/ hate crimes result from prejudice, murder can have other reasons/ murder is generally considered to be worse/ some murders are classed as hate crimes. **B** *For*: hatred of a criminal is not constructive/ reasons why the criminal committed the crime should be considered/ love and compassion are religious teachings that should extend even to criminals/ Christians and Buddhists believe in the importance of rehabilitation. *Against*: criminal actions can cause great harm and upset/ some victims never fully recover from a criminal action/ 'let everyone be subject to the governing authorities, for there is no authority except that which God established' (Romans 13:1 [NIV])/ crimes break Christian and Buddhist teachings and morality/ Buddhism teaches that hatred is never justified as it only creates more suffering.

9.4 **A *Retribution*: getting your own back/ the offender should receive the same (not greater) injuries and harm that their actions caused. *Deterrence*: putting people off from committing crimes/ the punishment should be severe enough to prevent repetition of the offence. *Reformation*: changing someone's behaviour for the better/ offenders are helped to change so they do not reoffend. B *For*:** severe punishment can help prevent future crimes/ the criminal deserves severe punishment for what they have done/ 'eye for an eye' means punishment should equal harm caused, so more serious crimes deserve severe punishment. *Against*: less severe punishment may lead more easily to repentance and change/ positive methods (e.g. reformation) are more likely to have a lasting effect/ 'Do not take revenge, my dear friends' (Romans 12:19 [NIV])/ Buddhists do not support violence, so severe punishment is not appropriate.

9.5 **A** 1: Christians believe suffering is a result of free will given by God/ Adam and Eve misused their free will to bring sin and suffering into the world/ suffering can be reduced by following the example and teachings of Jesus. 2: Buddhism teaches that suffering is an inevitable part of life (the first noble truth)/ Buddhists believe suffering can be overcome by following the Buddha's teachings to achieve enlightenment. **B** *Arguments for might include*: Buddhism teaches that all violence causes suffering/ violence is not loving and doesn't show respect, even in self-defence/ better to try to repair damage that has been done rather than responding with further violence/ Jesus taught people to turn the other cheek. *Against*: using violence in self-defence may cause less harm than allowing an attack to continue/ Buddhism suggests there may be some cases where using force or violence expresses compassion because it aims to protect others from harm.

9.6 **A** Christians oppose all punishment that causes harm to offenders/ corporal punishment has no element of reform/ Buddhists also oppose corporal punishment because it expresses violence and is not aimed at helping the person to correct their behaviour/ goes against the first moral precept. **B** *Arguments for*: 'eye for eye' suggests offenders who commit serious crimes should receive severe punishment. *Arguments against*: 'love your neighbour' suggests criminals should be treated well/ all humans are deserving of respect as they are created by God/ the parable of the Sheep and the Goats teaches that showing kindness to prisoners is good/ Buddhist teachings emphasise compassion and loving-kindness/ harming criminals goes against the first moral precept.

9.7 **A Many Christians believe that while forgiveness is important, it is still necessary to punish the criminal/ Buddhists emphasise the importance of apology and forgiveness and, when this happens, punishment is no longer necessary/ Christians practise forgiveness as an act of mercy/ because God expects them to forgive/ Buddhists practise forgiveness because if they continue to hold on to anger and resentment they will continue to suffer. B** *E.g. 'I agree that nobody should expect to be forgiven more than once because they should have learnt from their original mistake. If they were punished on the first occasion they should have used the chance to repent and promised not to offend again. On the other hand, Christians are taught they should forgive again. When asked how many times they should forgive, Jesus said, 'not seven times, but seventy-seven times.' Buddhists also believe forgiveness is important, even if it has to happen many times. Because of this, Christians and Buddhists should forgive as many times as necessary, even if the offender does not expect it. They should also try to help the offender not to commit offences in future.'*

9.8 **A** Some Bible passages agree with retribution (e.g. Genesis 9:6)/ others with reform (e.g. Ezekiel 33:11)/ 'You shall not murder' (Exodus 20:13 [NIV])/ the death penalty does not reform the offender, which Christians and Buddhists believe is an important aim/ does not respect the sanctity of life/ goes against the first moral precept. **B** The death penalty is not loving or compassionate/ may kill an innocent person by mistake/ life is sacred and only God has the right to take it/ evidence suggests that it does not deter/ a dead offender cannot be reformed/ the victim's family may not want it to happen/ the death penalty goes against the first moral precept/ killing is an unskilful action that causes suffering.

10 Religion, human rights and social justice

Please note that these are suggested answers to the Apply questions, designed to give you guidance, rather than being definitive answers.

10.1 **A** A fair trial/ education/ free elections/ family life/ life/ liberty/ security/ privacy/ marriage. **B** *For:* everyone is entitled to have rights/ they allow the more disadvantaged to be treated with justice and compassion/ promote equality/ allow people freedom to live their lives as they wish. *Against*: some people (e.g. murderers) do not deserve rights/ rights should be earned/ those who do not respect the rights of others should have no rights themselves/ it is sometimes best to restrict the rights of some people to ensure the welfare of others.

10.2 **A** *Similarity*: many Christians and Buddhists believe it is wrong to discriminate against someone based on their sexuality. *Difference*: some Christians believe homosexual relationships go against God's plan for humans, whereas the Buddhist moral precepts do not favour one form of sexuality over another. **B** *For*: leadership of the Christian Church has traditionally been male/ 'Women should remain silent in the churches' (1 Corinthians 14:34 [NIV])/ men and women should have different roles/ the *Aparimitayur Sutra* suggests women cannot achieve enlightenment. *Against*: there is no reason why women cannot make equally good leaders to men/ Jesus treated women as equal to men/ women can now become priests in the Church of England/ the Dalai Lama said there was no reason why a future Dalai Lama couldn't be a woman.

10.3 **A** Christianity supports freedom of religion, and encourages tolerance and harmony between different religions/ 'If it is possible […] live at peace with everyone' (Romans 12:8 [NIV])/ Buddhism also supports freedom of religion/ the Buddha encouraged people to listen to the teachers of other religions with respect. **B** *Points might include*: it is a basic human right to be allowed to follow a religion/ following any religion can only be helpful to a person and society as a whole/ *any reference to the answers in 10.3 A*/ some sects and interpretations of major religions may be harmful and so should be avoided/ people should follow the religion of their country to show patriotism.

10.4 **A** Christians oppose racism because they believe all people have been made equal in the image of God/ 'There is neither Jew nor Gentile […] for you are one in Christ Jesus' (Galatians 3:28 [NIV])/ Buddhists oppose racism because it does not express loving-kindness. **B** *E.g. 'I believe all discrimination is wrong because it can cause great harm to people. It is also completely unjust because Christians believe all humans are created by God, in his image, and with equal rights. Behaving in any other way shows no love and respect to others and makes them feel that they are in some way inferior and wrong through no fault of their own. However, positive discrimination is an exception because it is not harmful. This means to treat people of some minority groups better than others, for example by giving disabled people special areas of seating in sports stadiums and theatres. This allows them equal opportunity to see sports or arts performances because it removes problems with access. Christians see this as fulfilling the prophecy of Amos: 'Let justice roll on like a river and righteousness like a never-failing stream' (Amos 5:24).'*

10.5 **A** Christians believe God blesses people with wealth in response to their faithfulness/ excess wealth should be shared with those who have less/ wealth can be dangerous (1 Timothy 6:10)/ can cause neglect of the spiritual life (Matthew 6:24)/ Buddhism teaches that happiness is not achieved through craving wealth but through enlightenment/ craving wealth expresses greed (one of the three poisons) and leads to suffering/ wealth can be helpful when it allows people to demonstrate generosity and compassion. **B** *E.g. 'If giving to charity was compulsory, it is likely that charities would receive much more than they do at present, so could help more people in need throughout the world. This might help to fix many problems in society, which for Christians would demonstrate good stewardship and help in the pursuit of justice (Amos 5:24), and for Buddhists would show compassion and loving-kindness. However, perhaps it should only be compulsory for people who earn a certain amount of money, as otherwise it could contribute to forcing more people into poverty.'*

10.6 **A** Unemployment/ low wages/ high cost of living/ debt from loans or credit cards/ gambling/ addiction/ financial mismanagement. **B** *Arguments for might include*: if people have got into poverty through their own fault, they should take responsibility for getting out of poverty/ Buddhism teaches that people have a responsibility to create the conditions needed for a healthy life/ 'the one who is unwilling to work shall not eat' (2 Thessalonians 3:10 [NIV]). *Arguments against might include*: Christians and Buddhists believe it is important to show compassion to those in poverty and help them out of it if possible/ people living in poverty may not be able to get themselves out of it without the help of others.

10.7 **A** By not being paid fairly for the work they do/ by being forced to work in poor conditions/ by being charged excessive interest on loans/ by being exploited by people-traffickers. **B** *E.g. 'Developed countries that prefer to buy cheap goods do cause exploitation. In order to have cheap goods, the cost of making them has to be reduced to a minimum. This means exploiting workers by paying them next to nothing. If people in developed countries were prepared to pay a little more, the workers could be paid more. Exploitation goes against religious ideas of justice, compassion and love, and shows that Amos' vision that justice should flow like a river and righteousness like a stream has not yet been reached. However, another opinion is that it is the multinational companies that make the goods, and the shops that sell the goods, who are to blame. Designer goods are often made in poor countries by people who are exploited, yet they are expensive to buy because the producers and shops are keen to make ever bigger profits because they are so greedy. In 1 Timothy it says, 'the love of money is the root of all evil', so exploitation of poor countries is caused by the greed of rich people, not poor people who want to buy decent things at prices they can afford.'*

10.8 **A** Long-term aid educates people in skills such as literacy, numeracy and basic training to allow them to access work/ teaches them agricultural methods to grow their own crops/ provides assistance for setting up a small business to earn enough to provide for their needs. **B** *E.g. of an argument in favour: 'Aid sometimes does not get to the root of the problem. For example, aid might provide necessary supplies like food and clothing, but this does not address the underlying causes of poverty and so does not really change anything. Aid can also make a country dependent on whoever is giving out the aid, rather than encouraging the country to solve its problems by itself.' E.g. of an argument against: 'Long-term aid does help people to lift themselves out of poverty and become less dependent on aid. It does this by addressing the root causes of poverty, such as a lack of education. For example, educating farmers about more effective farming techniques means they can produce more food for their families, even after the aid has been withdrawn.'*

Exam practice answers

1 Christianity: beliefs and teachings

Test the 1 mark question
1.   B) Incarnation
2.   C) Benevolent

Test the 2 mark question
Suggested answers, other relevant answers would be credited. 1 mark for each correct point.

3.   Through good works/ through the grace of God/ through faith/ through Jesus' death/ through obeying the Ten Commandments/ through loving one's neighbour/ through prayer/ through worship/ through the Holy Spirit.

4.   Christians believe everyone will be raised from the dead (resurrection)/ face judgement of God/ immediately or at the end of time/ Judgement Day/ Second Coming of Christ/ Jesus rose from the dead/ people will be judged on how they lived their lives/ sent to heaven, hell or purgatory/ resurrection of the body/ restoration to glorified bodies.

Test the 4 mark question
Suggested answers, other relevant answers would be credited. 1 mark for each simple contrasting or similar point, another mark for developing each point, so a maximum of 4 marks for two developed points.

6.   Christians may show respect towards all of God's creation/ actively work for conservation/ show stewardship/ take practical steps like recycling/ be energy efficient.

Christians may treat others with respect/ all are created 'in imago dei' (in God's image)/ work for peace between people/ support charities that help people in need/ reflect God in all they do.

Christians may take care of themselves (both body and soul)/ adopt healthy lifestyles/ develop spiritual practices/ prayer/ worship/ meditation.

7.   Christians believe that because God is loving, God wants the best for them/ they accept God's will as being for their own benefit, even if it does not appear to be so/ they love others because God loves them.

God's greatest act of love was sending his Son Jesus/ to save people from sin/ to gain eternal life/ so they are grateful to God/ express their thanks through worship or praise.

God is love/ qualities of love described in Paul's letter to the Corinthians/ patient/ kind/ not easily angered/ Christians try to live according to these descriptions of love.

Test the 5 mark question
Suggested answers, other relevant answers would be credited. 1 mark for each simple contrasting or similar point, another mark for developing each point, so 4 marks for two developed points, 1 extra mark for a correct reference to a source of religious belief or teaching.

9.   Christians believe God is omnipotent (all-powerful)/ has supreme authority/ can do all things/ 'Nothing is impossible with God' (Luke 1:37 [NIV])/ is loving (benevolent)/ wants good for God's creation/ wants people to love God freely in return/ 'God so loved the world that he gave his one and only Son, that whoever believes in him shall not perish but have eternal life' (John 3:16 [NIV])/ is just (fair/righteous)/ wants people to choose good over evil/ punishes wrongdoing/ is the perfect judge of human character.

Christians believe there is only one God/ 'The Lord is our God, the Lord alone' (Deuteronomy 6:4 [NIV])/ but within God there is a Trinity of persons/ Father, Son (Jesus), Holy Spirit/ 'Our Father in heaven' (Lord's Prayer)/ the Spirit's presence at Jesus' baptism.

God is the creator of all that is/ 'In the beginning, God created the heavens and the earth' (Genesis 1:1 [NIV])/ the Spirit was present at creation/ the Word of God (the Son) was involved in creation too.

10.   Christians believe Jesus restored the relationship between God and humanity/ Jesus atoned for the sins of humankind/ God accepted his death as atonement for sin by raising Jesus from the dead/ 'Jesus Christ […] is the atoning sacrifice for our sins, and not only for ours but also for the sins of the whole world' (1 John 2:1–2 [NIV]).

Through the atonement of Jesus, humans can receive forgiveness for sin/ be able to get close to God/ gain eternal life/ sin has been defeated/ 'For the wages of sin is death, but the gift of God is eternal life in Christ Jesus our Lord' (Romans 6:23 [NIV]).

Jesus' death atoned for the original sin of Adam and Eve/ Adam chose to disobey God, but Jesus chose to offer his life as a sacrifice/ 'For since death came through a man, the resurrection of the dead also comes through a man. For as in Adam all die, so in Christ all will be made alive' (1 Corinthians 15:21 [NIV]).

Test the 12 mark question
Suggested answers shown here, but see page 10 for guidance on levels of response.

12.   **Arguments in support**
•   Hell is not a place/ exploration of the earth and space have not discovered a place where spirits are punished forever/ although hell is shown in paintings as a place of fire and torture ruled by Satan (the devil) somewhere beneath the earth, no such place exists.

- The idea of hell is inconsistent with a benevolent God/ Christians believe God is loving/ a loving God would never send anyone to eternal damnation in hell/ like a loving Father, God will give people another chance if they repent.
- The idea of hell is just a way of comforting those who want to see justice/ some people get away with many bad things and seem not to receive punishment in this life/ the idea of hell ensures the idea of justice being done, but it does not really exist.

Arguments in support of other views

- Today hell is more often thought to be an eternal state of mind being cut off from the possibility of God/ the state of being without God, rather than a place/ a person who did not acknowledge God or follow his teachings would necessarily end up without God in the afterlife.
- Christians believe God is just/ it is only fair that someone who has gone against God's laws should be punished eventually/ it is a just punishment for an immoral life.
- Jesus spoke about hell as a possible consequence for sinners/ 'But I tell you that anyone who is angry with a brother or sister will be subject to judgment [...] And anyone who says, 'You fool!' will be in danger of the fire of hell.' (Matthew 5:22 [NIV])/ 'If your right eye causes you to stumble, gouge it out and throw it away. It is better for you to lose one part of your body than for your whole body to be thrown into hell.' (Matthew 5:29 [NIV])/ 'For if God did not spare angels when they sinned, but sent them to hell, putting them in chains of darkness to be held for judgement' (2 Peter 2:4 [NIV]).

13. Arguments in support

- Salvation means deliverance from sin and admission to heaven brought about by Jesus/ saving one's soul/ sin separates people from God who is holy/ the original sin of Adam and Eve brought suffering and death to humankind/ so God gave the law so that people would know how to stay close to him/ Jesus' teaching takes the law even further.
- One way of gaining salvation is through good works/ by having faith in God and obeying God's laws/ obeying the Ten Commandments (Exodus 20:1–19) is the best way of being saved because by doing so Christians are avoiding sin/ following other Christian teachings such as the Beatitudes (Matthew 5:1–12) helps gain salvation through good works/ being merciful/ a peacemaker.
- Christians believe God gave people free will to make moral choices/ following God's law shows the person is willing to use their free will wisely.

Arguments in support of other views

- The best way of gaining salvation is through grace/ grace is a free gift of God's love and support/ it is not earned by following laws/ faith in Jesus is all a person needs to be saved/ 'For it is by grace you have been saved, through faith – and this is not from yourselves, it is the gift of God – not by works, so that no one can boast.' (Ephesians 2:8–9 [NIV]).
- Merely following the law is a legalistic approach/ it can hide sinfulness inside a person/ Jesus criticised the Pharisees for following the law but having evil hearts/ Jesus said, 'The teachers of the law and the Pharisees sit in Moses' seat. So you must be careful to do everything they tell you. But do not do what they do, for they do not practise what they preach.' (Matthew 23:2–3 [NIV]).
- Most Christians believe both good works and grace (through faith in Jesus) are needed to be saved/ you can't prove you have faith unless you show it in your outward behaviour/ a danger in believing in salvation through grace alone is that people can feel specially chosen so look down on others/ not feel they have to obey God's law as they are already 'saved'.

2 Christianity: practices

Test the 1 mark question

1.   D) Liturgical worship

2.   C) Christmas

Test the 2 mark question

Suggested answers, other relevant answers would be credited. 1 mark for each correct point.

3.   By setting up charities/ Christian Aid/ CAFOD/ Tearfund/ by raising or donating money/ by working overseas in poor countries/ by praying for justice for the poor/ by campaigning for the poor.

4.   Prayer helps Christians communicate with God/ develop and sustain their relationship with God/ thank God for blessings/ praise God/ ask God for help for oneself or others/ find courage to accept God's will in difficult times.

Test the 4 mark question

Suggested answers, other relevant answers would be credited. 1 mark for each simple contrasting or similar point, another mark for developing each point, so a maximum of 4 marks for two developed points.

6.   *Ways must be contrasting:*

Infant baptism: Catholic, Orthodox, Anglican, Methodist and United Reformed Churches baptise babies/ 'I baptise you in the name of the Father, and of the Son, and of the Holy Spirit'/ blessed water poured over the baby's head/ sign of cross on baby's forehead/ anointing with oil/ white garment/ candle/ godparents' and parents' promises.

Believers' baptism: others such as Baptist and Pentecostal Christians baptise those who are old enough to make their own decision about baptism/ baptise people who have made a commitment to faith in Jesus/ full immersion in pool/ minister talks about meaning of baptism/ candidates are asked if they are willing to change their lives/

Bible passage/ brief testimony from candidate/ baptised 'in the name of the Father, and of the Son, and of the Holy Spirit'.

7.   *Interpretations must be contrasting:*

Catholic, Orthodox and some Anglican Christians believe the bread and wine become the body and blood of Christ/ Jesus is fully present in the bread and wine/ a divine mystery/ those receiving become present in a mystical way at the death and resurrection of Christ/ receive God's grace/ Holy Communion is a sacrament.

Protestant Christians see Holy Communion as a reminder of Jesus' words and actions at the Last Supper/ bread and wine are symbols of Jesus' sacrifice/ they help them reflect on the meaning of Jesus' death and resurrection for their lives today/ it is an act of fellowship.

Test the 5 mark question

Suggested answers, other relevant answers would be credited. 1 mark for each simple contrasting or similar point, another mark for developing each point, so 4 marks for two developed points, 1 extra mark for a correct reference to a source of religious belief or teaching.

9.   Evangelism is spreading the Christian gospel/ by public preaching/ by personal witness.

Evangelism is considered a duty of Christians because of the Great Commission/ 'Therefore go and make disciples of all nations, baptising them in the name of the Father and of the Son and of the Holy Spirit, and teaching them to obey everything I have commanded you' (Matthew 28:19–20 [NIV])/ people have a desire to share the good news with others because they have experienced it themselves.

Christians believe they are called to do more than just know Jesus in their own lives/ they are called to spread the good news to non-believers that Jesus is the Saviour of the world.

When the early disciples received the Spirit at Pentecost they were given the gifts necessary to carry out the Great Commission/ the Spirit gives some people wisdom/ knowledge/ faith/ gifts of healing/ miraculous powers/ prophecy/ the ability to speak in tongues and understand the message of those who speak in tongues.

10.   Christians may work for reconciliation in their own lives by forgiving their enemies/ making up with people they have offended/ going to the sacrament of Reconciliation to be reconciled with God/ 'But I tell you, love your enemies and pray for those who persecute you' (Matthew 5:44 [NIV]).

Christians may work for reconciliation between political or religious groups through organisations/ e.g. through the Irish Churches Peace Project/ the Corrymeela Community/ which sought to bring Catholic and Protestant communities together in Northern Ireland/ through discussion and working on their differences together.

Christians could work for more global reconciliation through an organisation such as the Community of the Cross of Nails at Coventry Cathedral/ which works with partners in many countries/ to bring about peace and harmony in areas where conflict and violence are present.

Christians do this work because of Jesus' teaching and example/ as Paul says, 'For if, while we were God's enemies, we were reconciled to him through the death of his Son, how much more, having been reconciled, shall we be saved through his life!' (Romans 5:10 [NIV]).

Test the 12 mark question

Suggested answers shown here, but see page 10 for guidance on levels of response.

12.   Arguments in support

- A pilgrimage is a journey made for religious reasons/ to a holy place/ a place where Jesus or saints lived and died/ it can teach people more about their religion's history/ can strengthen faith as it increases knowledge about holy people/ Christians make pilgrimages to the Holy Land as it is where Jesus lived, preached, died and resurrected from the dead/ Christians can experience for themselves what it was like to live there/ they follow in the footsteps of Jesus/ meet others who share their faith.
- Some Christians go on pilgrimage to places where miracles are said to have occurred/ e.g. Lourdes in France/ they pray to be healed from sin/ mental or physical illness/ to thank God for a special blessing/ to help others who are disabled or ill, putting into practice love of neighbour.
- Some Christians go on pilgrimage to a remote place/ e.g. Iona in Scotland/ they go to have quiet time to pray/ read scriptures/ connect with God through nature/ reflect on their lives/ particularly if facing a big decision/ refresh their spiritual lives in today's busy world.

Arguments in support of other views

- Pilgrimage does not always bring people closer to God/ some places are very commercialised/ it can disappoint people who had a certain mental image of a place to see that it is touristy/ it can be very crowded so not a place for reflection/ some people on the pilgrimage may just see it as a holiday, making it hard to concentrate on God.
- Pilgrimage can be expensive/ not everyone can afford going abroad/ not everyone has time to make a pilgrimage, e.g. getting time off work/ family commitments.
- Other ways of becoming closer to God are better than pilgrimage/ daily prayer in one's own home can bring the peace of mind and heart the person needs/ receiving Holy Communion brings people closer to God than any journey/ going to the sacrament of Reconciliation can be done locally.

13.   Arguments in support

- The Church (meaning all Christians) has a mission to spread the good news/ that Jesus Christ is the Son of God/ came into the world to be its Saviour/ the Great

Commission/ 'Therefore go and make disciples of all nations, baptising them in the name of the Father and of the Son and of the Holy Spirit, and teaching them to obey everything I have commanded you' (Matthew 28:19–20 [NIV]).

• Christians believe they are called to do more than just know Jesus in their own lives/ they are called to spread the good news to non-believers that Jesus is the Saviour of the world.

• When the early disciples received the Spirit at Pentecost they were given the gifts necessary to carry out the Great Commission/ the Spirit gives some people wisdom/ knowledge/ faith/ gifts of healing/ miraculous powers/ prophecy/ the ability to speak in tongues and understand the message of those who speak in tongues/ Christians today receive the Holy Spirit at their Confirmation/ they are called to be disciples of Jesus, like the first disciples/ so they must spread the faith fearlessly as the disciples did.

Arguments in support of other views

• The main job of a Christian is to believe in Jesus/ follow the commandments/ worship God/ love one's neighbour as oneself/ live a good life in the hope of eternal life in heaven.

• Many Christians do not have the personality to preach to others about their faith/ do not have the time if working/ have family responsibilities/ are not public speakers/ do not want to antagonise people who are unsympathetic non-believers/ cannot go abroad to work as missionaries.

• There are other ways of showing one's faith to others without actually 'telling them'/ being a good neighbour/ helping those in need/ working with charities/ worshipping God/ showing integrity/ having high moral principles that make non-believers notice that faith makes a difference to the Christian believer.

3 Buddhism: beliefs and teachings

Test the 1 mark question

1. C) Not everyone suffers
2. A) Anicca

Test the 2 mark question

Suggested answers, other relevant answers would be credited. 1 mark for each correct point.

3. Generosity/ morality/ patience/ energy/ meditation/ wisdom.

4. Because he had become too weak to meditate/ asceticism did not help to answer the question of why people suffer/ help Siddhartha to achieve enlightenment/ 'it was to him like a time of intertwining the sky with knots' (the *Jataka*, vol. 1, p. 67).

Test the 4 mark question

Suggested answers, other relevant answers would be credited. 1 mark for each simple contrasting or similar point, another mark for developing each point, so a maximum of 4 marks for two developed points.

6. Learning about the first three sights makes Buddhists aware of suffering/ the fact that everyone grows old, gets ill and dies/ this helps them to accept suffering as a fact of existence.

Learning about the first three sights influences Buddhists' awareness of impermanence (anicca)/ helps Buddhists to realise all things are impermanent/ which helps them to reduce their attachment to things/ craving of things.

The fourth sight (a holy man) gives Buddhists faith that a meaningful spiritual life is possible/ that all people are able to achieve enlightenment/ this inspires them to follow the Buddha's teachings.

7. An Arhat is a 'perfected person'/ who has overcome the main sources of suffering (the three poisons) to become enlightened/ when someone becomes an Arhat they are no longer reborn when they die/ the goal for Theravada Buddhists/ achieved by following the Eightfold Path.

A Bodhisattva sees their own enlightenment as being bound up with the enlightenment of all beings/ they choose to remain in the cycle of samsara to help others achieve enlightenment/ they combine being compassionate with being wise/ the goal for Mahayana Buddhists/ achieved by practising the six perfections.

Test the 5 mark question

Suggested answers, other relevant answers would be credited. 1 mark for each simple contrasting or similar point, another mark for developing each point, so 4 marks for two developed points, 1 extra mark for a correct reference to a source of religious belief or teaching.

9. The Buddha gained knowledge of all his previous lives/ understood the repetitive cycle of birth, death and rebirth (samsara).

He understood how beings are reborn according to their kamma/ unskilful actions lead to suffering and an unfavourable rebirth/ skilful actions lead to happiness and a favourable rebirth.

He understood that nothing has a fixed essence (anatta)/ there is no fixed part of a person that does not change/ illustrated by the story of Nagasena and the chariot.

He understood that beings suffer because of desire and attachment/ 'it is this craving which leads to renewed existence' (the *Samyutta Nikaya*, vol. 5, p. 421)/ suffering can be overcome by following the Eightfold Path/ 'the noble eightfold path leading to the cessation of suffering' (the *Dhammapada*, verse 191).

10. Mahayana Buddhists believe in sunyata/ the idea that nothing has a fixed nature or essence/ everything arises in dependence on conditions/ e.g. a tree has no essence but depends on rain, sunlight and soil to survive and grow/ similar to the teaching of anatta but applies to all things rather than just human beings.

Some Mahayana Buddhists believe in the idea of Buddha-nature/ everyone has the essence or nature of a Buddha inside them/ the potential to become enlightened/ this is hidden by desires, attachments, ignorance, negative thoughts/ when a person truly understands the Buddha's teachings they experience their inner Buddha nature/ the *Uttaratantra Shastra* compares Buddha-nature to honey hidden by a swarm of bees.

The goal of Mahayana Buddhism is to become a Bodhisattva/ an enlightened being who helps others achieve enlightenment/ achieved by practising the six perfections.

Test the 12 mark question

Suggested answers shown here, but see page 10 for guidance on levels of response.

12. **Arguments in support**

• The main practice of Pure Land Buddhism is to recite Amitabha's name/ Pure Land Buddhists believe that by having faith in Amitabha, they will be reborn in Sukhavati/ this does not require Buddhists to live ethically or follow many religious rules/ once reborn in Sukhavati, Amitabha will teach Buddhists and help them to achieve enlightenment/ there is no suffering or any of the other problems that stop people from achieving enlightenment/ this makes achieving enlightenment easier.

• The Buddha taught it is possible for anyone to achieve enlightenment/ many Buddhists are said to have already achieved enlightenment/ e.g. many of the Buddha's disciples became Arhats/ which means it cannot be that difficult to become enlightened.

• The human realm is said to be the best realm in which to achieve enlightenment/ this world provides all the conditions necessary to achieve enlightenment/ e.g. the ability to make ethical choices/ e.g. the Buddha's teachings/ which means achieving enlightenment is not as difficult as it would be in other worlds/realms.

Arguments in support of other views

• It can take many lifetimes to become enlightened/ e.g. the Buddha spoke about his previous lives/ so it must be difficult if it is not possible to achieve in one lifetime.

• Theravada Buddhism emphasises ordination in the monastic community/ which requires Buddhists to dedicate their whole lives to following the path of enlightenment/ so it must be difficult if it requires this level of commitment.

• The Eightfold Path and five moral precepts encourage behaviour that Buddhists might find difficult/ e.g. always speaking kindly about others/ e.g. not harming any other living beings/ e.g. not drinking alcohol.

• The six perfections may also be difficult to follow/ e.g. giving freely without expecting anything in return/ e.g. being patient with others.

• Buddhists are expected to develop compassion and loving-kindness towards all people, even people who have wronged them or caused them to suffer, which some may find very difficult.

• Meditation requires a concentration and focus that is difficult to develop/ enlightenment requires a deep understanding about the nature of reality that is hard to achieve.

13. **Arguments in support**

• For Theravada Buddhists, a person becomes enlightened by achieving a deep understanding of the nature of reality/ obtaining wisdom and overcoming ignorance/ as indicated in the 'wisdom' section of the Eightfold Path (right understanding and right intention)/ all other aspects of the Eightfold Path contribute to this goal.

• Vipassana meditation is an important type of meditation in Theravada Buddhism/ the aim is to gain insight into the nature of reality/ and understand how all things are characterised by the three marks of existence/ i.e. to overcome ignorance.

• Ignorance is one of the three poisons/ which keep Buddhists trapped in the cycle of samsara/ the Buddha taught that craving (another one of the three poisons) is rooted in ignorance/ craving leads to hatred (the last of the three poisons)/ therefore by overcoming ignorance, Buddhists can overcome craving and hatred/ it is not possible to overcome craving and hatred unless you understand how to/ so overcoming ignorance is how to break free of the three poisons and the cycle of samsara/ how to achieve enlightenment.

Arguments in support of other views

• Mahayana Buddhism teaches that compassion is equally important for achieving enlightenment/ it is not possible to develop wisdom without developing compassion/ e.g. by learning to give freely without expecting anything in return (one of the six perfections)/ e.g. by developing loving-kindness towards all people/ 'one should cultivate […] loving-kindness towards all the world' (the *Sutta Nipata*, verses 149–150).

• The Buddha taught that one of the main causes of suffering is craving/ 'it is this craving which leads to renewed existence' (the *Samyutta Nikaya*, vol. 5, p. 421)/ therefore it is equally important to overcome attachment/craving/desire.

• Hatred is also important to overcome/ as it is one of the three poisons/ the Buddha's teachings about forgiveness and loving-kindness emphasise this.

4 Buddhism: practices

Test the 1 mark question

1. D) Stupa
2. C) Insight

Test the 2 mark question

Suggested answers, other relevant answers would be credited. 1 mark for each correct point.

3. By giving freely without expecting anything in return/ showing generosity/ giving material goods/ giving protection from fear/ giving the Dhamma/ by living ethically/ by following the five moral precepts/ by showing patience/ by enduring

suffering/ by developing mental energy and strength/ by practising meditation/ by studying the Buddha's teachings.

4. Temple/ monastery/ vihara/ gompa/ in the home/ at a shrine.

Test the 4 mark question

Suggested answers, other relevant answers would be credited. 1 mark for each simple contrasting or similar point, another mark for developing each point, so a maximum of 4 marks for two developed points.

6. The first moral precept encourages Buddhists not to harm or kill any being, including animals/ for this reason many Buddhists are vegetarian or vegan/ the second moral precept encourages Buddhists to abstain from taking what is not freely given/ this influences them to not steal or exploit other people/ the third moral precept encourages Buddhists to abstain from sexual misconduct/ this influences them to not take part in harmful sexual activity/ the fourth moral precept encourages Buddhists to abstain from wrong speech/ this influences them to speak truthfully, kindly and helpfully/ the fifth moral precept is to abstain from taking intoxicants/ for this reason many Buddhists do not drink alcohol or take drugs.

7. Buddhists might celebrate Wesak by lighting up homes with candles, lamps, paper lanterns/ as light is an important symbol of hope/enlightenment/overcoming darkness/ they may make offerings to a shrine of the Buddha/ as the festival celebrates three major events in the Buddha's life/ they may attend the local temple or monastery to take part in worship and meditation/ listen to sermons on the Buddha's teachings and life/ in Singapore they may take part in ceremonies where caged animals are released/ as a symbol of liberation.

Test the 5 mark question

Suggested answers, other relevant answers would be credited. 1 mark for each simple contrasting or similar point, another mark for developing each point, so 4 marks for two developed points, 1 extra mark for a correct reference to a source of religious belief or teaching.

9. Metta is one of the four sublime states/ a loving, kind, friendly attitude towards oneself and others/ a desire for others to be happy/ 'Just as compassion is the wish that all sentient beings be free of suffering, loving-kindness is the wish that all may enjoy happiness' (the Dalai Lama)/ Buddhists aim to develop metta towards themselves and others/ this reduces the tendency to act out of negative emotions/ makes a person more caring/ leads to a feeling of peace/ helps Buddhists to overcome suffering/ can be developed through loving-kindness meditation/ where Buddhists aim to develop loving-kindness towards themselves and then everyone else in the world/ 'one should cultivate an unbounded mind towards all beings, and loving-kindness towards all the world' (the *Sutta Nipata*, verses 149–150).

10. Kamma is an ethical principle that explains how a person's actions lead to happiness or suffering/ it affects a person's happiness in this life and their future lives/ a person will be reborn into one of six realms depending on their kamma/ it teaches that the intention behind an action is very important/ generosity, compassion and understanding lead to skilful actions, which results in happiness/ craving, hatred and ignorance lead to unskilful actions, which results in suffering/ a person cannot escape the consequences of their actions/ 'Not in the sky, not in the middle of the sea, not entering an opening in the mountains is there that place on earth where standing one might be freed from evil action' (the *Dhammapada*, verse 127)/ it is central to Buddhist ethics/ it motivates Buddhists to behave in a way that will increase their own and other's happiness.

Test the 12 mark question

Suggested answers shown here, but see page 10 for guidance on levels of response.

12. **Arguments in support**

• Through vipassana meditation, Buddhists gain insight into the nature of reality/ come to understand how all things are characterised by the three marks of existence/ develop wisdom/ which is essential for achieving enlightenment (the Buddhist goal).

• In samatha meditation the meditator is only supposed to focus on one simple, neutral object or process/ such as breathing or a candle flame/ whereas in vipassana meditation everything can be considered and explored/ which is important for understanding the true nature of everything.

• Samatha meditation is often seen as a preparation for vipassana meditation/ which suggests that vipassana meditation is more important/ samatha meditation does not develop wisdom.

Arguments in support of other views

• Samatha meditation calms the mind and leads to a more tranquil, restful mental state/ e.g. by practising mindfulness of breathing/ or focusing on a simple, neutral object that does not arouse any strong emotions in the meditator.

• Samatha meditation helps a person to develop focus and concentration/ e.g. by focusing on one object and bringing their attention back to it whenever their mind wanders/ 'Whenever your mind becomes scattered, use your breath as the means to take hold of your mind again' (Thich Nhat Hanh).

• It is not possible to objectively/mindfully contemplate the nature of reality without a calm and tranquil mind/ concentration and focus is needed to practise vipassana meditation/ therefore it would not be possible to successfully practise vipassana meditation without first doing samatha meditation/ so both are equally important.

13. **Arguments in support**

• According to kamma, a person's actions influence their rebirth/ unskilful actions lead to suffering and an unfavourable rebirth/ e.g. perhaps in the realm of animals/tormented beings/hungry ghosts/ skilful actions lead to happiness and a favourable rebirth.

• An unfavourable rebirth leads to increased suffering/ makes it harder to achieve enlightenment/ e.g. the Buddha taught that the human realm is the best one in which to achieve enlightenment.

• The five moral precepts guide Buddhists in how to act skilfully/ therefore help them to achieve a favourable rebirth and progress towards enlightenment/ which is the ultimate Buddhist goal.

Arguments in support of other views

• Not all Buddhists today believe in the concept of rebirth, but may still want to practise the moral precepts.

• Buddhists also want to practise the precepts out of concern for others/ to help make a positive contribution to the world/ to show compassion towards others/ as compassion is an important quality for many Buddhists/ e.g. the first moral precept is to not cause harm to any other living being/ e.g. the fourth moral precept is to abstain from wrong speech, so encourages Buddhists to speak kindly about others.

5 Relationships and families

Test the 1 mark question

1. D) Stability
2. B) A couple and their children

Test the 2 mark question

Suggested answers, other relevant answers would be credited. 1 mark for each correct point.

3. Christians believe all people are created equal by God/ 'love your neighbour' applies to everyone/ Christians follow Jesus' example in treating women with equal value/ 'There is neither Jew nor Gentile, neither slave nor free, nor is there male and female, for you are all one in Christ Jesus' (Galatians 3:28 [NIV])/ men and women can have different roles in the family but this does not mean they are not equal in God's sight/ Christian marriage is an equal partnership.

Many Buddhists today believe men and women should have equal status/ gender discrimination expresses a lack of loving-kindness/ many Buddhists believe men and women are equal in their ability to achieve enlightenment/ some Buddhists believe women must be reborn as men in order to achieve enlightenment.

4. Christians who oppose sex before marriage think cohabitation is wrong/ Catholic and Orthodox Churches believe a sexual relationship should only take place within marriage/ many Anglican and Protestant Christians accept that although marriage is best, people may live together in a faithful, loving, committed way without being married.

Buddhist teachings do not oppose sex before marriage or cohabitation.

Test the 4 mark question

Suggested answers, other relevant answers would be credited. 1 mark for each simple contrasting or similar point, another mark for developing each point, so a maximum of 4 marks for two developed points.

6. *Beliefs must be contrasting:*

Christians believe marriage is for life/ vows made in the presence of God should not be broken/ Jesus taught that anyone who divorced and remarried was committing adultery (Mark 10:11–12)/ except in the case of adultery (Matthew 5:32)/ for Catholics marriage is a sacrament that is permanent/ cannot be dissolved by civil divorce/ Catholics can separate but cannot marry someone else while their partner is still alive/ for some Christians divorce is the lesser of two evils/ Protestant Churches accept civil divorce and allow remarriage in church.

In Buddhism there is no teaching that states divorce is wrong/ societies where Buddhism is prevalent tend to disapprove of divorce, which is seen as a last resort/ clinging to an attachment that produces suffering goes against the Buddha's teachings/ divorce is acceptable when it is not possible to reconcile the relationship, and it is the only way to reduce the couple's suffering.

7. *Beliefs must be contrasting:*

Many Christians believe heterosexual relationships are part of God's plan for humans/ God created male and female/ told them to 'be fruitful and increase in number' (Genesis 1:28 [NIV])/ sex expresses a deep, life-long union best expressed in marriage/ some Christians oppose homosexual relationships because they go against God's plan/ the Catholic Church teaches that homosexual sex is a sinful activity/ some Christians think loving, faithful homosexual relationships are just as holy as heterosexual ones.

Buddhists do not necessarily favour one form of sexuality over another/ for Buddhists the most important principle is to not harm others through sexual activity/ 'There is a middle way wherein sexuality is fully acknowledged and regarded compassionately without the need to indulge in actions which lead to suffering' (Daishin Morgan)/ Buddhist teachings do not oppose homosexual relationships or marriage/ many Buddhists believe homosexual relationships are not morally different from heterosexual ones.

Test the 5 mark question

Suggested answers, other relevant answers would be credited. 1 mark for each simple contrasting or similar point, another mark for developing each point, so 4 marks for two developed points, 1 extra mark for a correct reference to a source of religious belief or teaching.

9. For Christians, procreation is an important purpose/ procreation is part of God's plan for humanity/ God created man and woman, blessed them and said, 'Be fruitful and increase in number; fill the earth and subdue it' (Genesis 1:28 [NIV])/ protection

of children is an important purpose/ educating children about Christian values is an important purpose/ 'Children thrive, grow and develop within the love and safeguarding of the family' (The Church of England website).

In Buddhism there are no religious pressures or expectations to have children/ educating children about Buddhist beliefs and practices is an important purpose for most Buddhist parents/ they will usually involve their children in religious ceremonies and gatherings/ some may send their children to monasteries to be educated.

10. The Christian Church teaches that both parents and children have responsibilities in a family/ the commandment to 'Honour one's father and mother' (Exodus 20:12 [NIV]) applies to children of all ages/ it includes the respect and care given to the elderly members of the family/ children should obey their parents/ 'Children, obey your parents in everything, for this pleases the Lord' (Colossians 3:20 [NIV]).

In Buddhist families, the usual role of children is to obey their parents/ love and respect their parents/ preserve the traditions of the family and of Buddhism/ support and care for their parents when they get older.

Test the 12 mark question

Suggested answers shown here, but see page 10 for guidance on levels of response.

12. Arguments in support

• Most Christians think marriage is the proper place to enjoy a sexual relationship/ sex expresses a deep, loving, life-long union that first requires the commitment of marriage/ it is one of God's gifts at creation/ 'That is why a man leaves his father and mother and is united to his wife, and they become one flesh' (Genesis 2:24 [NIV]).

• Having sex is part of the trust between partners in a marriage/ sex should not be a casual, temporary pleasure/ 'The sexual act must take place exclusively within marriage. Outside of marriage it always constitutes a grave sin' (Catechism 2390).

• Paul urged sexual restraint: 'Flee from sexual immorality. All other sins a person commits are outside the body, but whoever sins sexually, sins against their own body. Do you not know that your bodies are temples of the Holy Spirit, who is in you, whom you have received from God? You are not your own' (1 Corinthians 6:18–19 [NIV]).

• Marriage brings security/ protects each partner's rights/ the rights of children/ provides a stable environment in which to raise a family.

Arguments in support of other views

• Society has changed/ many people do not see sex as requiring the commitment of marriage/ contraception has reduced the risk of pregnancy before marriage/ many people engage in casual sexual relationships.

• The cost of marriage prevents some people from marrying immediately/ some couples want to see if the relationship is going to work before marrying/ some people do not think a marriage certificate makes any difference to their relationship.

• Some Christians accept that for some people sex before marriage is a valid expression of their love for each other/ some Christians may accept cohabitation, particularly if the couple is committed to each other/ more liberal Christians may accept that people may live together in a faithful, loving and committed way without being married.

• Buddhists don't believe sex is sacred/ for Buddhists, marriage is not a sacred or religious act/ so it is not against Buddhist principles to have sex before marriage/ the important principle is not to harm others through sexual activity.

13. Arguments in support

• The Orthodox and Catholic Churches teach that using artificial contraception within marriage is wrong/ against natural law/ against the purpose of marriage to have children/ having children is God's greatest gift to a married couple/ 'Every sexual act should have the possibility of creating new life' (*Humanae Vitae*, 1968).

• God will not send more children than a couple can care for/ if Catholic couples wish to plan their families they should use a natural method, such as the rhythm method.

Arguments in support of other views

• Other Christians accept the use of artificial contraception provided it is not used to prevent having children altogether/ by mutual consent of the couple.

• Its use may allow a couple to develop their relationship before having children/ prevent sexually transmitted infections/ help reduce the population explosion.

• The Church of England approved the use of artificial contraception at the Lambeth Conference in 1930/ 'The Conference agrees that other methods may be used, provided that this is done in the light of Christian principles.'

• Most Buddhists believe it is acceptable to use artificial contraception that prevents conception/ some believe contraception that prevents a fertilised egg from developing is a form of killing and breaks the first moral precept, so is not acceptable/ having children is not considered an obligation.

6 Religion and life

Test the 1 mark question

1. C) A painless death

2. D) The theory of evolution

Test the 2 mark question

Suggested answers, other relevant answers would be credited. 1 mark for each correct point.

3. Christians believe the world is on loan to humans, who have been given the responsibility by God to look after it (Genesis 1:28)/ the parable of the Talents (Matthew 25:14–30) warns that God will be the final judge about how responsible

humans have been in looking after the earth/ pollution is not loving towards others – Jesus teaches Christians to 'love your neighbour' (Luke 10:27 [NIV]).

Most Buddhists are keen to reduce pollution because it causes harm to living creatures and so contradicts the first moral precept/ dependent arising means all life is interconnected, so pollution affects all life.

4. Christians believe animals were created by God for humans to use and care for/ humans are more important than animals but should still be treated kindly/ God gave animals to humanity to use for food, so it is fine to eat meat.

Most Buddhists believe animals should be treated with kindness and compassion/ the principle of kamma teaches that causing harm to animals is unskilful and will lead to suffering/ the Eightfold Path teaches Buddhists should not make a living from activities that cause harm to others, including animals/ many Buddhists are vegetarian or vegan to reduce harm caused to animals.

Test the 4 mark question

Suggested answers, other relevant answers would be credited. 1 mark for each simple contrasting or similar point, another mark for developing each point, so a maximum of 4 marks for two developed points.

6. *Beliefs must be similar*:

Most Christians believe animal experimentation can be justified to help save human lives/ Christians believe humans have dominion/are more important than animals, so they can use animals for this purpose.

Some Buddhists believe animal experimentation is acceptable if it is the only way to save many human lives/ although the suffering of the animals should be reduced as far as possible, as causing harm to animals goes against the first moral precept.

7. *Beliefs must be contrasting*:

Christians believe the Earth is a priceless gift from God, loaned to humans as a result of his love/ the earth's resources should be used responsibly so the world still has value for future generations.

Buddhists value the world because it provides and sustains life/ it also provides Buddhists with all the conditions needed to achieve enlightenment.

Test the 5 mark question

Suggested answers, other relevant answers would be credited. 1 mark for each simple contrasting or similar point, another mark for developing each point, so 4 marks for two developed points, 1 extra mark for a correct reference to a source of religious belief or teaching.

9. Christians believe stewardship means humans have a responsibility to look after the earth on behalf of God/ God put Adam into the Garden of Eden 'to work it and take care of it' (Genesis 2:15 [NIV])/ it is an act of love to protect the earth for future generations.

Buddhists believe that although the world belongs to nobody, it is everybody's responsibility to look after it/ if humans misuse the environment they will cause suffering for themselves and others/ this contradicts the five moral precepts/ Buddhists aim to develop loving-kindness and compassion, which extends towards the earth/ 'I believe that not only should we keep our relationship with our other fellow human beings very gentle and non-violent, but it is also very important to extend that kind of attitude to the natural environment' (the Dalai Lama).

10. Christians believe the universe was designed and made by God out of nothing/ Genesis 1 says that God made the universe and all life in it in six days/ 'In the beginning God created the heavens and the earth' (Genesis 1:1 [NIV])/ some Christians believe God used the Big Bang to create the universe.

Buddhists do not generally believe in a creator of the universe/ instead they have a cyclical vision of the universe in which there is no beginning or end/ understanding the origins of the universe is generally not considered to be important/ instead it is more important to focus on understanding the way out of suffering/ this is supported by the parable of the man hit by a poisoned arrow.

Test the 12 mark question

Suggested answers shown here, but see page 10 for guidance on levels of response.

12. Arguments in support

• The mother has to carry the baby, give birth to it and bring it up, so she should have the right to choose whether to continue with the pregnancy/ some Buddhists might argue that having an abortion should be a matter of personal choice – not dictated by the law.

• Life doesn't start until birth (or from the point when the foetus can survive outside the womb), so abortion does not involve killing.

• It is cruel to allow a severely disabled child to be born/ if the child would have a very poor quality of life then abortion may be the lesser of two evils/ some Christians and Buddhists would agree with this view.

Arguments in support of other views

• The current law is the best compromise between sides who support abortion and those that don't/ there is a reasonable balance between the rights of the mother and the unborn child.

• Many Christians believe abortion doesn't respect the sanctity of life/ Christians who believe life begins at the moment of conception think abortion is wrong, as it is taking away life given by God.

• Many Buddhists see abortion as a form of killing which goes against the first moral precept and so is unskilful/ those involved in abortions will suffer owing to kamma either in this or a future life.

• Disabled children can enjoy a good quality of life/ unwanted children can be adopted into families that will care for them/ those who choose abortion can suffer from depression and guilt afterwards.

13. Arguments in support

• A minority of Christians believe humans were given dominion over the earth so can do what they want with it/ 'Rule over the fish in the sea and the birds in the sky and over every living creature that moves on the ground' (Genesis 1:28 [NIV]).

• If resources are destroyed or used up, scientists will develop alternatives.

• Humans need natural resources to sustain their way of life.

Arguments in support of other views

• Most Christians believe humans were put on the earth as stewards to look after it on behalf of God for future generations/ God put Adam into the Garden of Eden 'to work it and take care of it' (Genesis 2:15 [NIV])/ it is wrong to destroy something that belongs to someone else (i.e. God).

• Many of the earth's natural resources are non-renewable so there is only a limited supply of them/ using them up too quickly will probably make life much harder for future generations/ this shows a lack of love and respect for others.

• Many Buddhists believe using the earth's resources irresponsibly expresses greed (one of the three poisons) and a lack of compassion for others, including future generations.

7 The existence of God and revelation

Test the 1 mark question

1. C) Theist
2. B) Mortal

Test the 2 mark question

Suggested answers, other relevant answers would be credited. 1 mark for each correct point.

3. William Paley/ Isaac Newton/ Thomas Aquinas/ F.R. Tennant.

4. Disobedience of Adam and Eve/ misuse of freewill/ nature/ punishment/ evil/ to allow people to do good in response/ craving and attachment.

Test the 4 mark question

Suggested answers, other relevant answers would be credited. 1 mark for each simple contrasting or similar point, another mark for developing each point, so a maximum of 4 marks for two developed points.

6. *Beliefs must be contrasting:*

Christians believe miracles are events performed by God which appear to break the laws of nature/ *an example of such an event/* they confirm God's existence/ they show God is at work in the world.

They are not real/ they are lucky coincidences that have nothing to do with God/ may be made up for fame or money/ healing miracles may be mind over matter or misdiagnosis/ can be explained scientifically in a way we don't yet know.

For Buddhists, miracles do not prove the existence of God/ they are usually not interpreted literally/ they are to be understood symbolically.

7. *Beliefs must be similar:*

Comes through ordinary human experiences/ seeing God's creative work and presence in nature/ Christians believe God is revealed through his creation to be creative, clever and powerful/ comes through worship or scripture/ the Bible can help to reveal what God is like and how he wants people to live/ scriptures can help Buddhists to understand the nature of reality.

Test the 5 mark question

Suggested answers, other relevant answers would be credited. 1 mark for each simple contrasting or similar point, another mark for developing each point, so 4 marks for two developed points, 1 extra mark for a correct reference to a source of religious belief or teaching.

9. For Christians, a way of God revealing something about himself/ direct experience of God in an event, such as a vision or prophecy/ e.g. Moses receiving the Ten Commandments/ Mary finding out she is pregnant from the angel Gabriel/ Saul's vision/ can have a great influence on people's lives.

For Buddhists, a way to help people understand the nature of reality/ e.g. a Buddhist may have a vision of a Buddha or Bodhisattva while meditating, who communicates something to them about how to achieve enlightenment.

10. Omnipotent/ omniscient/ benevolent/ immanent/ transcendent/ personal/ impersonal/ creator/ *any ideas in scripture related to creation, possibility of relationship with God through prayer, incarnation of Jesus, work of Holy Spirit.*

Test the 12 mark question

Suggested answers shown here, but see page 10 for guidance on levels of response.

12. Arguments in support

• Christians believe miracles are events with no natural or scientific explanation that only God could perform.

• If they occur as a response to prayer, they are a response to asking God for something/ prove that God is listening and responding to prayers.

• They are usually good and God is the source of all that is good.

• The fact that some people convert to Christianity after experiencing a miracle is proof of God's existence.

• 69 healing miracles have officially been recognised as taking place at Lourdes.

• Miracles exist and are caused by God, therefore God exists.

Arguments in support of other views

• Miracles are lucky coincidences and nothing to do with God.

• Whether something counts as a miracle is a matter of interpretation.

• They may have scientific explanations we haven't yet discovered.

• Healings could be mind over matter or misdiagnosis.

• Some miracles are made up for fame or money.

• If God is involved in miracles, this means he is selective and unfair (as only a few people experience them)/ but God cannot be selective and unfair/ therefore he cannot be involved in miracles.

• If miracles don't exist or have other explanations, they are nothing to do with God, so do not prove he exists.

13. Arguments in support

• A loving God would not allow people to suffer.

• God should be aware of evil and suffering because he is omniscient/ if so, he should use his powers to prevent it because he is omnipotent/ because God does not do this, he cannot exist.

• If God made all of creation to be perfect then there would not be earthquakes, droughts, etc./ suffering caused by the natural world is an example of poor design, which no God would be responsible for.

Arguments in support of other views

• It is unfair to blame God for suffering because he doesn't cause it.

• Suffering is a result of the disobedience of Adam and Eve/ the result of humans misusing their free will.

• If there was no evil, no one would be able to actively choose good over bad/ learn from their mistakes/ show compassion and kindness towards others who are suffering.

• Humans are in charge of looking after the earth and God chooses not to interfere.

• The existence of evil doesn't necessarily prove God does not exist, but could suggest he is not all-loving or all-powerful.

8 Religion, peace and conflict

Test the 1 mark question

1. C) Justice
2. D) Conventional weapons

Test the 2 mark question

Suggested answers, other relevant answers would be credited. 1 mark for each correct point.

3. Just cause/ correct authority/ good intention/ last resort/ reasonable chance of success/ proportional methods used.

4. For Christians violent protest goes against Jesus' teachings not to use violence/ goes against the commandment 'Do not kill'/ does not show 'love of neighbour'/ goes against the sanctity of life/ goes against 'So in everything, do to others what you would have them do to you, for this sums up the Law and the Prophets' (Matthew 7:12 [NIV]).

For Buddhists it goes against the first moral precept/ increases suffering.

Test the 4 mark question

Suggested answers, other relevant answers would be credited. 1 mark for each simple contrasting or similar point, another mark for developing each point, so a maximum of 4 marks for two developed points.

6. *Beliefs must be contrasting:*

Christians who support pacifism (e.g. The Religious Society of Friends/Quakers) believe that war can never be justified/ all killing is wrong/ it breaks the commandment 'You shall not murder' (Exodus 20:13 [NIV])/ Jesus taught 'Blessed are the peacemakers, for they shall be called children of God' (Matthew 5:9 [NIV])/ conflicts should be settled peacefully.

Christians who do not support pacifism believe that war is sometimes necessary as a last resort/ they would fight in a 'just war'/ to stop genocide taking place/ to defend one's country or way of life/ to help a weaker country defend itself from attack.

Buddhists support pacifism because the first moral precept teaches Buddhists should not harm or kill any living being/ peace and non-violence are core Buddhist beliefs/ the principle of compassion (karuna) is important/ right action (part of the Eightfold Path) means violence to others must be avoided/ a Buddhist should not act out of hatred.

7. *Beliefs must be similar:*

Forgiveness is showing grace and mercy/ pardoning someone for what they have done wrong/ Christians believe forgiveness is important as in the Lord's Prayer it says 'Forgive us our sins as we forgive those who sin against us'/ this means God will not forgive if Christians do not forgive others/ Christians believe God sets the example by offering forgiveness to all who ask for it in faith.

Buddhists believe that forgiveness is important because it allows a person to let go of anger and hatred/ so they do not harbour feelings of resentment and anger/ forgiveness also expresses loving-kindness/ forgiveness creates peace for the person who is forgiven and for the person who forgives.

Test the 5 mark question

Suggested answers, other relevant answers would be credited. 1 mark for each simple contrasting or similar point, another mark for developing each point, so 4 marks for two developed points, 1 extra mark for a correct reference to a source of religious belief or teaching.

9. Some Christians believe in the just war theory/ it is right to fight in a war if the cause is just/ war can be the lesser of two evils/ it can be justified if its purpose is to stop atrocities/ people have a right to self-defence/ 'If there is a serious injury, you are to take life for life, eye for eye, tooth for tooth' (Exodus 21:23–24 [NIV])/ 'Love your neighbour as yourself' (Matthew 22:39 [NIV]) demands protection of weaker allies through war.

10. Reconciliation is a sacrament in the Catholic Church/ Christians believe it is important to ask God for forgiveness for sins/ reconciliation restores a Christian's relationship with God and other people/ it is when individuals or groups restore friendly relations after conflict or disagreement/ it is important to build good relationships after a war so conflict does not break out again/ justice and peace must be restored to prevent further conflict/ to create a world which reflects God's intention in creation/ Christians believe they must be reconciled to others before they can worship God properly/ 'Therefore, if you are offering your gift at the altar and there remember that your brother or sister has something against you, leave your gift there in front of the altar. First go and be reconciled to them; then come and offer your gift.' (Matthew 5:23–24 [NIV])/ for Buddhists, letting go of blame and resentment is important in reconciliation.

Test the 12 mark question

Suggested answers shown here, but see page 10 for guidance on levels of response.

12. Arguments in support

• Some religious people believe in the concept of a holy war/ a holy war is fighting for a religious cause or God/ probably controlled by a religious leader/ these believers think that it is justifiable to defend their faith from attack.

• Religion has been a cause of such wars in the past/ e.g. the Crusades, wars between Christians and Muslims, were fought over rights to the Holy Land/ in the Old Testament there are many references to God helping the Jews settle in the Promised Land at the expense of those already living there.

• There are many examples of conflicts that involve different religious groups/ e.g. Catholics and Protestants in Northern Ireland during the 'Troubles'/ Israeli–Palestinian conflict/ conflict in India and Pakistan between Muslims and Hindus.

• Some atheists claim that without religion, many conflicts could be avoided/ religiously motivated terrorism would cease.

Arguments in support of other views

• Religion is not the main cause of wars: greed, self-defence and retaliation are all more common causes/ academic studies have found that religion plays a minor role in the majority of conflicts/ most wars have many causes/ e.g. opposition to a government/ economic reasons/ objection to ideological, political or social systems/ e.g. political differences played a greater role in the conflict in Northern Ireland than religion.

• Christians today believe they should defend their faith by reasoned argument, not violence/ many Christians think no war can be considered 'holy' when there is great loss of life/ "Put your sword back in its place," Jesus said, 'for all who draw the sword die by the sword" (Matthew 26:52 [NIV])/ 'You have heard that it was said to the people long ago, 'You shall not murder […] But I tell you that anyone who is angry with a brother or sister will be subject to judgement" (Matthew 5:21–22 [NIV]).

• Buddhism strongly promotes pacifism/ Most Buddhists believe war cannot be justified in any circumstances/ so most Buddhists would never use violence to defend their faith from attack.

13. Arguments in support

• Religious people should be the main peacemakers because of their beliefs/ e.g. Christians believe in 'love your neighbour'/ the sanctity of life/ equality/ justice/ peace/ forgiveness/ reconciliation/ Jesus taught 'Blessed are the peacemakers'/ Buddhists believe it is important to reduce suffering/ respond to violence peacefully/ reconcile people and groups together.

• Prayer and meditation can bring inner peace to individuals/ this helps avoid quarrels with others/ peacemaking begins with each person/ 'We can never obtain peace in the outer world until we make peace within ourselves' (the Dalai Lama).

• Many religious people are engaged in peacemaking in today's world/ e.g. the Anglican Pacifist Fellowship works to raise awareness of the issue of pacifism/ the 'Peace People' (Mairead Corrigan, Betty Williams and Ciaran McKeown) in Northern Ireland work to bring the Catholic and Protestant communities together to stop violence/ Thich Nhat Hanh is a Buddhist monk who promotes non-violent protest and engaged Buddhism.

Arguments in support of other views

• Religious people should be peacemakers, but not the main ones/ the problems of global conflict require global solutions that are beyond any individual to solve/ the United Nations should be the main peacekeeping organisation/ only large organisations or governments with powerful resources can hope to affect peacemaking in the world.

• Religious people can be peacemakers in their own families and support justice and peace groups locally, but they cannot take the lead as peacemakers/ their main duty is to their family/ people have jobs that do not allow them to stop violence across the world/ the most they can do is contribute to organisations which help.

• Everyone should take equal responsibility for helping to contribute towards peace, whether they are religious or not/ some situations might benefit from peacemakers who are not religious.

9 Religion, crime and punishment

Test the 1 mark question

1. A) Corporal punishment

2. C) Happiness

Test the 2 mark question

Suggested answers, other relevant answers would be credited. 1 mark for each correct point.

3. Retribution/ deterrence/ reformation/ protection.

4. Poverty/ upbringing/ mental illness/ addiction/ greed/ hate/ opposition to an unjust law.

Test the 4 mark question

Suggested answers, other relevant answers would be credited. 1 mark for each simple contrasting or similar point, another mark for developing each point, so a maximum of 4 marks for two developed points.

6. *Beliefs must be contrasting:*

Approved of by most Christians and Buddhists/ as allows offenders to make up for what they have done wrong/ helps to reform and rehabilitate offenders/ may involve counselling, treatment or education/ may include an opportunity to apologise to the victim/ no harm is done to the offender.

Some people disapprove of community service as it is not a sufficient deterrent/ there is no element of retribution/ it is too soft a punishment.

7. *Beliefs must be similar:*

Most Christians oppose retribution because it does not show forgiveness/ it is not as positive as reformation/ 'Do not be overcome by evil, but overcome evil with good' (Romans 21:21 [NIV])/ Jesus taught his followers to 'turn the other cheek'.

Most Buddhists oppose retribution because it is a form of violence/ does not show forgiveness/ causing suffering to someone goes against Buddhist principles/ reformation is more positive/ 'We should not seek revenge on those who have committed crimes against us' (the Dalai Lama).

Test the 5 mark question

Suggested answers, other relevant answers would be credited. 1 mark for each simple contrasting or similar point, another mark for developing each point, so 4 marks for two developed points, 1 extra mark for a correct reference to a source of religious belief or teaching.

9. Christians are expected to forgive those who offend against them and if they do God will forgive them/ forgiveness is not a replacement for punishment/ it should be unlimited/ 'not seven times, but seventy-seven times' (Matthew 18:22 [NIV])/ Jesus forgave those who crucified him and Christians should follow his example/ 'Father forgive them, for they do not know what they are doing' (Luke 23:34 [NIV]).

Buddhism teaches that if people do not forgive they will suffer/ people should forgive others for the sake of their own health and welfare/ forgiving a criminal does not mean their actions will not have consequences, because of kamma/ a person should confess and apologise before hoping for forgiveness/ "He abused me, he struck me, he overcame me, he robbed me." Of those who wrap themselves up in it hatred is not quenched' (the *Dhammapada*, verse 3).

10. Hate crimes are condemned by Christianity and Buddhism/ hate crimes target individuals and groups perceived to be different/ Christians believe God created all humans equal in his image/ 'There is neither Jew nor Gentile, slave nor free man, male nor female, for you are all one in Christ Jesus' (Galatians 3:28 [NIV])/ hate crimes are not loving ('love your neighbour').

Hatred is one of the three poisons in Buddhism/ and the direct opposite of loving-kindness and compassion/ so there is no justification for hate crimes in Buddhism.

Test the 12 mark question

Suggested answers shown here, but see page 10 for guidance on levels of response.

12. Arguments in support

• Use of the death penalty means there is a chance of killing an innocent person.

• There is little evidence it is an effective deterrent.

• It is never right to take another person's life/ this does not show forgiveness or compassion.

• Society can still be protected by imprisoning criminals instead of executing them.

• For Christians, sanctity of life means life is sacred and special to God, and only he has the right to take it away/ Ezekiel 33:11 teaches that wrongdoers should be reformed/ 'I take no pleasure in the death of the wicked, but rather that they turn away from their ways and live' (Ezekiel 33:11 [NIV]).

• For Buddhists, the death penalty breaks the first moral precept/ makes revenge part of the criminal justice system/ does not allow the possibility of rehabilitation.

Arguments in support of other views

• The death penalty should be allowed as retribution for people who commit the worst possible crimes.

- It protects society by removing the worst criminals so they cannot cause harm again.
- It may deter others from committing murder.
- It creates happiness for the greatest number of people (the principle of utility).
- Teachings from the Old Testament seem to support it/ 'Whoever sheds human blood, by humans shall their blood be shed' (Genesis 9:6 [NIV]).

13. Arguments in support

- Committing crime is wrong whatever the reason/ all crime causes someone to suffer.
- People should obey the law/ God put the system of government in place to rule every citizen so it is his law that is being broken (Romans 13:31).
- Christians and Buddhists believe it is wrong to commit crime because of poverty/ people should focus on creating a fairer society where the need to steal because of poverty is removed.
- Those who commit crime through illness or addiction should be provided with treatment so they have no reason to commit crimes.
- People who want to protest against an unjust law can do so legally, e.g. through a peaceful protest.

Arguments in support of other views

- Society is not fair so crimes because of need/poverty are justified in some circumstances/ e.g. it may be better to steal food than allow a child to starve.
- Some laws are unjust and the only way to change them is to break them/ peaceful protest is not always powerful enough to change the law.
- All humans have a tendency to do bad things, including crime, because of original sin.
- Those who commit crime because of addiction/mental illness cannot help it.

10 Religion, human rights and social justice

Test the 1 mark question

1. C) Unfairly judging someone before the facts are known
2. A) Promoting tolerance

Test the 2 mark question

Suggested answers, other relevant answers would be credited. 1 mark for each correct point.

3. Unfair pay/ bad working conditions/ bad housing/ poor education/ high interest rates on loans or credit cards/ people trafficking/ modern slavery.

4. Give to the Church/ help people in need/ donate to charities/ use it to keep themselves safe/ give offerings to monks or nuns/ provide pleasure and satisfaction for themselves, their family and friends.

Test the 4 mark question

Suggested answers, other relevant answers would be credited. 1 mark for each simple contrasting or similar point, another mark for developing each point, so a maximum of 4 marks for two developed points.

6. *Beliefs must be contrasting:*

Christianity teaches that prejudice is always wrong because it is unjust to single out individuals or groups for inferior treatment/ some Christians think homosexual relationships are unnatural and against the Bible/ cannot lead to the 'natural' creation of a child/ other Christians believe any relationship based on love should be cherished.

Buddhists believe that no form of sexuality is more ethical than any other/ any kind of prejudice expresses hatred and so does not agree with the principle of loving-kindness/ the important thing is not to harm others through sex.

7. *Beliefs must be similar:*

The Bible stresses the importance of providing human rights to all people/ which includes creating a more just society/ 'Let justice roll on like a river' (Amos 5:24)/ Christians believe it is not loving to deny people their rights/ rights are written into law, and the law is inspired by God so must be obeyed/ Christians have a responsibility to help provide human rights/ 'faith without deeds is useless' (James 2:20 [NIV]).

The Buddha taught that while suffering is inevitable, people should strive to alleviate suffering where possible/ which includes helping to provide human rights for all/ Engaged Buddhism is a movement that uses the Buddha's teachings to tackle social issues and help make sure everyone has access to human rights.

Test the 5 mark question

Suggested answers, other relevant answers would be credited. 1 mark for each simple contrasting or similar point, another mark for developing each point, so 4 marks for two developed points, 1 extra mark for a correct reference to a source of religious belief or teaching.

9. Poverty is sometimes caused by injustice and Christians must combat injustice/ poverty involves suffering and Christians are expected to help relieve suffering/ e.g. the parable of the Sheep and the Goats/ people have God-given talents that they should use to help overcome poverty/ e.g. the parable of the Talents/ tackling poverty is good stewardship/ Jesus' teaching to 'love your neighbour' encourages Christians to help those in poverty.

Buddhists believe that all poverty deserves compassion/ it is important to help overcome the root causes of poverty/ e.g. through the movement of Engaged Buddhism/ Buddhism also recognises that each person has a responsibility to help themselves out of poverty/ sometimes poverty results from unskilful habits/ Buddhism emphasises using one's wealth to benefit others.

10. Christianity teaches that wealth can lead to traits such as greed and selfishness/ 'the love of money is a root of all sorts of evil' (1 Timothy 6:10 [NIV])/ focusing on wealth brings the danger of ignoring God and neglecting the spiritual life/ 'You cannot serve both God and money' (Matthew 6:24 [NIV]).

For Buddhists, the pursuit of wealth can strengthen the tendency towards greed/ which is one of the three poisons and leads to suffering/ pursuing wealth may lead people to exploit others/ which goes against the second moral precept (to abstain from taking what is not freely given)/ focusing too much on wealth can distract a person from working towards enlightenment/ 'By action, knowledge and Dhamma, by virtue and noble way of life – By these are mortals purified, not by lineage or wealth' (the *Majjhima Nikaya*, vol. 3, p. 262).

Test the 12 mark question

Suggested answers shown here, but see page 10 for guidance on levels of response.

12. Arguments in support

- Discrimination is an action that can cause physical and psychological harm/ goes against the ideas of equality/justice/human rights.
- Christianity teaches that all people should be treated equally because they are all made in God's image/ 'There is neither Jew nor Gentile, neither slave nor free, nor is there male and female, for you are all one in Christ Jesus' (Galatians 3:28 [NIV]).
- Buddhism teaches that discrimination expresses hatred/ and causes suffering to others/ it is more important to show compassion and loving-kindness instead/ and to work towards equality for everyone/ e.g. through the movement of Engaged Buddhism.
- Positive discrimination is still a form of discrimination/ it would be better to treat all people equally.

Arguments in support of other views

- Positive discrimination helps to make up for centuries of negative discrimination against minority groups/ helps to make people aware of the need to rectify negative discrimination against minority groups.
- Positive discrimination helps those with disabilities to live more equally alongside people without disabilities/ shows love and compassion to people who are suffering/ so it can be supported by Christian and Buddhist teachings.
- It is important to differentiate between the needs of different people/ not everyone is the same/ some people are better suited to certain roles than others.

13. Arguments in support

- Freedom of religion is a basic human right/ 'Everyone has the right to freedom of thought, conscience and religion' (The United Declaration of Human Rights)/ in the UK the law allows people to follow whichever faith they choose.
- It is wrong to try to force someone to follow a religion/ or to prevent them from following a religion/ it should be a matter of personal choice/ this makes choosing to follow a particular religion more significant/meaningful.
- Forcing people to follow a religion or preventing them from following a religion could lead to more conflict and fighting between different religions.
- Being a Christian is a choice that any person can make/ Christians believe religious freedom is important/ Jesus taught people to show tolerance and harmony.
- The Buddha encouraged his followers to listen to teachers of other religions with respect/ 'I always say that every person on this earth has the freedom to practise or not practise religion. It is all right to do either' (the Dalai Lama).

Arguments in support of other views

- If a religion teaches hatred and intolerance, there should be limits on how it can be taught or practised/ people should not be allowed to join it for the wrong reasons.
- Some people might argue that to show patriotism, a person should follow the main religion in their country.
- Some people might argue that when people are allowed to join any religion, this can lead to conflict and tension between different religious groups, whereas if everyone followed the same religion then there would be more harmony between people.
- Some people might unintentionally harm/upset others through choosing a particular religion/ e.g. by choosing a religion that is different to their parents'/ so perhaps it should not be so easy to switch from one religion to another.
- Everybody also has the right not to follow any religion.